The South West Bus Handbook

British Bus Publishing

Body codes used in the Bus Handbook series:

Type:
A	Articulated vehicle
B	Bus, either single-deck or double-deck
BC	Interurban - high-back seated bus
C	Coach
M	Minibus with design capacity of 16 seats or less
N	Low-floor bus (*Niederflur*), either single-deck or double-deck
O	Open-top bus (CO = convertible; PO = partial open-top)

Seating capacity is then shown. For double-decks the upper deck capacity is followed by the lower deck.

Door position:
C	Centre entrance/exit
D	Dual doorway.
F	Front entrance/exit
R	Rear entrance/exit (no distinction between doored and open)
T	Three or more access points

Equipment:
L	Lift for wheelchair	TV		Training vehicle.
M	Mail compartment	RV		Used as tow bus or engineer's vehicle.
T	Toilet	w		Vehicle is withdrawn and awaiting disposal.

e.g. - B32/28F is a double-deck bus with thirty-two seats upstairs, twenty-eight down and a front entrance/exit.
N43D is a low-floor bus with two or more doorways.

Re-registrations:
Where a vehicle has gained new index marks, the details are listed at the end of each fleet showing the current mark, followed in sequence by those previously carried starting with the original mark.

Regional books in the series:
The Scottish Bus Handbook
The Ireland & Islands Bus Handbook
The North East Bus Handbook
The Yorkshire Bus Handbook
The North West Bus Handbook
The East Midlands Bus Handbook
The West Midlands Bus Handbook
The Welsh Bus Handbook
The Eastern Bus Handbook
The London Bus Handbook
The South East Bus Handbook
The South West Bus Handbook

Annual books are produced for the major groups:
The Stagecoach Bus Handbook
The Go-Ahead Bus Handbook
The First Bus Handbook
The Arriva Bus Handbook
The National Express Handbook (bi-annual)
Most editions for earlier years are available direct from the publisher.

Associated series:
The Hong Kong Bus Handbook
The Malta Bus Handbook
The Leyland Lynx Handbook
The Model Bus Handbook
The Postbus Handbook
The Overall Advertisement Bus Handbook - Volume 1
The Toy & Model Bus Handbook - Volume 1 - Early Diecasts
The Fire Brigade Handbook (fleet list of each local authority fire brigade)
The Police Range Rover Handbook

Some earlier editions of these books are still available. Please contact the publisher on 01952 255669.

Contents

A Bus	5
APL Travel	7
Alexcars	8
Andybus	9
Applegates	10
Arleen	11
Axe Valley Mini Travel	12
Bakers Dolphin	13
Barnes	16
Barry's	17
K W Beard Ltd	18
Beaumont Travel	19
Beeline	20
Bennetts	21
Berkley	23
Berrys	24
Bluebird	25
Blue Iris	26
The Blue Motors	27
Brean & Berrow	27
Buglers	28
Caradon Riviera Tours	29
Carmel Coaches	31
Castleways	32
Centurian Travel	33
Citytour	34
Coach House Travel	35
Cooks Coaches	36
Coombs Travel	38
Cottrell's	40
Country Bus	41
Currian	42
D A C Coaches	43
Dartline	44
Dawlish Coaches	46
C J Down	47
Dukes Travel	48
Eagle of Bristol	49
Eastwood	50
Ebley	51
Eurotaxis	52
Excelsior Coaches	54
Faresaver	55
Filer's	57
Geoff Willetts	58
Glenvic	59
Grey Cars	60
Hamblys of Kernow	61
Hatts Europa	62
Hookways	64
Hopley's of Mount Hawke	67
James Bevan	68
Marchants	69
Peter Carol	73
Plymouth Citybus	74
Polperro Tram Co	77
Pulham's	78
Quantock Motor Services	79
River Link	83
Roselyn Coaches	84
Safeway Services	86
Sewards	87
Shaftesbury & District	88
Somerbus	90
South Gloucestershire	90
St Ives Mini Bus Co	97
Sureline	98
Swanbrook	99
Tally Ho!	100
Target Travel	102
Taw & Torridge	104
Taylors	106
Thamesdown	107
Tilley's	110
Trathens	111
Truronian	113
Turners	115
Turner's Tours	117
Weaverbus	118
Webberbus	119
Wessex Bus	121
Western Greyhound	122
Westward Travel	124
F T Williams Travel	125
Yellow Buses	127
Vehicle index	**130**

The South West Bus Handbook

This third edition of the Bus Handbook covering England's South West region and is part of a series that details the fleets of bus and express coach operators from across Britain. Operations by the national fleets of Stagecoach and First along with Arriva and Go-Ahead fleets have their own books. A list of current editions is shown on page 2. The operators included in this edition cover those who provide tendered and commercial services in the counties and unitary area within the region. Also included are a number of operators who provide significant coaching activities.

Quality photographs for inclusion in the series are welcome, for which a fee is payable. Unfortunately the publishers cannot accept responsibility for any loss and request you show your name on each picture or slide.

To keep the fleet information up to date we recommend the Ian Allan publication, *Buses*, published monthly, or for more detailed information, the PSV Circle monthly news sheets. The writer and publisher would be glad to hear from readers should any information be available which corrects or enhances that given in this publication.

Series Editor: Bill Potter
Principal Editor for *The South West Bus Handbook:* Simon Nicholas

Acknowledgments:
We are grateful to David Donati, Robert Edworthy, Dave Godley, Simon Jennings, Tom Johnson, John Madge, Alan Walker, Steve White, the PSV Circle and the operating companies for their assistance in the compilation of this book.

The cover photographs are by Mark Bailey, Robert Edworthy and Phillip Stephenson, Frontispiece is by Tom Johnson.

Earlier editions of the area covered by the South West Bus Handbook:

1st Edition - 1997   ISBN 1-897990-42-1
2nd Edition - 2001   ISBN 1-897990-64-2

ISBN 1 904875 52 1   (3rd Edition)
Published by *British Bus Publishing Ltd*
16 St Margaret's Drive, Wellington, Telford, TF1 3PH

Telephone: 01952 255669 - Facsimile 01952 222397 - www.britishbuspublishing.co.uk
© British Bus Publishing Ltd, March 2005

A BUS

L C Munden & Sons Ltd, 6-7 Freestone Road, St Phillips, Bristol, BS2 0QH
S J & J M Munden, 6-7 Freestone Road, St Phillips, Bristol, BS2 0QH
A J Peters, 104 Winchester Road, Brislington, Bristol, BS4 3NL

w	NFB113R	Bristol VRT/SL3/6LXB	Eastern Coach Works	B43/33F	1977	City Line, 1993
w	KOO792V	Bristol VRT/SL3/6LXB	Eastern Coach Works	B39/31F	1980	First Cityline, 2000
w	AHW198V	Bristol VRT/SL3/6LXB	Eastern Coach Works	B43/27D	1980	First Bristol, 2000
w	KOO791V	Bristol VRT/SL3/6LXB	Eastern Coach Works	B39/31F	1980	First Bristol, 1998
	KOO793V	Bristol VRT/SL3/6LXB	Eastern Coach Works	B39/31F	1980	First Bristol, 1998
	AVK142V	Leyland Atlantean AN68A/2R	Alexander AL	B49/37F	1980	Stagecoach, 2004
	AVK156V	Leyland Atlantean AN68A/2R	Alexander AL	B49/37F	1980	Stagecoach, 2004
	EJR118V	Leyland Atlantean AN68A/2R	Alexander AL	B49/37F	1980	Stagecoach, 2004
	STW33W	Bristol VRT/SL3/6LXB	Eastern Coach Works	B39/31F	1980	First Bristol, 2000
	EWS739W	Bristol VRT/SL3/6LXB	Eastern Coach Works	B43/31F	1981	First Cityline, 2000
	XHK221X	Bristol VRT/SL3/6LXB	Eastern Coach Works	B39/31F	1981	First Cityline, 2000
	XHK222X	Bristol VRT/SL3/6LXB	Eastern Coach Works	B39/31F	1981	First Cityline, 2000
	RBO506Y	Leyland Olympian ONLXB/1R	East Lancs	B43/31F	1983	Cardiff Bus, 1998
	RBO508Y	Leyland Olympian ONLXB/1R	East Lancs	B43/31F	1983	Cardiff Bus, 1998
	B892UAS	Leyland Olympian ONLXB/1R	Alexander RL	B45/32F	1985	Stagecoach, 2004
	B893UAS	Leyland Olympian ONLXB/1R	Alexander RL	B45/32F	1985	Stagecoach, 2005
	B895UAS	Leyland Olympian ONLXB/1R	Alexander RL	B45/32F	1985	Stagecoach, 2005
	B896UAS	Leyland Olympian ONLXB/1R	Alexander RL	B45/32F	1985	Stagecoach, 2004
	B899UAS	Leyland Olympian ONLXB/1R	Alexander RL	B45/32F	1985	Stagecoach, 2004

A Bus was the first operator of a low-floor double-deck bus in Britain beating Travel West Midlands by just a few hours. The vehicle achieving this was Optare Spectra R222AJP, seen here operating the principal service from Bristol to Keynsham. *Phillip Stephenson*

J80BUS is the only Iveco double-deck bus in the country. It originally operated in north Devon where it plied between Ilfracombe and Barnstaple for Filer's of Ilfracombe. Since then it has seen operation in Rochdale and Bristol before joining A Bus. The vehicle carries an adaptation of Alexander's RH design. *Robert Edworthy*

J80BUS	Iveco 480.10.21	Alexander RH	B52/31F	1991	Somerbus, Bristol, 2002
M248NNF	Iveco TurboDaily 59.12	Marshall C31	B25F	1994	First Somerset, 2003
M413RND	Iveco TurboDaily 59.12	Marshall C31	B25F	1995	First Somerset, 2004
R222AJP	DAF DE02RSDB250	Optare Spectra	N51/30F	1998	
S111AJP	DAF DE02RSDB250	Optare Spectra	N50/27F	1998	
V444AJP	DAF DE02RSDB250	Alexander ALX400	N45/24F	1999	
AP03BUS	Optare Solo M850	Optare	N29F	2003	
AP03BUZ	Optare Solo M850	Optare	N29F	2003	
AP53BUS	DAF DE02PSDB250	Optare Spectra	N50/27F	2003	
AP04BUS	DAF DE02PSDB250	Optare Spectra	N47/27F	2004	
BU54AJP	Scania N94UD 10.6m	East Lancs OmniDekka 4.4m	N(86)F	On order	

Special event vehicles:

UHY384	Bristol KSW6G	Eastern Coach Works	B32/28RD	1955	New to Bristol
969EHW	Bristol Lodekka LD6G	Eastern Coach Works	B33/25RD	1959	New to Bath Tramways
972EHW	Bristol Lodekka LD6B	Eastern Coach Works	B33/25R	1959	New to Bristol

Depots: Freestone Road, Bristol and Kingsland Sidings, Bristol
Note: Several non pcv minibuses are also operated under the Guyan Minibuses fleetname.

APL TRAVEL

APL Travel Ltd, 1 Pear Tree Cottage, Crudwell, SN16 9ES

A342MWD	Leyland Tiger TRCTL11/3R	Plaxton Paramount 3200 E	C53F	1983	Coachstyle, Nettleton, 2004
MIL5237	Mercedes-Benz 811D	Optare StarRider	B26F	1989	Hatts Europa, Foxham, 2005
K205GMX	Dennis Javelin 12m	Plaxton Première 320	C49FT	1993	Southlands, Swanley, 2004
M259CDE	Mercedes-Benz 811D	Mellor	BC31F	1994	Curtis, Brislington, 2001
N9LON	Dennis Javelin 12m	Berkhof Excellence 2000	C53F	1996	Hodgson, Barnard Castle, 2004
P76VWO	Mercedes-Benz 814D	Autobus Nouvelle	BC33F	1997	Bebb, Llantwit Fardre, 1999
P296JHE	Mercedes-Benz Vario 0814	Plaxton Cheetah	C29F	1997	Summerdale Cs, Letterston, 2005
S853PKH	Mercedes-Benz Vario 0814	Plaxton Beaver 2	B31F	1998	Turner, Bristol, 2004
S762XYA	Iveco TurboDaily 59.12	Marshall C19	B29F	1999	Bodmans, Worton, 2004
T623KFH	Mercedes-Benz Vario 0814	Autobus Nouvelle 2	C33F	1999	Cross Country, Castle Eaton, 2004
YJ54UCA	Optare Solo M850	Optare	N26F	2004	

Previous registrations:

A342MWD	A211SAE, 420GAC, A224NAC, MJI3751		P296JHE	P296JHE, P2JPT
MIL5237	F35CWY			

Special livery: Blue (Wiggleybus) YJ54UCA
Depot: Station Road, Christian Malford.

A new low floor Optare Solo, purchased by the Council but operated on its behalf by APL Travel of Christian Malford, provides a timetabled service. The bus also stops for pre-booked request passengers, and can deviate into many of the smaller villages, either side of the A4 trunk road, on request. YJ54UCA is seen on the service. *Optare*

ALEXCARS

Alexcars Ltd, 11 Love Lane, Cirencester, GL7 1YG

B888PDY	Bedford YNV Venturer	Plaxton Parramount 3200 II	C57F	1985	Rambler, Hastings, 1992
ACH53A	MAN 10.180	Caetano Algarve	C35F	1991	Wray's, Harrogate, 1999
672DYA	Toyota Coaster HDB30R	Caetano Optimo II	C21F	1991	Hearn, Harrow Weald, 2001
TIL1858	Toyota Coaster HDB30R	Caetano Optimo II	C21F	1991	Peruffo, Kimbolton, 2000
NUI5155	Scania K93CRB	Plaxton Première 320	C53F	1992	PPH, St Albans, 2004
LUI5601	Dennis Javelin 12m	Wadham Stringer Vanguard II	BC70F	1992	MoD (74KK99), 2001
ACH80A	Dennis Javelin 12m	Wadham Stringer Vanguard II	BC70F	1993	MoD (75KK32), 2004
M702HBC	Dennis Javelin 12m	Marcopolo Continental 330	C51F	1995	Hancock, Southey Green, 2002
M887WWB	Dennis Javelin 10m	Plaxton Première 320	C43F	1995	Clegg & Brooking, M Wallop, 2001
M549XHC	Dennis Javelin 11m	Plaxton Première 320	C57F	1995	Gatwick Parking, Horley, 2002
N4RDC	Dennis Javelin 12m	Berkhof Excellence 1000	C57F	1996	Mitchell, Plean, 2002
P97TTX	Toyota Coaster HZB50R	Caetano Optimo I	C21F	1996	Easyway, Pencoed, 2003
R851SDT	MAN 11.220	Irizar MidiCentury	C35F	1997	Channel Coachways, Bow, 2001
R464YDT	Scania L94IB	Irizar InterCentury 12.32	C53F	1998	Shire Coaches, St Albans, 2004
516ACH	MAN 18.310	Noge Catalan 350	C51FT	1999	Solent, Newport, 2002
T446HRV	Dennis Dart SLF	Caetano NimBus	N44F	1999	
ODW459	Scania L94IB	Irizar InterCentury 12.32	C49FT	1999	Dunn-Line, Nottingham, 2003
W31SBC	Toyota Coaster BB50R	Caetano Optimo III	C21F	2000	
Y69HHE	Scania L94IB	Irizar InterCentury 12.32	C53F	2001	
Y10RAD	Scania L94IB	Irizar InterCentury 12.32	C53F	2001	Radley, Brigg, 2003

Previous registrations:

516ACH	T810RDL	M549XHC	M785NBA, A15GPC
672DYA	J310KFP	M702HBC	M702HBC, M2WMT
ACH53A	H172EJF	NUI5155	J292NNC
ACH80A	K451PHY	ODW459	T47CNN
B888PDY	B888PDY, ACH69A	TIL1858	J303KFP, FIW748, J990JKN
LUI5601	K279PHT		

Caetano is the third bodybuilder to have occupied the site in Waterlooville following on from Wadham Stringer and UVG. The current model is the Caetano NimBus shown here on Dennis Dart T446HRV, the only low-floor vehicle operated by Alexcars. *Robert Edworthy*

ANDYBUS

Andrew James - Andybus

A R James, Ferris Farm, Olivemead Lane, Dauntsey, Chippenham, SN16 9LU

Reg	Chassis	Body	Layout	Year	History
WYV820T	Bedford YLQ	Duple Dominant II	C45F	1979	G&M, Lampeter, 2002
E318STG	Mercedes-Benz 811D	Optare StarRider	B33F	1988	Cruisers, Redhill, 2001
G782XAE	Leyland Tiger TRCTL11/3RZM	Plaxton Derwent	BC70F	1990	MOD (03KJ48) 2002
K112XRU	Ford Transit VE6	Ford	M8	1992	Miles, Stratton, 2003
K30ARJ	Iveco TurboDaily 59.12	Mellor	B29F	1993	Hatts Coaches, Foxham, 2002
K803WFJ	Iveco TurboDaily 59.12	Mellor	B29F	1993	Stagecoach Devon, 2002
M93BOU	Toyota Coaster HZB50R	Caetano Optimo III	C21F	1994	AMB, Bristol, 2003
N3ARJ	Bova FLC12.280	Bova Futura Club	C53F	1995	
M30ARJ	Dennis Dart 9.8m	Plaxton Pointer	BC40F	1995	Castleways, Winchcombe, 2002
N30AJRJ	Optare Excel L1000	Optare	N36F	1997	Tillingbourne, Cranleigh, 2001
R30ARJ	Dennis Dart SLF	Marshall Capital	N37F	1997	Isle of Man Transport, 2003
R57JSG	Mercedes-Benz Vario O810	Plaxton Beaver 2	B33F	1998	
N222LFR	MAN NL222FR	East Lancs Spryte	N43F	1998	MAN demonstrator, 2001
WR02XXO	Bova Futura FHD12.340	Bova Futura	C51FT	2002	
WP52YXA	Mercedes-Benz Vario O814	Plaxton Beaver 2	BC33F	2002	Somerbus, Bristol, 2004
WU03ZPS	Mercedes-Benz Vario O814	Plaxton Beaver 2	BC33F	2003	
WU03ZPY	Mercedes-Benz Vario O814	Plaxton Beaver 2	BC33F	2003	
AJ04BUS	TransBus Javelin	TransBus Profile	C57F	2004	

Special event vehicle:

Reg	Chassis	Body	Layout	Year	History
SNT925H	Bedford VAL70	Plaxton Panorama Elite II	C53F	1970	Sanders, Holt, 2000

Ancillary vehicle:

Reg	Chassis	Body	Layout	Year	History
D726VAM	Dodge Commando G13	Marshall Campaigner	B39F	1986	MOD (80KF63), 1996

Previous registrations:

K30ARJ	K714UTT	R30ARJ	R822JHJ, DMN18R
M30ARJ	M151KDD	WP52YZA	620UKM
N30ARJ	P446SWX, TIL6877	WYV820T	249D193

Web: www.andrew-james.co.uk; **Depot:** 6 Whitewalls, Easton Grey, Malmesbury

Carrying a specially selected Preston mark, to closely represent the chassis designation, the former MAN demonstrator is now in service with Andybus names. It is seen in Swindon. *Dave Heath*

APPLEGATES

E F Applegate, Heathfield Garage, Heathfield, Alkington, Berkeley, GL13 9PL

Reg	Chassis	Body	Seats	Year	History
YPL420T	Leyland National 10351B/1R (Cummins)		B41F	1978	Arriva Southern Counties, 2000
BFR958Y	Mercedes-Benz L307D	Cheshire Conversions	M12	1983	Grantley & Cole, Sharpness, 1998
PHT885Y	Setra S215HD	Setra	C49FT	1983	Ball, Felixstowe, 1994
OHV707Y	Leyland Titan TNLXB2RR	Leyland	B44/26D	1983	Sovereign, 1997
A610THV	Leyland Titan TNLXB2RR	Leyland	B44/26D	1984	London Central, 2001
A19EFA	Neoplan N722/3	Plaxton Paramount 4000 II	C53/18CT	1986	Durham Travel, Hetton-le-Hole, 1995
C312NRC	Volvo Citybus B10M-50	Northern Counties	B49/35D	1985	City of Nottingham, 2004
C314NRC	Volvo Citybus B10M-50	Northern Counties	B49/35D	1985	City of Nottingham, 2003
G340KWE	Neoplan Skyliner N122/3	Neoplan	C57/18CT	1990	Home James, Totton, 2000
A16EFA	LAG Panoramic G355Z	LAG	C49FT	1990	Streets Coachways, Chivenor, 2001
K590VBC	DAF SB3000KS601	Caetano Algarve II	C49FT	1992	Mannion, Gildersome, 2002
A18EFA	Scania K113TRB	Irizar Century 12.35	C51FT	1995	Silver Choice, East Kilbride, 1997
Y7JMJ	Neoplan Starliner N516/3	Neoplan	C44FT	2001	P W Jones, Burley Gate, 2004
BA02EFA	MAN 18.310	Noge Catalan 350	C49FT	2002	
FE52HFR	Irisbus Agora Line	Irisbus	N42F	2003	Irisbus demonstrator, 2003
AA52EFA	Mercedes-Benz O404	Hispano Vito	C49FT	2002	
BX53OMD	Toyota Coaster BB50R	Caetano Optimo V	C26F	2003	Toyota demonstrator, 2004

Previous registrations:
A16EFA	G485KBD, WJI3814		G340KWE	G340KWE, HJI8686
A18EFA	M26XSC		K590VBC	K590VBC, 800XPC
A19EFA	C220CWW, RIB4320		PHT885Y	CPA477Y, 6348ED

Web: www.applegates.co.uk

After a period out of the United Kingdom full-length bus market, Iveco now part of Irisbus, returned in 2003. Another constituent of Irisbus is Renault and the group is now the second largest manufacturer of coaches and buses in Europe. The full-length single-deck model is the Agora Line, and FE52HFR is seen here with Applegates. *Robert Edworthy*

ARLEEN

Arleen Coach Hire & Services Ltd, 14 Bath Road, Peasedown St John, Bath, BA2 8DH

Reg	Chassis	Body	Seating	Year	History
NYC398V	Bedford YMT	Duple Dominant II	C53F	1980	South West Cs, Wincanton, 2002
YDP396X	Bedford YNT	Plaxton Supreme VI	C44FT	1982	JVA, Midsomer Norton, 2004
BYC828B	Leyland Tiger TRCTL11/3R	Plaxton Supreme V	C53F	1982	Chivers, Stratton on Fosse, 1988
XBZ4253	Bova EL28-581	Duple Calypso	C53F	1986	Park's of Hamilton, 1986
RIL4022	DAF MB200DKFL600	Duple Laser 2	C53F	1985	Adams, Walsall, 1999
660FHU	DAF SB3000DHS585	Plaxton Paramount 3200 II	C53F	1986	Clapton, Haydock, 2000
RIL7643	Leyland Tiger TRCTL11/3LZ	Wadham Stringer Vanguard	BC68F	1985	MoD (37AC37), 1999
XBZ4254	Mercedes-Benz 811D	Optare StarRider	BC29F	1988	
RIL2102	DAF MB230LB615	Plaxton Paramount 3500 III	C53F	1988	City Tour, Langridge, 2002
XBZ4256	DAF SB2305DHS585	Van Hool Alizée	C51FT	1989	Cropper, Kirkstall, 2001
RIL7644	Dennis Javelin 12m	Plaxton Paramount 3200 III	C53F	1989	Martin, Kettering, 2000
CLZ8307	Mercedes-Benz O303-15R	Mercedes-Benz	C49FT	1990	
L948CTT	Ford Transit VE6	Ford	M14	1994	-, 2000
M311EEA	DAF 400	Walsall Motor Bodies	M16	1995	AMB, Bristol, 2001
152EKH	EOS E180Z	EOS 90	C49FT	1995	Peter Carol, Bristol, 2000
YBZ9558	EOS E180Z	EOS 90	C49FT	1995	Berkeley, Hemel Hempstead, 2001
P7ARL	Mercedes-Benz 814D	Autobus Nouvelle	C33F	1996	
S462VWB	Neoplan Cityliner N116/2	Neoplan	C48FT	1997	Cummer, Galway, 2001
V689OJW	Mercedes-Benz 410D	Excel	M16	1998	-, 2001
W506EOL	Mercedes-Benz 410D	Excel	M16	1999	Woods, Tillicoultry, 2001
YR02UNY	Neoplan Euroliner N316SHD	Neoplan	C49FT	2002	

Previous registrations:

152EKH	M801RCP		
660FHU	C310UFP, SIB7515	S462VWB	99G1436
BYC828B	SND711X	XBZ4253	A800JAY
CLZ8307	G884WHY	XBZ4254	E468YUM
RIL2102	E647KCX	XBZ4256	F256RJX
RIL4022	B915TKV	YBZ9558	M604RCP
RIL7644	G411VAY	YDP396X	TPN750X, 194WHT, YDP396X, PJI6084, JVA1

Web: www.arleen.co.uk

The latest coach for Arleen is YR02UNY which carries large vinyls proclaiming the coach model Euroliner in the livery. The integral Euroliner is the successor to the Transliner body which was supplied to the UK on MAN and Dennis chassis. The standard power unit is the Mercedes 11-litre with an option of a MAN unit.
Robert Edworthy

AXE VALLEY MINI TRAVEL

F M Searle, Bus Depot, 26 Harbour Road, Seaton, EX12 2NA

GBU8V	MCW Metrobus DR101/6	MCW	B43/30F	1979	Arriva The Shires, 2000
GYE557W	MCW Metrobus DR101/14	MCW	B43/28D	1981	Arriva Southern Counties, 2001
KYV685X	MCW Metrobus DR101/14	MCW	B43/28D	1981	Billingshurst Coaches, 2002
ANA155Y	MCW Metrobus DR102/23	MCW	B43/34F	1982	Meadowhall, Garston, 2003
B87WUV	Leyland Titan TNLXB/2RR	Leyland	B44/26D	1984	London Central, 2001
J622HMH	Optare MetroRider MR03	Optare	B28F	1992	First London, 2003
K164FYG	Optare MetroRider MR03	Optare	B29F	1992	Stagecoach Busways, 2002
K331RCN	Iveco TurboDaily 59-12	Dormobile Routemaker	B29F	1992	Mike Halford, Bridport, 2001
L810TFY	Optare MetroRider	Optare	B22F	1994	Glenvale, Liverpool, 2003

Axe Valley started as a minibus operation, though half the fleet is now double-deck. Pictured on Seaton sea-front is Metrobus ANA155Y, one of two in the fleet new to Greater Manchester. *Richard Godfrey*

BAKERS DOLPHIN

Bakers Coaches Ltd, 88 High Street, Weston-super-Mare, BS23 1HT

#	Reg	Chassis	Body	Type	Year	History
1	P725JYA	Volvo B10M-62	Van Hool Alizée HE	C44FT	1997	
2	R372XYD	Volvo B10M-62	Van Hool T9 Alizée	C46FT	1998	
3	R373XYD	Volvo B10M-62	Van Hool T9 Alizée	C46FT	1998	
4	Y227NYA	Volvo B10M-62	Van Hool T9 Alizée	C48FT	2001	
5	T761JYB	Volvo B10M-62	Van Hool T9 Alizée	C48FT	1999	
6	T762JYB	Volvo B10M-62	Van Hool T9 Alizée	C48FT	1999	
7	340MYA	Volvo B10M-60	Van Hool Alizée	C49FT	1990	Shearings, 1993
8	SIL6716	Volvo B10M-62	Jonckheere Deauville 45	C49FT	1994	Wallace Arnold, 1999
9	SIL6715	Volvo B10M-62	Jonckheere Deauville 45	C49FT	1994	Wallace Arnold, 1999
10	Y228NYA	Volvo B10M-62	Van Hool T9 Alizée	C48FT	2001	
11	7740KO	Volvo B10M-61	Van Hool Alizée	C49FT	1983	Rowe, Muirkirk, 1986
12	Y229NYA	Bova FHD 12.370	Bova Futura	C48FT	2001	
14	791WHT	Volvo B10M-62	Van Hool Alizée	C46FT	1996	
15	UJI3791	Volvo B10M-61	Van Hool Alizée	C49FT	1988	Bow Belle of Devon, 1997
16	UPV487	Volvo B10M-62	Van Hool Alizée	C46FT	1996	
17	WJI6880	Volvo B10M-60	Van Hool Alizée	C49FT	1992	Metroline (Brents), Watford, 1996
18	NIL4981	Volvo B10M-61	Van Hool Alizée	C49FT	1988	Edwards Bros, Tiers Cross, 1997
19	N308OGJ	Dennis Javelin 12m	Plaxton Première 320	C48FT	1996	Epsom Coaches, 2003
20	194WHT	Iveco EuroRider 395E.9.27	Beulas Stergo ε	C35F	1998	Waterhouse, Polegate, 2003
21	WJI2321	Volvo B10M-60	Van Hool Alizée	C53F	1989	Clarkes of London, 1998
22	958VKM	Volvo B10M-61	Van Hool Alizée	C53F	1989	Park's of Hamilton, 1994
23	NIL4982	Volvo B10M-61	Van Hool Alizée	C53F	1988	Clarkes of London, 1997
24	NIL5381	Volvo B10M-61	Van Hool Alizée	C53F	1988	Clarkes of London, 1997
25	NIL5382	Volvo B10M-61	Van Hool Alizée	C53F	1988	Clarkes of London, 1997
26	YXI2730	Volvo B10M-61	Van Hool Alizée	C53F	1989	Shearings, 1996
27	YXI2732	Volvo B10M-61	Van Hool Alizée	C53F	1989	Shearings, 1996
28	S102KJF	Iveco EuroRider 395E.9.27	Beulas Stergo ε	C35F	2003	
29	WJI6879	Volvo B10M-60	Van Hool Alizée	C53F	1989	Clarkes of London, 1998
30	M638KVU	Volvo B10M-62	Van Hool Alizée HE	C53F	1995	Shearings, 2003
31	NIL4983	Volvo B10M-61	Plaxton Paramount 3200 II	C53F	1986	Shearings, 1993
32	NIL4984	Volvo B10M-61	Plaxton Paramount 3200 II	C53F	1986	Whitehead, Conisbrough, 1993
33	NIL4985	Volvo B10M-61	Plaxton Paramount 3200 II	C53F	1986	East Surrey, Godstone, 1993

Typifying the Bakers Dolphin fleet is the Van Hool Alizée on Volvo chassis. Illustrating the type is 105, 315MWL, which was new to the fleet in 1996. Recent arrivals have included the new T9 model, six of which are now owned. *Robert Edworthy*

Two examples of the Iveco EuroRider joined the fleet in 2003 and these carry the Beulas Stergo ε body. Seating just thirty-five, 102, S102KJF, is used on executive duties and was pictured at Ascot. *Dave Heath*

34	NIL4986	Volvo B10M-61	Plaxton Paramount 3200 II	C53F	1986	Shearings, 1993
35	T708UOS	Volvo B10M-62	Plaxton Expressliner 2	C53F	1999	Park's of Hamilton, 2003
36	T721UOS	Volvo B10M-62	Plaxton Expressliner 2	C53F	1999	Park's of Hamilton, 2003
37	XIL8422	Volvo B10M-62	Plaxton Excalibur	C49FT	1999	Excelsior, Bournemouth, 2004
38	XIL8423	Volvo B10M-62	Plaxton Excalibur	C49FT	1999	Excelsior, Bournemouth, 2004
39	XIL8424	Volvo B10M-62	Plaxton Première 320	C49FT	1999	Excelsior, Bournemouth, 2004
40	XIL8425	Volvo B10M-62	Plaxton Première 320	C49FT	1999	Excelsior, Bournemouth, 2004
41	WJI3491	Leyland Tiger TRCTL11/3LZM	Plaxton Derwent	BC52F	1987	MoD (82KF26), 1998
42	WJI3492	Leyland Tiger TRCTL11/3LZM	Plaxton Derwent	BC52F	1987	MoD (82KF22), 1998
43	WJI3493	Leyland Tiger TRCTL11/3LZM	Plaxton Derwent	BC52F	1987	MoD (82KF19), 1998
44	WJI3490	Leyland Tiger TRCTL11/3LZM	Plaxton Derwent	BC52F	1987	MoD (82KF24), 1998
45	XJI6331	Leyland Tiger TRCTL11/3LZM	Plaxton Derwent	BC54F	1987	Beeline, Warminster, 1999
46	WJI3496	Leyland Tiger TRCTL11/3LZM	Plaxton Derwent	BC52F	1987	MoD (82KF23), 1998
48	XJI6330	Leyland Tiger TRCTL11/3LZM	Plaxton Derwent	BC52F	1987	MoD (87KF48), 1998
52	XJI5459	Leyland Tiger TRCTL11/3LZM	Plaxton Derwent	BC68F	1987	MoD (87KF36), 1998
53	XJI5458	Leyland Tiger TRCTL11/3LZM	Plaxton Derwent	BC68F	1987	MoD (82KF37), 1998
54	XJI6332	Leyland Tiger TRCTL11/3LZM	Plaxton Derwent	BC68F	1987	Turner, Bristol, 1999
55	XJI6333	Leyland Tiger TRCTL11/3LZM	Plaxton Derwent	BC68F	1987	MoD (87KF42), 1998
57	XJI5457	Leyland Tiger TRCTL11/3LZM	Plaxton Derwent	BC68F	1987	MoD (87KF48), 1998
58	WJI3494	Leyland Tiger TRCTL11/3LZM	Plaxton Derwent	BC68F	1987	MoD (82KF18), 1998
59	WJI3495	Leyland Tiger TRCTL11/3LZM	Plaxton Derwent	BC68F	1987	MoD (82KF31), 1998
60	WJI3497	Leyland Tiger TRCTL11/3LZM	Plaxton Derwent	BC68F	1987	MoD (82KF30), 1998
61	RJI5716	Volvo B10M-53	Van Hool Astral	C51/25CT	1985	
65	P726JYA	Volvo B12T	Van Hool Astrobel	C53/14CT	1997	
66	R632VYB	Volvo B12T	Van Hool Astrobel	C51/16CT	1998	
72	R778MFH	Mercedes-Benz Atego O1120L	Optare/Ferqui Solera	C35F	1998	
73	C432VGX	Mercedes-Benz L608D	Rootes	C19F	1985	Crystals, Dartford, 1990
75	IUI4360	Mercedes-Benz 609D	Olympus	C24F	2000	MCH, Uxbridge, 1997
81	YRY1Y	Bedford YMT	Plaxton Supreme IV	C53F	1982	King of the Road, Worthing, 1991
82	TAY888X	Bedford YMT	Plaxton Supreme IV	C53F	1981	King of the Road, Worthing, 1991
83	HHU146V	Bedford YMT	Plaxton Supreme IV	C53F	1980	Barnes, Puriton, 1991
86	KAU573V	Bedford YMT	Plaxton Supreme IV Express	C53F	1980	Barton, 1988
88	VBC984X	Bedford YNT	Plaxton Supreme IV	C53F	1982	Mountford, Manchester, 1992
89	NUI1602	Bedford YMT	Plaxton Supreme IV	C53F	1981	Capital, West Drayton, 1992

The three double-deck coaches in the Bakers Dolphin fleet are all Van Hool-bodied Volvos. Two are based on the B12 chassis, while 61, RJI5716, has an Astral body built on a B10M chassis fitted with a trailing third axle.
Dave Heath

93	LTY553X	Bedford YNT	Plaxton Supreme V Express	C53F	1982	Rochester & Marshall, 1990
102	XLH570	Volvo B10M-61	Van Hool Alizée	C57F	1989	Park's of Hamilton, 1994
104	T920LEU	Volvo B7R	Plaxton Prima	C57F	1999	
105	315MWL	Volvo B10M-62	Van Hool Alizée HE	C53F	1996	
108	VJY921V	Volvo B58-61	Plaxton Supreme IV	C57F	1980	Smith, Buntingford, 1991
110	T398VHO	Volvo B10M-62	Plaxton Première 350	C53F	1999	Excelsior, Bournemouth, 2004
115	FN02VCF	Iveco EuroRider 395E.9.27	Beulas El Mundo	C48FT	2002	Diamond Holidays, Morriston, 2005
116	FN02VCK	Iveco EuroRider 395E.9.27	Beulas El Mundo	C48FT	2002	Diamond Holidays, Morriston, 2005

Previous registrations:

194WHT	S101KJF	SIL6716	L956NWW
315MWL	N203DYB	T398VHO	A10EXC
340MYA	C342GSD, RJI5716	T708UOS	LSK473
791WHT	N804DYB	T721UOS	LSK824
958VKM	F758ENE	UJI3791	E634BFJ
7740KO	USD224Y	UPV487	N205DYB
HHU146V	DKG271V, 315MWL	VJY921V	VJY921V, 958VKM
IUI4360	N698SPK	WJI2321	F672TFH
NIL4981	E622UNE	WJI6879	F552TMH
NIL4982	E220JJF	WJI6880	J461HDS, KSK501, J690LGE
NIL4983	C345DND	XIL8422	A6EXC, T442VHO
NIL4984	C347DND	XIL8423	A3EXC, T451VHO
NIL4985	C349DND	XIL8424	A14EXC, T443VHO
NIL4986	C355DND	XIL8425	A17EXC, T445VHO
NIL5381	E222LBC	XJI6331	03KJ22, G514XWS
NIL5382	E224LBC	XJI6332	82KF28, D76JHY
NUI1602	SLH42W	XLH570	F753ENE, LSK510, F276MGB
RJI5716	G868RNC, 340MYA	YXI2730	F730ENE
SIL6715	L962NWW	YXI2732	F732ENE

Livery: Blue, white, yellow and green
Depots: Locking Road, Weston; Esplanade, Weston; Cattle Market, Bath Road, Bridgwater; Outstation: Nailsea
Web: www.bakersdolphin.com

BARNES

Barnes Coaches Ltd, 15 The Square, Aldbourne, Marlborough, SN8 2DU

VIB3903	Volvo B10M-60	Plaxton Paramount 3200 III	C57F	1989	Excelsior, Bournemouth, 1994
JIB1451	Volvo B10M-60	Plaxton Paramount 3200 III	C57F	1989	Excelsior, Bournemouth, 1995
UIB9492	Volvo B10M-60	Jonckheere Deauville	C51F	1990	
RIB7874	Volvo B10M-60	Jonckheere Deauville	C51F	1991	
WIB1444	Bova FHD12-290	Bova Futura	C55F	1991	
NBZ1360	Bova FHD12-290	Bova Futura	C51F	1992	
MIL6804	Volvo B10M-62	Jonckheere Deauville 45	C49FT	1994	Worthing Coaches, 1999
SIB7515	DAF DE33WSSB3000	Berkhof Excellence 2000	C51F	1995	
LIL9168	Volvo B10M-62	Berkhof Excellence 2000	C49FT	1996	
NIB5595	Volvo B10M-62	Van Hool Alizée HE	C48FT	1997	
TIB9471	Volvo B10M-61	Berkhof Axial 50	C49FT	1998	
OJI4672	Volvo B10M-62	Van Hool T9 Alizée	C49FT	1998	
MIB6310	Volvo B10M-62	Van Hool T9 Alizée	C49FT	1998	
XIB3421	Volvo B10M-62	Van Hool T9 Alizée	C49FT	1999	
HIB7178	Bova FHD12-370	Bova Futura	C49FT	2000	
LIB3903	Bova FHD12-370	Bova Futura	C49FT	2000	
Y221NYA	Bova FHD12-370	Bova Futura	C49FT	2001	
WJ02VRV	Bova FHD12-370	Bova Futura	C49FT	2002	
WJ02KDO	Volvo B10M-62	Van Hool T9 Alizée	C49FT	2002	
WJ02VRO	Volvo B10M-62	Van Hool T9 Alizée	C49FT	2002	
WJ52MTO	Volvo B12M	Van Hool T9 Alizée	C49FT	2002	
WA03HPZ	Volvo B12M	Van Hool T9 Alizée	C49FT	2003	
WA04EWL	Volvo B12M	Van Hool T9 Alizée	C49FT	2004	
WA04EWV	VDL Bova FHD14-430	VDL Bova Futura	C63F	2004	
WA54KTT	VDL Bova FHD14-430	VDL Bova Futura	C63F	2005	

Special event vehicle:

BJV590	Bedford OB	Duple Vista	C24F	1950	Addison, Callander, 2000

Previous registrations:

HIB7178	W151RYB		
JIB1451	F454WFX	RIB7874	J530JNH
LIB3903	W557RYC	RIL1578	K812HUM
LIL9168	P717EJM	SIB7515	M86SRD
MIB6310	S751XYA	TIB9471	R995FBL
MIL6804	L742YGE	UIB9492	H41VNH
NBZ1360	J550BWE	VIB3903	F452WFX
NIB5595	P310PYA	WIB1444	H622FUT
OJI4672	R377XYD	XIB3421	T522PYD

Web: www.barnescoaches.co.uk

With the foundation of 'Metaalindustrie en Constructiewerkplaats P. van der Leegte' in 1953, the basis was laid for what was later to become the VDL Groep. Towards the end of 2003 Bova joined the Group which also includes VDL Jonckheere and VDL Bus, the successor to DAF Bus. Representing Barnes is 14-metre Futura WA04EWV.
Dave Heath

BARRY'S

Barry's Coaches Ltd, 9 Cambridge Road, Granby Ind Est, Weymouth, DT4 9TJ

Reg	Chassis	Body	Layout	Year	History
B209REL	Leyland Tiger TRCTL11/3RH	Duple Laser 2	C51F	1984	Wilts & Dorset, 2004
B477UNB	Volvo B10M-61	Van Hool Alizée	C53F	1985	Wilts & Dorset, 2004
362KHT	Leyland Tiger TRCTL11/3R	Plaxton Paramount 3200 II	C53F	1985	Wilts & Dorset, 2003
LAZ2370	Leyland Tiger TRCTL11/3RZ	Plaxton Paramount 3200 III	C53F	1987	Dorset CC, 2000
TIL2506	Volvo B9M	Plaxton Paramount 3200 III	C53F	1987	Wilts & Dorset, 2003
4708RU	Dennis Javelin 12m	Plaxton Paramount 3200 III	C51FT	1989	Price, Halesowen, 2000
YSV645	Dennis Javelin 8.5m	Plaxton Paramount 3200 III	C35F	1989	Dewar, Falkirk, 1997
LUI1519	Mercedes-Benz 811D	Optare StarRider	BC29F	1989	BAA Gatwick, 2001
G38KAK	Mercedes-Benz 609D	Whittaker	BC19F	1989	Bluebird, Weymouth, 2002
G517MYD	Dennis Javelin 12m	Caetano Algarve	C53F	1989	Redwood, Hemyock, 2002
G501XOR	Leyland Tiger TRCTL11/3ARZM	Plaxton Paramount 3200	C53F	1989	Coach Services, Thetford, 2001
VJI9417	LAG G355Z	LAG Panoramic	C49FT	1989	Turners, Wickham St Paul, 2004
F441DUG	Volvo B10M-60	Plaxton Paramount 3200 III	C53F	1989	Ousey, Bryanston, 2004
PJI7002	Volvo B10M-60	Plaxton Paramount 3200 III	C57F	1990	Wilts & Dorset, 2004
H672ATN	Toyota Coaster HB31R	Caetano Optimo	C21F	1990	Safeguard, Guildford, 2001
LUI5812	Dennis Javelin 12m	Plaxton Paramount 3200	C51F	1990	Whittle, Kidderminster, 2001
H655DKO	Ford Transit VE6	Dormobile	B16F	1990	Devon CC, 1998
SBZ8075	Volvo B10M-60	Van Hool Alizée	C49FT	1991	Associated, Stansted, 2002
K977RLW	Ford Transit VE6	Advanced	M14	1993	British Airways, Heathrow, 1998
K809WPF	Talbot Pulman	TBP	B10F	1993	Surrey CC, 1998
LUI4653	Volvo B10M-60	Van Hool Alizée	C49FT	1993	Chambers, Bures, 2001
M321VET	Scania K113CRB	Van Hool Alizée HE	C49FT	1995	Dunn-Line, Nottingham, 2003
OIL5267	Scania K113CRB	Van Hool Alizée HE	C49FT	1995	Dunn-Line, Nottingham, 2003
N512MWV	Iveco Daily 49-10	Bedwas	B24FL	1996	Hampshire CC, 2004
N860XMO	Dennis Javelin 12m	Berkhof Excellence 1000	C53F	1996	Limebourne, Battersea, 1999
R500GSM	MAN 11.220	Berkhof Excellence 1000	C33FT	1997	APT Coaches, Rayleigh, 2004
LEN616	Scania L94IB	Irizar Century 12.35	C49FT	1998	Bus Eireann, 2002
YHA320	Scania L94IB	Irizar Century 12.35	C49FT	1998	Bus Eireann, 2001
298HPK	Scania L94IB	Irizar Century 12.35	C49FT	1998	Bus Eireann, 2004

Pictured in Weymouth, Barry's Optare StarRider LUI1519 illustrates the narrow-door version of the StarRider normally fitted with high-back seating. *Tony Wilson*

471BET	Scania K113TRB		Irizar Century 12.37	C53F	1998	Acton Holidays, 2004
S903NPO	LDV Convoy		LDV	M16	1999	-, 2004

Previous registrations:

298HPK	S348SET, 99D10575		LUI5812	G111JNP, URH341, G111JNP
362KHT	B909SPR, XAM152, B909SPR		OIL5267	M325VET
471BET	P103GHE		PJI7002	G507EFX, A8EXC, G391GJT
4708RU	F797GFD, XXI8950, F797GFD		R500GSM	R500GSM, H19AND
G517MYD	G517MYD, USV562		SBZ8075	H166DVM
LAZ2370	D153HML		TIL2506	E700HKV
LEN616	R471YDT		VJI9417	G953GRP, IIL1953
LUI1519	G590SNJ		YHA320	R474YDT, 98D41101
LUI4653	K103VJT, A4XEL, K103VJT		YSV645	F902BLS

K W BEARD LTD

K W Beard Ltd, Valley Road, Cinderford, GL14 2PD

WDD17X	Bedford YNT	Plaxton Supreme VI Express	C53F	1982	
RIL9864	Leyland Tiger TRCTL11/3RZ	Plaxton Paramount 3500 II	C53F	1984	Shearings, 1989
RIL9865	DAF MB230DKVL615	Duple 340	C49FT	1986	Yorkshire European, 1997
CHZ4714	Volvo B10M-61	Plaxton Paramount 3200 III	C53F	1987	Ashton, St Helens, 1995
F167UDG	Leyland Tiger TRCTL11/3RZ	Plaxton Paramount 3200 III	C53F	1989	
BHZ8804	Bova FHD12-290	Bova Futura	C55F	1990	Dawlish Coaches, 2002
KLZ1148	DAF SB3000DKV601	Van Hool Alizeé DH	C51FT	1992	Moxon's, Oldcotes, 2001
KLZ1149	Volvo B10M-60	Jonckheere Deauville	C51FT	1992	Elcock Reisen, Telford, 2000
R5WGT	Bova FHD12-340	Bova Futura	C51FT	1998	Thomas-Rhondda, 2003
X564CUY	Mercedes-Benz Vario 0814	Onyx	C24F	2000	

Previous registrations:

BHZ8804	G897NYC		KLZ1149	K321AUX
CHZ4714	E318UUB		RIL9864	B502UNB
KLZ1148	J813KHD, 5711MT, J813KHD		RIL9865	C645LVH, A2YET, C604FWW

From the fleet of K W Beard is Bova Futura R5WGT. It is one of two currently operated. *Robert Edworthy*

BEAUMONT TRAVEL

Beaumont Travel Ltd, City Plaza, Market Parade, Gloucester, GL1 1RL

RUA458W	Bristol VRT/SL3/6LXB	Eastern Coach Works	B43/31F	1981	Bennetts, Gloucester, 2004
PRA604X	Leyland Olympian ONLXB/1R	Eastern Coach Works	B45/32F	1981	Stagecoach, 2004
CLV85X	Leyland Olympian ONLXB/2R	East Lancs	B51/37F	1982	Warrington, 2004
C637LFT	Leyland Olympian ONLXB/1R	Alexander RH	B45/31F	1985	Stagecoach, 2004
E300BWL	Mercedes-Benz 709D	Reeve Burgess Beaver	BC25F	1988	Swanbrook, Cheltenham, 2001
E303BWL	Mercedes-Benz 709D	Reeve Burgess Beaver	BC25F	1988	Swanbrook, Cheltenham, 2001
G921WGS	Mercedes-Benz 709D	Reeve Burgess Beaver	B23F	1989	Yorkshire Coastliner, 2000
G170FJC	Mercedes-Benz 709D	Reeve Burgess Beaver	BC25F	1989	Tyrer, Trawden, 2002
G176FJC	Mercedes-Benz 709D	Reeve Burgess Beaver	BC25F	1989	Tyrer, Trawden, 2002
J173CNU	Mercedes-Benz 709D	Reeve Burgess Beaver	B25F	1991	City of Nottingham, 2002
J210KTT	Mercedes-Benz 709D	Reeve Burgess Beaver	B25F	1991	First, 2004
J348GKH	Dennis Dart 9.8m	Plaxton Pointer	B40F	1991	Travel Dundee, 2001
L376JBD	Mercedes-Benz 709D	Alexander Sprint	B25F	1993	Stagecoach, 2005
L378JBD	Mercedes-Benz 709D	Alexander Sprint	B25F	1993	Stagecoach, 2005
L379JBD	Mercedes-Benz 709D	Alexander Sprint	B25F	1993	Stagecoach, 2005
M198TKJ	Ford Transit VE6	Devon Conversions	M16	1995	Kent CC, 2002
M960TKL	Ford Transit VE6	Devon Conversions	M16	1995	Kent CC, 2002
P525UDG	Ford Transit VE6	Minibus Options	M14	1996	
R54OCK	Dennis Dart SLF 10m	East Lancs Spryte	N35F	1998	A2B, Prenton, 2001
V181FVU	Mercedes-Benz Vario O814	Onyx	BC24F	1999	
X96AHU	Renault Master	Rohill	B16F	2001	Swanbrook, Cheltenham, 2003
Y882HAE	Renault Master	Rohill	B16F	2001	Swanbrook, Cheltenham, 2003
Y883HAE	Renault Master	Rohill	B16F	2001	Swanbrook, Cheltenham, 2003
Y683LDF	Ford Transit	Ford	M7	2001	
VX51RDO	Dennis Dart SLF 9.8m	Alexander ALX200	N33F	2001	Mistral, 2002
YU04XJK	Mercedes-Benz Vario O814	Plaxton Beaver 2	B29F	2004	
YN54LKC	Optare Alero AL03	Optare	N14F	2004	
YN54LKV	Optare Alero AL03	Optare	N14F	2004	

Depot: Quedgeley Industrial Estate, Bristol Road, Gloucester.
Web: www.beaumont-travel.com

Beaumont Travel operates a low-floor Dennis Dart. This vehicle, VX51RDO, carries Alexander ALX200 bodywork and is shown here operating in Cirencester while heading for Moreton-in-Marsh. *Mark Bailey*

BEELINE

R&R Coaches Ltd, Bishopstrow Road, Warminster, BA12 9HQ

ANZ3607	Volvo B10M-61	Plaxton Paramount 3500 II	C53F	1986	Cropley, Fosdyke, 2000
NIL9886	Volvo B10M-61	Plaxton Paramount 3500 II	C53F	1986	Eastbourne, 1997
XIB1907	Volvo B10M-56	Plaxton Paramount 3200 II	C53F	1986	Smith's, Tring, 1998
VIL6840	Volvo B10M-56	Plaxton Paramount 3200 II	C53F	1987	-, 2002
832JYA	Volvo B10M-61	Plaxton Paramount 3500 II	C50FT	1987	Burtons, Haverhill, 2000
RIL1203	Volvo B10M-61	Plaxton Paramount 3500 III	C50FT	1987	Bluebird, Weymouth, 2000
BNZ4922	Volvo B10M-61	Plaxton Paramount 3500 III	C50FT	1987	Burtons, Haverhill, 2000
YAZ8922	Volvo B10M-61	Plaxton Paramount 3500 III	C50FT	1987	AD Coaches, Witheridge, 1997
RJI8602	Volvo B10M-61	Plaxton Paramount 3500 III	C53FT	1988	Allison's Coaches, Dunfermline, 1997
E323UUB	Volvo B10M-61	Plaxton Paramount 3500 III	C53F	1988	James Bevan, Lydney, 2003
SCZ9766	Dennis Javelin 8.5m	Duple 320	C35F	1988	John Millner, Combe Down, 2005
JLZ3043	Volvo B10M-61	Plaxton Paramount 3500 III	C53F	1989	Burtons, Haverhill, 2003
DNZ5043	Volvo B10M-60	Plaxton Première 350	C50F	1992	Safeguard, Guildford, 2003
L694JEC	Mercedes-Benz 609D	Concept	C24F	1993	Perruzza & Daughters, Kendal, 1998
N270KAM	Mercedes-Benz 811D	Plaxton Beaver	B33F	1995	
N271KAM	Mercedes-Benz 811D	Plaxton Beaver	B33F	1995	
N272KAM	Mercedes-Benz 811D	Plaxton Beaver	B33F	1995	
N273KAM	Mercedes-Benz 811D	Plaxton Beaver	B33F	1995	
N274KAM	Mercedes-Benz 811D	Plaxton Beaver	B33F	1995	
XCZ4146	Mercedes-Benz 811D	Plaxton Beaver	B33F	1995	
XCZ4147	Mercedes-Benz 814D	Plaxton Beaver	B33F	1995	
N123DNV	Mercedes-Benz 711D	Plaxton Beaver	C25F	1995	Country Lion, Northampton, 1998
XCZ4148	Mercedes-Benz 814D	Autobus Classique Nouvelle	C33F	1995	Maynes, Buckie, 1997
XCZ4149	Mercedes-Benz 814D	Autobus Classique Nouvelle	C33F	1996	Costello, Dundee, 1997

Beeline's coach fleet is dominated by Volvo B10Ms with Plaxton Paramount bodies. The majority of these are the higher 3500 of which 832JYA is one. *Robert Edworthy*

In 1995 Beeline added several Mercedes-Benz 811minibuses to the fleet. These carry Plaxton Beaver bodies and the delivery is represented by N276KAM seen here on school duties. *Richard Godfrey*

YSV739	Mercedes-Benz 711D	Plaxton Beaver	BC25F	1996	Taylor, Tintinhull, 2001	
P691LKL	LDV Convoy	Jaycas	M16	1997	Jaycrest, Sittingbourne, 2003	
P689VHU	LDV Convoy	LDV	M16	1997		
R767HOY	LDV Convoy	LDV	M16	1997		
V116GWP	Mercedes-Benz Vario 0814	Onyx	BC24F	1999		
X46CNY	Volvo B10M-62	Plaxton Paragon Expressliner	C49FT	2000	Bebb, Llantwit Fardre, 2004	
X541HJM	LDV Convoy	LDV	M16	2000	Hertz, 2003	
RK51KNV	LDV Convoy	LDV	M16	2001	Hertz, 2004	

Previous registrations:

832JYA	D68VJC	RJI8602	E828EUT
6220WY	-	SCZ9766	E149AGG, 7178KP, E149AGG
ANZ3607	B505CGP	VIL6840	D999FYL
BNZ4922	D287UDM, VLT229, VLT149, D328UTU	XCZ4147	N276KAM
DNZ5043	J745CWT, DSK558, 247FCG	XCZ4148	N460KMW
JLZ3043	F102CCL	XCZ4149	N604ADC
N123DNV	A19CLN, L10NKK	XIB1907	C24KBH
NIL9886	C580KNO	YAZ8922	D202LWX, WVT818, D326GCD
RIL1203	E312OMG	YSV739	N806CRJ

BENNETTS

P, R A, & D Bennett and P A Lane, Eastern Avenue, Gloucester, GL4 4LP

SJR617Y	Leyland Olympian ONLXB/1R	Eastern Coach Works	B43/32F	1983	Go Tyneside, 2000
OFS701Y	Leyland Olympian ONTL11/2R	Eastern Coach Works	B50/31D	1983	Lothian Buses, 2000
OFS702Y	Leyland Olympian ONTL11/2R	Eastern Coach Works	B50/31D	1983	Lothian Buses, 2000
B7BEN	Leyland Olympian ONLXB/1R	Eastern Coach Works	B45/32F	1985	Arriva North East, 2000
G293CLE	DAF SB220LC590	Hispano	B66F	1990	Capital, West Drayton, 1999

The South West Bus Handbook

Seen at Gloucester cattle market is Bennetts X83AAK, a low-floor example of the Ikarus Polaris single-deck body that was introduced to the UK by MAN as an alternative to the Alexander ALX300, then the only option for the chassis. Though it was initially used by Stagecoach as seed vehicle, further orders for the group continued to be placed with Alexanders. The remaining British examples of this Ikarus product have all been bought by Bennetts. *Richard Godfrey*

	H203LOM	Scania N113CRB	Alexander RH	B45/31F	1990	Travel West Midlands, 2002
	H207LOM	Scania N113CRB	Alexander RH	B45/31F	1990	Travel West Midlands, 2002
	J21GCX	DAF SB2305DHS585	Plaxton Paramount 3200 III	C53F	1991	Yorkshire European, Harrogate, 1992
	K712RNR	DAF SB2700HDS585	Caetano Algarve II	C53F	1993	Perrett, Shipton Oliffe, 2000
	K424WUT	DAF SB2700HDS585	Caetano Algarve II	C53F	1993	Paul S Winson, Loughborough, 1997
	K589VBC	DAF SB3000DKS601	Caetano Algarve II	C53F	1993	Bailey, Newbury, 2004
	L519EHD	DAF SB2700HDS585	Van Hool Alizée	C53F	1994	Enfield Transport, Co. Meath, 1998
	L463RDN	DAF SB2700HS585	Van Hool Alizée	C51F	1994	Deros, Killarney, 1995
	M809RCP	DAF SB3000WS601	Van Hool Alizée HE	C53F	1995	Redwood, Hemyock, 1996
	R179GNR	DAF DE33WSSB300	Van Hool T9 Alizée	C53F	1998	North Kent Express, 2003
	T419PDG	DAF DE02GSSB220	Ikarus CitiBus	N43F	1999	
14	X83AAK	MAN 11.220	Ikarus Polaris	B42F	2000	MAN demonstrator, 2001
	Y200BCC	Neoplan Euroliner N316SHD	Neoplan	C49FT	2001	
	Y300BCC	Neoplan Euroliner N316SHD	Neoplan	C49FT	2001	
	Y400BCC	Neoplan Euroliner N316SHD	Neoplan	C49FT	2001	
	YR02UMU	Neoplan Euroliner N316SHD	Neoplan	C49FT	2002	
	YN03AXS	Neoplan Euroliner N316SHD	Neoplan	C49FT	2003	
	VN03XXG	MAN 14.220	Ikarus Polaris	B42F	2003	MAN demonstrator, 2004
10	VO03DZD	MAN 14.220	Ikarus Polaris	B42F	2003	
11	VO03DZC	MAN 14.220	Ikarus Polaris	B42F	2003	
12	VO03DZE	MAN 14.220	Ikarus Polaris	B42F	2003	
	YK04KWA	Optare Solo M1020	Optare	N37F	2004	
	YK04KWB	Optare Solo M1020	Optare	N37F	2004	
	YK04KWC	Optare Solo M1020	Optare	N37F	2004	
	YK04KWD	Optare Solo M1020	Optare	N37F	2004	
	BX54EBD	Mercedes-Benz Citaro O530	Mercedes-Benz	N42F	2004	
	BX54EBF	Mercedes-Benz Citaro O530	Mercedes-Benz	N42F	2004	
	BX54EBG	Mercedes-Benz Citaro O530	Mercedes-Benz	N42F	2004	

Previous registrations:
B7BEN	B256RAJ	L519EHD	L519EHD, 94MH306
G293CLE	TIB393Z(Singapore)	L463RDN	94KY1609
K424WUT	K10PSW		

Special livery: Blue (Park & Ride) YK04KWA-D, BX54EBD/F/G.

BERKELEY

Berkeley Coach & Travel Ltd, Ham Lane, Paulton, Bristol, BS39 7PL

C110DWR	Volvo B10M-61	Plaxton Paramount 3500	C53F	1986	Rapsons, Inverness, 1999
C112DWR	Volvo B10M-61	Plaxton Paramount 3500	C53F	1986	Rapsons, Inverness, 1999
D35ALR	Bedford YMP	Plaxton Paramount 3200 III	C41F	1986	Anning, Peterchurch, 2004
E42ODE	Volvo B10M-61	Plaxton Paramount 3500 III	C53F	1988	Jones, Login, 1994
LIB6445	Volvo B10M-60	Duple 340	C57F	1989	Skills, Nottingham, 1996
YJI4610	Volvo B10M-60	Plaxton Paramount 3200 III	C57F	1990	Hodson, Gisburn, 2003
L2POW	Volvo B10M-60	Van Hool Alizée	C53F	1994	
P2POW	Volvo B10M-62	Plaxton Excalibur	C49FT	1997	
R2POW	Volvo B10M-62	Plaxton Excalibur	C53F	1998	
R4POW	Volvo B10M-62	Plaxton Excalibur	C49FT	1998	
R201WYD	Volvo B9M	Van Hool Alizée HE	C28FT	1998	Armchair, Brentford, 2004
T4POW	Volvo B10M-62	Plaxton Excalibur	C53F	1999	
W107RTC	Volvo B10M-62	Plaxton Panther	C49FT	2000	
WR02RVX	Volvo B10M-62	Plaxton Panther	C49FT	2002	

Previous registrations:
C110DWR	C110DWR, ESK930	LIB6445	F28LTO
C112DWR	C112DWR, ESK932	YJI4610	G801XLO
E42ODE	E327TUB, 834TDE		

The newest coach in Berkeley livery is Plaxton Panther-bodied Volvo B10M, WR02RVX. The vehicle is shown at its Paulton base with sister vehicle, W107RTC, parked alongside. *Robert Edworthy*

BERRYS

Berry's Coaches (Taunton) Ltd, Cornishway West, New Wellington Road, Taunton, TA1 5NA

Reg	Chassis	Body	Seating	Year	History
B910SPR	Volvo B10M-61	Plaxton Paramount 3200 II	C53F	1985	Excelsior, Bournemouth, 1987
C219FMF	Volvo B9M	Plaxton Paramount 3200 II	C41F	1986	Richmond, Barley, 2002
SIB9313	Volvo B10M-61	Jonckheere Jubilee P599	C51FT	1986	
D260HFX	Volvo B10M-61	Plaxton Paramount 3200 III	C53F	1987	Excelsior, Bournemouth, 1989
PIB4019	Volvo B10M-61	Van Hool Alizée	C53FT	1987	
E131KGM	Volvo B9M	Plaxton Paramount 3200 III	C41F	1987	Gerry, Plymouth, 2001
SIB8398	Volvo B10M-61	Van Hool Alizée	C55F	1988	Avalon Coaches, Glastonbury, 1995
PIB2470	Volvo B10M-53	Van Hool Astral	C51/13DT	1988	
PIB3360	Volvo B10M-61	Van Hool Alizée	C53F	1988	
F476WFX	Volvo B10M-60	Plaxton Paramount 3200 III	C53F	1989	Excelsior, Bournemouth, 1989
SIB9309	Volvo B10M-60	Van Hool Alizée	C49FT	1989	
G46RGG	Volvo B9M	Plaxton Paramount 3200 III	C41F	1990	Holmeswood Coaches, 2003
J819EYC	Volvo B10M-60	Jonckheere Deauville	C51FT	1992	
L238OYC	Volvo B10M-60	Van Hool Alizée HE	C53F	1993	
M201TYB	Volvo B12(T)	Van Hool Astrobel	C57/14CT	1994	
N320BYA	Volvo B12(T)	Van Hool Astrobel	C57/14CT	1995	
N758CYA	Volvo B10M-62	Van Hool Alizée HE	C49FT	1996	
N199DYB	Volvo B10M-62	Van Hool Alizée HE	C49FT	1996	
P727JYA	Volvo B12(T)	Van Hool Astrobel	C57/14CT	1997	
R380XYD	Volvo B12(T)	Van Hool Astrobel	C57/14CT	1998	
R199WYD	Volvo B10M-62	Van Hool T9 Alizée	C49FT	1998	
R202WYD	Volvo B10M-62	Van Hool T9 Alizée	C49FT	1998	
T766JYB	Volvo B10M-62	Van Hool T9 Alizée	C49FT	1999	
W161RYB	Volvo B10M-62	Van Hool T9 Alizée	C49FT	2000	
YN51WGX	Volvo B12M	Plaxton Panther	C49FT	2001	
WA03EYD	Volvo B12M	Van Hool T9 Alizée	C49FT	2003	
WA04MHF	Volvo B12M	Van Hool T9 Alizée	C49FT	2004	

Previous registrations:

C219FMF	C219FMF, 851FYD	PIB4019	D547OYD
E131KGM	WSV478	PIB5767	JYC794Y
G46RGG	G46RGG, SIA327	SIB8398	E272XYA
PIB2470	E22XYD	SIB9309	F121GYB
PIB3360	E63XYC	SIB9313	C785HYA

Web: www.berrycoaches.co.uk

Another example of the Van Hool Astral is Berrys' PIB2470. Based on the Volvo B10M chassis, the model boasts a lower saloon to the rear of the third axle and thus features two staircases. Other Van Hool double-decks in the fleet are the Astrobel which is built on the rear-engined Volvo B12 and in contrast has a lower deck at the front.
Robert Edworthy

24

BLUEBIRD

Bluebird Coaches (Weymouth) Ltd, 83 The Esplanade, Weymouth, DT4 7AA

Reg	Chassis	Body	Type	Year	History
URU650X	Volvo B10M-56	Plaxton Supreme V	C53F	1982	Westbus, Hounslow, 2002
A693TPO	Volvo B10M-56	Plaxton Paramount 3200 Express	C53F	1984	Tillingbourne, Cranleigh, 2000
UCT838	Volvo B10M-61	Van Hool Alizée	C53F	1984	Black Prince, Morley, 1991
654JHU	Volvo B10M-61	Van Hool Alizée	C53F	1985	Tellings-Golden Miller, Byfleet, 1988
C680KDS	Volvo B10M-61	Caetano Algarve	C53F	1986	AERE, Winfrith, 1993
YJI8595	Volvo B10M-61	Plaxton Paramount 3200 III	C53F	1988	Sovereign, 1995
A14FRX	Volvo B10M-62	Plaxton Première 320	C53F	1994	Frames Rickards, London, 2001
A15FRX	Volvo B10M-62	Plaxton Première 320	C53F	1994	Frames Rickards, London, 2001
YJI8594	Volvo B10M-62	Plaxton Première 350	C49FT	1994	
YJI8596	Volvo B10M-62	Plaxton Première 350	C49FT	1994	
M685MRP	Volvo B10M-62	Plaxton Première 350	C53F	1994	Amport & District, Thruxton, 2002
M590GRY	Toyota Coaster HZB50R	Caetano Optimo IV	C21F	1994	Venture, Harrow, 2002
M740RCP	DAF DE33WSSB3000	Van Hool Alizée HE	C55F	1995	North Kent Express, 2001
M741RCP	DAF DE33WSSB3000	Van Hool Alizée HE	C55F	1995	North Kent Express, 2001
P4BBC	Volvo B10M-62	Van Hool Alizée HE	C49FT	1997	
S659ETT	LDV Convoy	G&M	M16	1998	
T7BBC	Bova FHD 12.340	Bova Futura	C49FT	1999	
W2BBC	MAN 18.350	Neoplan Transliner	C49FT	2000	
BC51BBC	Neoplan Euroliner N316SHD	Neoplan	C49FT	2002	
YN03AWY	Neoplan Euroliner N316SHD	Neoplan	C49FT	2003	Bowers, Chapel-en-le-Frith, 2004
BC04BBC	VDL Bova FHD13-340	VDL Bova Futura	C53FT	2004	

Previous registrations:
654JHU	C335FSU			
A14FRX	M428WAK		UCT838	A191MNE
A15FRX	M429WAK		YJI8594	L947CRU
A693TPO	A489YGL, TBC658, A475JPB, HFB89, MIL4687		YJI8595	E310OMG
M685MRP	M685MRP, A16CLN		YJI8596	L948CRU

Depot: Chickerell Road, Chickerell, Weymouth.   **Web:** www.bluebirdcoaches.com

The Neoplan Transliner was produced on Dennis and MAN chassis. Bluebird's W2BBC is one of the latter seen during a visit to London. The Dorset to London daily express service formerly provided by Bere Regis and District, and then for a time by First, is now operated by Bluebird. *Dave Heath*

BLUE IRIS

Tarhum Limited, 25 Clevedon Road, Nailsea, Bristol, BS19 1EH

Reg	Chassis	Body	Seating	Year	Previous owner
L18LUE	Toyota Coaster HZB50R	Caetano Optimo IV	C21F	1994	Haldane, Glasgow, 2001
M18LUE	Scania K113TRB	Irizar Century 12.37	C51FT	1995	Capital, West Drayton, 1999
N18LUE	Toyota Coaster HZB50R	Caetano Optimo IV	C18F	1995	
N895VEG	Mercedes-Benz 811D	Marshall C	B33F	1996	Turner, Bristol, 2003
N88LUE	Volvo B10M-62	Plaxton Excalibur	C49FT	1996	Tillingbourne, Cranleigh, 2001
R18LUE	Toyota Coaster HZB50R	Caetano Optimo IV	C18F	1997	
R872SDT	Scania L94IB	Irizar Century 12.35	C53F	1998	Bus Eireann, 2001
S344SET	Scania L94IB	Irizar Century 12.35	C53F	1998	Bus Eireann, 2001
T568SUF	Toyota Coaster BB50R	Caetano Optimo V	C22F	1998	Toyota demonstrator, 2001
T18LUE	Toyota Coaster BB50R	Caetano Optimo V	C24F	1999	
V28LUE	Scania L94IB	Van Hool T9 Alizée	C49FT	2000	Chambers, Bures, 2002
V888LUE	Scania L94IB	Van Hool T9 Alizée	C49FT	2000	Chambers, Bures, 2002
SN53RXC	Scania K114IB4	Irizar Century 12.35	C49FT	2003	DWA, Gorebridge, 2005
SN53RXD	Scania K114IB4	Irizar Century 12.35	C49FT	2003	DWA, Gorebridge, 2005
WX54PEO	Toyota Coaster BB50R	Caetano Optimo V	C22F	2004	

Special event vehicle:

Reg	Chassis	Body	Seating	Year	Previous owner
708RHN	Neoplan Cityliner N216H	Neoplan	C49FT	1982	Kinsman, Bodmin, 1998

Previous registrations:

708RHU	SFV667X	S344SET	98D54644(EI)
L18LUE	M898CNS	SN53RXC	B14DWA
N88LUE	A6XEL, N984THO, MIL8584	SN53RXD	B15DWA
P88LUE	-	V28LUE	V5CCH, CNZ3834
R872SDT	98D10285(EI)	V888LUE	V4CCH, CNZ3831

Web: http://www.blueiris.co.uk

A simple blue iris motif is applied to Van Hool Alizée V28LUE. The coach is one of two Scania L94s in the fleet to feature this body, both examples arriving during 2002. *Robert Edworthy*

THE BLUE MOTORS

M Babb, Blue Motors, Oakdene, Loxhore Cott, EX31 4ST

JDV754	Bedford OB	Duple Vista	C23F	1947	preservation, 1998
AUP651L	Bedford VAS5	Plaxton Embassy	C29F	1973	Mid Devon, Crediton, 1998
FVM191V	Bedford CFL	Plaxton Mini Supreme	C17F	1979	Mayo, Kings Stanley, 1999
B234RRU	DAF SB2300DHS585	Plaxton Paramount 3200	C53F	1985	JG Coaches, Heathfield, 2004
C930LMW	Mercedes-Benz L608D	Plaxton Mini Supreme	C25F	1986	Watts, Oxhey, 2003
D504NDA	Freight Rover Sherpa	Carlyle Citybus	B19F	1987	Forward, Tiverton, 2003
D825PUK	Freight Rover Sherpa	Carlyle Citybus	B20F	1987	Ridler, Dulverton, 2001
L6ABC	Optare MetroRider MR09	Optare	B22F	1993	ABC Travel, Aintree, 2003

Previous registration:
C930LMW   C930LMW, WSU485

Depot: Scarlet Garage, Mart Road, Minehead. **Named Vehicles:** JDV794 *Exmoor Beauty*; AUP651L *Exmoor Heather* and FVM191V *Exmoor Deer*.

BREAN & BERROW

Brean & Berrow Ltd, Martin's Hill Farm, Red Road, Berrow, Burnham-on-Sea, TA8 2QT

OFS912M	Leyland Atlantean AN68/1R	Alexander AL	O45/33F	1973	Guide Friday, Stratford-u-Avon, 2003
XIL8505	Setra S210H	Setra	C28FT	1989	Freedom Travel, Piltdown, 2004
G330XRE	Mercedes-Benz 811D	PMT Ami	B28F	1989	Collinson, Rochester, 2004
OAZ1372	Volvo B10M-60	Jonckheere Deauville	C51FT	1989	Hills, Wolverhampton, 2004
P665ECJ	Renault Master	Jubilee	M15	1997	Newbury Coaches, Ledbury, 2003

Previous registration:
OAZ1372   G263UAS, ESK985, G806XAS   XIL8505   TSU612

Web: www.allyouneed-somerset.co.uk/Transport/Transport.htm

After a period on Merseyside, MetroRider L6ABC now operates Blue Motor's town service in Minehead. The fleet also includes an operational Bedford OB coach.
Bill Potter

BUGLERS

Bugler Coaches Ltd, 100 School Road, Brislington, Bristol, BS4 4NF

Reg	Chassis	Body	Layout	Year	History
XWY475X	Leyland Olympian ONLXB/1R	Eastern Coach Works	B43/32F	1982	Isle of Man Transport, 2001
F432OBK	Mercedes-Benz 811D	Robin Hood	BC28FL	1988	
586PHU	Mercedes-Benz 811D	Robin Hood	C29F	1988	
HIL3471	Dennis Javelin 12m	Plaxton Paramount 3200 III	C53DL	1988	Mayne's, Buckie, 1991
TAZ6963	Volvo B10M-60	Van Hool Alizée	C53F	1989	Clarke's of London, 1998
280OHT	Leyland Swift ST2R44C97T5	Elme Orion	C37DL	1990	Gosling, Redbourn, 1991
426VNU	Dennis Javelin 12m	Plaxton Paramount 3200 III	C53DL	1990	Denslow, Chard, 1992
HAZ2963	Dennis Javelin 12m	Plaxton Paramount 3200 III	C57DL	1990	Bakers, Biddulph, 1994
WDR145	Volvo B10M-62	Van Hool Alizée HE	C53DL	1995	APCOA, Copthorne, 2000
M845CWS	Mercedes-Benz 711D	Marshall C19	C18FL	1995	
P9MCT	Dennis Javelin 12m	Marco Polo Explorer	C47FLT	1997	MCT, Motherwell, 2005
P536YEU	Dennis Javelin 12m	UVG Cutlass	C41F	1997	Western Welsh, Ystradowen, 2001
R814LFV	Mercedes-Benz Vario 0810	Plaxton Beaver 2	B27FL	1997	Fitzsimmons, Marker, 2001
TRX615	Mercedes-Benz Vario 0814	Plaxton Beaver 2	B27F	1999	
	Optare Solo M850	Optare	N29F	On order	operated for Bristol City Council
	Optare Solo M850	Optare	N29F	On order	operated for Bristol City Council

Previous registrations:

280OHT	G647KBV		
426VNU	G366PYB	TAZ6963	F167RJF
586PHU	F251OPX	TRX615	T565RFS
HAZ2963	G653EBF, 3379RU, G143FRF	WDR145	M210UYD
HIL3471	F640PSE	XWY475X	XWY475X, DMN81H

Web: www.buglercoaches37.freeserve.co.uk

New to Clarkes of London, TAZ6963 was almost back home when pictured in Battersea. Now in Buglers' colours the Volvo B10M has the T8 version of the Van Hool Alizée body, and along with most other vehicles in the fleet features facilities for disabled passengers. *Dave Heath*

CARADON RIVIERA TOURS

J K Deeble, The Garage, Upton Cross, Liskeard, PL14 5AX

VJI8684	Bedford YMT	Plaxton Supreme IV Express	C53F	1979	Stagecoach East Midland, 2001
BVA787V	Leyland Leopard PSU3F/5R	Plaxton Supreme IV Express	C49F	1980	Millmans, Newton Abbot, 2001
LUI9952	Leyland Leopard PSU3E/4R	Plaxton Supreme IV	C53F	1980	Ford, Street, 1994
LUI9954	Leyland Leopard PSU5D/4R	Plaxton P'mount 3200 III (1987)	C53F	1980	Solus, Fazeley, 2004
LUI9955	Leyland Leopard PSU5D/4R	Plaxton P'mount 3200 III (1987)	C53F	1980	Eastbond, Tamworth, 2004
LIB1180	Leyland Leopard PSU5D/4R	Plaxton Paramount 3200 (1988)	C53F	1980	Mulley, Ixworth, 2003
NKU962X	Leyland Tiger TRCTL11/3R	Plaxton Supreme IV	C57F	1981	Chivers, Wallington, 2003
HIL7621	Leyland Tiger TRCTL11/3R	Duple Dominant IV	C57F	1982	Liskeard & District, 2001
LUI9953	Leyland Tiger TRCTL11/2RP	Alexander TE	C53F	1983	Stagecoach Bluebird, 2001
LUI9961	Leyland Tiger TRCTL11/3R	Plaxton Paramount 3200 III	C53F	1983	Ham's Diplomat, Flimwell, 2003
JBZ4909	Leyland Tiger TRCTL11/3R	Plaxton Paramount 3200 III	C53F	1983	Ball, Plymouth, 2004
LUI9962	Leyland Tiger TRCTL11/3R	Plaxton Paramount 3200	C57F	1984	Lambkin, Queenborough, 2002
LUI9966	Leyland Tiger TRCTL11/3R	Plaxton Paramount 3200 Express	C57F	1984	Matthews Country Chickens, 2002
GSU344	Leyland Tiger TRCTL11/2RH	Alexander TC	C47F	1985	Stagecoach Fife, 1999
761CRT	Leyland Tiger TRCTL11/2RP	Alexander TC	C51F	1985	Liskeard & District, 2001
C849CSN	Leyland Royal Tiger RTC	Leyland Doyen	C49F	1986	Meadway, Birmingham, 2001
C660JAT	Leyland Tiger TRCTL11/3R	Duple 340	C49FT	1986	Ball, Plymouth, 2004
C122PNV	Leyland Tiger TRCTL11/3RP	Plaxton Paramount 3200 II	BC70F	1986	Holmeswood Coaches, 2004
D241OOJ	Freight Rover Sherpa	Carlyle	B20F	1987	Henderson, Penygraig, 1997
E402TVC	MCW MetroRider MF150/52	MCW	B23F	1988	Llynfi Coaches, Maesteg, 1997
LUI9956	Leyland Tiger TRBTL11/2RP	East Lancs	BC47F	1989	Rossendale, 2001
LUI9957	Leyland Tiger TRBTL11/2RP	East Lancs	B51F	1989	Boseley, Widnes, 2001
LUI9958	Leyland Tiger TRBTL11/2RP	East Lancs	B51F	1989	Liskeard & District, 2001
LUI9959	Leyland Tiger TRBTL11/2RP	East Lancs	B51F	1989	Rossendale, 2001

Pictured operating route 77 in Plymouth while on hire to Liskeard & District, Caradon's K427HWY is an Optare MetroRider. This bus works alongside two earlier MetroRiders built by MCW. *Mark Bailey*

Shown here outside The Garage in Upton Cross, Leyland Leopard LUI9955 illustrates the Plaxton Paramount 3200 body added in 1987. The coach carries an earlier index mark, AAL303A that it received on rebodying it was one of a batch of National Welsh Leopards so treated after two were burnt out in a fire at Barry. *Mark Bailey*

751CRT	MCW MetroRider MF154/10	MCW		C29F	1989	Meyers, Llanpumpsaint, 2002
924CRT	Leyland Tiger TRCTL11/3RZM	Plaxton Paramount 3200 III		C57F	1991	Eagle Coaches, Bristol, 2002
LUI9967	Dennis Javelin 12m	Wadham Stringer Vanguard II		BC70F	1992	MoD (75KK06), 2003
K427HWY	Optare MetroRider MR03	Optare		B26F	1993	Alanways, Heathfield, 2004
K104PHW	Dennis Javelin 8.5m	Wadham Stringer Vanguard II		B36F	1993	MoD (21KL12), 2004
LUI9964	Dennis Javelin 11m	Wadham Stringer Vanguard II		BC46F	1993	MoD (74KK59), 2004
LUI9965	Dennis Javelin 8.5m	Wadham Stringer Vanguard II		BC30F	1994	MoD (47KL54), 1994
L969UHU	DAF 400	G&M		M16	1994	James, Rawnsley, 2003
LUI9968	Dennis Javelin 12m	Wadham Stringer Vanguard II		BC70F	1995	Go-Goodwins, Eccles, 2003
R623JDV	LDV Convoy	LDV		M16	1998	-, 2004

Previous registrations:

751CRT	F114UEH, 565LON, F481WFA	LUI9955	BUH226V, AAL303A
761CRT	B328LSA, TSV718, B328LSA	LUI9956	F92XBV
924CRT	J888ALL	LUI9957	F93XBV
BVA787V	BVA787V, LIL3066	LUI9958	F94XBV
C660JAT	C119GKH, 926BWV	LUI9959	F95XBV
C849CSN	C816BTS, WLT784	LUI9960	-
E402TVC	E142TBO, VJI8684	LUI9961	A90SHW
GSU344	B210FFS	LUI9962	A816NNC, PIW4791, A816NNC
HIL7621	WFA210X	LUI9963	D309PEJ, TJI6875, D309PEJ
JBZ4909	RNY309Y, VFN53, JUB675Y	LUI9964	L492XOU
K104PHW	K432XPE	LUI9965	L166XUS, L779XCV
LIB1180	BUH225V, AAL468A	LUI9966	A152EPA
LUI9952	LUA276V, 751CRT	LUI9967	K341GRC
LUI9953	A120GLS, WLT976, A663WSU	LUI9968	CX72AA, M255ATC, WSV550
LUI9954	BUH222V, AAL404A	VJI8684	FTO550V

Depots: The Garage, Upton Cross; South Hill Road, Callington; Culverland Road, Liskeard and Perch Garage, St Breock, Wadebridge.

CARMEL

A G Hazell, Station Road, Northlew, Okehampton, EX20 3BN

	L225BUT	Dennis Javelin 12m	Plaxton Première 350	C53F	1994	Flowerdew, Fleggburgh, 2000
	L552EHD	DAF SB3000DKV601	Van Hool Alizée	C55F	1993	Weavaway, Newbury, 2003
w	N998KUS	Mercedes-Benz 814D	Mellor	BC33F	1995	DAC, St Ann's Chapel, 2002
	N991FWT	DAF DE33WSSB3000	Van Hool Alizée HE	C51FT	1996	Galloway, Mendlesham, 2002
	P100SYD	Iveco TurboDaily 59-12	UVG City Star	B27F	1996	Crockernwell Motor Works, 2002
	R616BWO	Iveco TurboDaily 59-12	UVG City Star	B29F	1997	Barnacle, Cleveleys, 2004
	R43ADV	Toyota Coaster BB50R	Caetano Optimo IV	C21F	1997	AD Coaches, Witheridge, 2003
	R632VNN	Dennis Javelin 12m	Marcopolo Explorer	C53F	1998	Llynfi Coaches, Maesteg, 2002
	R987PFT	Bova FHD12.300	Bova Futura	C53F	1998	Andy Jarnes, Tetbury, 2003
	W913BEC	Scania L94IB	Irizar Century 12.35	C49FT	2000	Quantock MS. Wiveliscombe, 2004
	X89CNY	Mercedes-Benz Vario 0814	Autobus Nouvelle 2	BC31F	2001	Hutchinson, Easingwold, 2004
	SF51PVU	Mercedes-Benz Vario 0814	Plaxton Beaver 2	B27F	2001	Patterson, Birmingham, 2001
	WA04EWP	Mercedes-Benz Vario 0815	Sitcar Beluga	C29F	2004	

Special event vehicle:
| | LOD495 | Albion Victor FT39N | Duple | FC31F | 1950 | preservation, 1994 |

Previous registrations:
L552EHD	L552EHD, LUI9692		R987PFT	R987PFT, R30ARJ
N991FWT	N991FWT, 6037PP			

Web: www.carmelcoaches.co.uk

Carmel operates three of the Mercedes-Benz Vario model, each featuring a different body builder. Pictured with The *Bizzy Bus* logo, SF51PVU has a Plaxton Beaver 2 body. It is seen in North Tawton while operating route 318 into Okehampton. *Mark Bailey*

CASTLEWAYS

Castleways (Winchcombe) Ltd, Castle House, Greet Road, Winchcombe, Cheltenham, GL54 5PU

J688MFE	Setra S215HR	Setra Rational	C53F	1992	
J689MFE	Setra S215HR	Setra Rational	C53F	1992	
86JBF	Setra S210HD	Setra	C35F	1995	
TJF757	Setra S250	Setra Special	C53F	1996	Travellers, Hounslow, 1998
P200TCC	Setra S250	Setra Special	C48FT	1997	Travellers, Hounslow, 1999
V200DCC	Setra S315GT-HD	Setra	C48FT	2000	
W391JOG	Toyota Coaster BB50R	Caetano Optimo IV	C22F	2000	
BX02CME	Mercedes-Benz Citaro O530	Mercedes-Benz	N38F	2002	
VU02UVM	Dennis Dart SLF 8.8m	Plaxton Pointer MPD	N31F	2002	
YN03NJE	Volvo B7R	Plaxton Profile	BC70F	2003	

Previous registrations:
86JBF   N325MFE   TJF757   N205PUL

Web: www.castleways.co.uk

Integral buses are more common in continental Europe than in Britain and Ireland where body on chassis has dominated. The introduction of the right-hand drive Citaro from Mercedes-Benz and the OmniCity from Scania is slowly developing the integral market. Castleways operates a 12-metre O530 Citaro on its route 606 from Cheltenham to Willersey, which was pictured in Broadway in September 2004. *Mark Bailey*

CENTURION TRAVEL

Centurion Travel - Economy Travel

Centurion Travel Ltd, West End Garage, Welton, Midsomer Norton, BA3 2TP

BYC802B	Bedford YMT	Plaxton Supreme IV	C53F	1979	Arleen, Peasedown, 1998
XIB8381	DAF MB200DKTL600	Plaxton Supreme IV	C57F	1982	Arleen, Peasedown, 1998
XIB8380	Bova FHD12-280	Bova Futura	C49F	1984	Arleen, Peasedown, 1995
A675DCN	Leyland Tiger TRCTL11/3R	Plaxton Paramount 3500	C51F	1984	Hoskins, Easlington, 2003
B45DNY	Bedford YNT	Duple Laser	C53F	1985	Tourmaster, Crowland, 2003
XIB8385	Bedford YNT	Duple Laser	C53F	1985	Metrobus, Orpington, 1993
XIB8387	Bedford YNT	Duple Laser	C53F	1985	Metrobus, Orpington, 1993
B991YTC	Bedford YNT	Plaxton Paramount 3200 II	C53F	1985	Winford Queen, Winford, 1998
RIB8819	DAF MB230DKFL615	Duple 340	C61F	1987	Arleen, Peasedown, 1996
RIB8816	DAF MB230LT615	Van Hool Alizée	C49FT	1989	Moxon, Oldcotes, 2000
RIB8817	DAF MB230LT615	Van Hool Alizée	C49FT	1989	Moxon, Oldcotes, 2000
RIB8809	Leyland Tiger TRCTL11/3ARZ	Duple 320	C53F	1992	Arleen, Peasedown, 1996
J211DYL	Mercedes-Benz OH1628L	Jonckheere Jubilee	C53F	1992	Curtis, Brislington, 2000
J412LLK	Sanos S315-21	Sanos Charisma	C49FT	1992	TW, South Molton, 2001
J734KBC	Dennis Javelin 12m	Plaxton Paramount 3200 III	C57F	1992	Lawman, Kettering, 2003
L667PWT	Mercedes-Benz 814D	Optare StarRider	BC29F	1994	Andy James, Tetbury, 1999
R627VNN	Dennis Javelin 12m	Marcopolo Explorer	C53F	1998	
WV02ANX	Mercedes-Benz Vario O814	Autobus Nouvelle	C29F	2002	
WP52WBZ	Mercedes-Benz Sprinter 413Cdi	Onyx	M16	2003	
WX03UXT	Mercedes-Benz Atego O1120L	Optare/Ferqui Solero	C39F	2003	
OO04MJS	Bova FHD14-430	Bova Futura	C63FT	2004	

Previous registrations:

A675DCN	A30FVN, GSU346	RIB8817	F252RJX, FIL7887, F252RJX
B991YTC	B115NSS	RIB8819	D801GHU
BYC802B	XHE759T	XIB8380	B720MBC
J412LLK	J412LLK, TTL262	XIB8381	VBC469X
RIB8809	G793RNC	XIB8387	B47DNY
RIB8816	F251RJX, 166YHK, F251RJX	XIB8385	B43DNY

Web: www.centuriontravel.co.uk

Built on a Dennis Javelin chassis by a Portugese subsidiary of a Brazilian company, the Marcopolo Explorer is no longer in production. All Marcopolo products for the British market are now supplied on MAN chassis. This operator is connected with Arleen of Peasedown St John. *Robert Edworthy*

CITYTOUR / RYANS

M J; C & N Ryan, Watersmeet Cottage, Langridge, Bath, BA1 8AJ

NUD106L	Bristol VRT/SL2/6LX	Eastern Coach Works	O41/27F	1973	Thames Transit, 1989
TNJ995S	Bristol VRT/SL3/6LXB	Eastern Coach Works	CO43/27D	1977	Stephenson, Rochford, 1994
TNJ996S	Bristol VRT/SL3/6LXB	Eastern Coach Works	CO43/27D	1977	Brighton & Hove, 1990
TNJ998S	Bristol VRT/SL3/6LXB	Eastern Coach Works	CO43/27D	1977	Stephenson, Rochford, 1994
UWV619S	Bristol VRT/SL3/6LXB	Eastern Coach Works	CO43/31F	1978	Brighton & Hove, 1999
AHW199V	Bristol VRT/SL3/6LXB	Eastern Coach Works	B43/27D	1980	Brewers, 1994
ANA565Y	Leyland Atlantean AN68D/1R	Northern Counties	O43/32F	1982	GM Buses, 1991
HIL3451	Leyland Tiger TRCTL11/3RZ	Plaxton Paramount 3500 III	C53F	1987	Shearings, 1992
RIL2103	DAF MB230LB615	Plaxton Paramount 3500 III	C53F	1988	Metroline (Brents), 1997
J243MFP	Dennis Javelin 11SDA1921	Plaxton Paramount 3200 III	C53F	1992	Smith, Liss, 1998
R275LDE	Dennis Javelin	Plaxton Première 320	C57F	1998	Davies Bros, Pencader, 1999
S698RWG	Volvo B7R	Plaxton Première 320	C57F	1998	Parkna, Mallusk, 2003
WJI3726	Mercedes-Benz 814D	Reeve Burgess Beaver	BC33F	1989	Bee Line, Warminster, 1999
Y446AUY	Mercedes-Benz Vario 0814	Onyx	BC24F	2001	
Y138RDG	Mercedes-Benz Vario 0814	Onyx	BC24F	2001	
Y139RDG	Mercedes-Benz Vario 0814	Onyx	BC24F	2001	

Previous registrations:

HIL3451	D595MVR		WJI3726	G70GHG
RIL2103	E64SJS			

Depot: Lockswood Road, Bath

Open-top sight-seeing tours in Bath are undertaken by Citytour and City Sightseeing, the latter now part of the Ensign fleet and detailed in the Eastern Bus Handbook. The Ryan family operates Citytour using a fleet of dual-doored convertible open-top Bristol VRs which are represented here by TNJ996S. *Robert Edworthy*

COACH HOUSE TRAVEL

Coach House Travel Ltd, 16 Poundbury Ind Est, Poundbury Road, Dorchester, DT1 2PG

F875RFP	Dennis Javelin 12m	Duple 320	C53F	1989	McDougall, Bayswater, 1999
F425DUG	Volvo B10M-60	Plaxton Paramount 3200 III	C-F	1989	Hearn, Harrow Weald, 2002
F254MGB	Volvo B10M-60	Van Hool Alizée	C49FT	1989	Courtney, Bracknell, 2000
G250CPS	Dennis Javelin 11m	Plaxton Paramount 3200 III	C53F	1989	Windsorian, Bedfont, 2001
G907VKJ	Ford Transit VE6	Crystals	B8FL	1990	Kent CC, 1996
H347CKP	Ford Transit VE6	Crystals	B8FL	1990	Kent CC, 1996
J571PRU	Ford Transit VE6	Dormobile	B16F	1992	West Dorset HA, 1994
J93UBL	Dennis Javelin 10m	Berkhof Excellence 1000L	C35FT	1992	Hughes, Ashford, 2002
J61NJT	Volvo B10M-60	Plaxton Excalibur	C47FT	1992	Jones, Market Drayton, 1997
K526EFL	Iveco Daily 49-10	Marshall C29	B23F	1993	Stagecoach Midland Red, 1999
M39LOA	Iveco Daily 49-10	Jubilee	BC19F	1995	
N791WNE	LDV 400	Concept	M16	1995	
N232HWX	Volvo B10M-60	Plaxton Première 350	C50F	1995	Sunline Tours, Flimwell, 2002
R974MGB	Mercedes-Benz Vario 0814	Mellor	BC33F	1998	
S640MGA	Mercedes-Benz Vario 0814	Mellor	BC33F	1999	A1A, Birkenhead, 2003
T480RCE	LDV Convoy	LDV	M16	1999	Budget Self Drive, 2002
V600CBC	Mercedes-Benz Vario 0814	Marshall Master	B31F	1999	Coakley Bus, Motherwell, 2002
MX51TJY	LDV Convoy	Concept	M16L	2001	

Previous registrations:

F254MGB	F767ENE, LSK507	J61NJT	A4XEL
N232HWX	N232HWX, 969LKE		

Depots: Poundbury Road, Dorchester and Marabout Ind Est, Dorchester

Coach House Travel currently operates some Dorchester town services on tender to the Dorset authority. Seen in the town is V600CBC, a Mercedes-Benz Vario with Marshall Master bodywork. *Tony Wilson*

COOKS COACHES

Cooks Coaches - Kilmington Coaches

Landylines Ltd, Victor House, Greenham Business Park, Wellington, Somerset TA21 0LR

Reg	Chassis	Body	Type	Year	History
VIB9378	Leyland Tiger TRCTL11/3R	Plaxton Paramount 3200	C57F	1984	Chalkwell, Sittingbourne, 2000
BAZ7326	Volvo B10M-61	Plaxton Paramount 3200 II	C57F	1985	Richmond, Barley, 2000
H476UYD	Mercedes-Benz 811D	Reeve Burgess Beaver	BC25F	1990	
PIL9537	Mercedes-Benz 814D	Plaxton Beaver	BC33F	1990	Kent Coach Tours. Ashford, 1998
K338FYG	Mercedes-Benz 410D	G&M	M16	1992	Brenton, Plymouth, 1999
SIL4465	Dennis Javelin 12m	Berkhof Excellence 1000	C51FT	1993	Tally Ho!, Kingsbridge, 2005
L32OKV	Mercedes-Benz 410D	G&M	M16	1993	van, 1997
L360ANR	Mercedes-Benz 410D	G&M	M16	1994	van, 1998
M842TYC	LDV 400	Autobus Classique	M16	1994	
M843TYC	Mercedes-Benz 410D	Autobus Classique	M15	1994	
M968TYG	Mercedes-Benz 410D	G&M	M5FL	1994	van, 1999
M345UVX	Mercedes-Benz 811D	Plaxton Beaver	B31F	1994	Silverwing, Bristol, 2001
M289CAM	Mercedes-Benz 709D	G&M	BC24F	1994	private owner, 1999
M91JHB	Mercedes-Benz 709D	Wadham Stringer Wessex	B29F	1995	Phil Anslow, Pontypool, 2001
M582KTG	Mercedes-Benz 711D	G&M	BC24F	1995	Carmel, Northlew, 2001
N344OBC	Mercedes-Benz 709D	Alexander Sprint	B27F	1995	Arriva Midlands, 2003
HBZ4676	Mercedes-Benz 814D	Plaxton Beaver	BC33F	1996	Cooper, Dukinfield, 2001
N614DKR	Mercedes-Benz 811D	Plaxton Beaver	B31F	1996	Kent Coach Tours, Ashford, 2001
N917LRL	LDV 200	LDV	M8	1996	White, Torpoint, 2001
NIL7278	Mercedes-Benz 814D	G&M	BC24F	1996	van. 2000
N456VOD	Mercedes-Benz 709D	Alexander Sprint	B25F	1996	Lancashire United, 2002
N457VOD	Mercedes-Benz 709D	Alexander Sprint	B25F	1996	Lancashire United, 2002
N614DKR	Mercedes-Benz 811D	Plaxton Beaver	B31F	1996	Kent Coach Tours, Ashford, 1996
HAZ3346	Mercedes-Benz 711D	Onyx	BC23F	1996	Spencer, Broughton, 2001
P158BFJ	LDV Convoy	G&M	M16	1996	van, 1999
P944GEG	LDV Convoy	Walsall Motor Bodies	M16	1996	Horn, East Finchley, 2000
P848REU	LDV Convoy	Walsall Motor Bodies	M16	1996	Horn, East Finchley, 2000
P494RHU	LDV Convoy	G&M	M16	1996	van, 1998
P210JKK	Mercedes-Benz 709D	Plaxton Beaver	B27F	1996	Arriva Cymru, 2002
P211JKK	Mercedes-Benz 709D	Plaxton Beaver	B27F	1996	Arriva Southern Counties, 2002
P232NKK	Mercedes-Benz 811D	Plaxton Beaver	B31F	1997	Kent Coach Tours, Ashford, 2001
P306HWG	LDV Convoy	Onyx	M16	1997	Holloway, Scunthorpe, 2001
P117KBL	LDV Convoy	G&M	M16	1997	van, 1999
P110HCH	Mercedes-Benz Vario O814	Alexander ALX100	B29F	1997	Arriva Midlands, 2003
P115HCH	Mercedes-Benz Vario O814	Alexander ALX100	B29F	1997	Arriva Midlands, 2003
R501BUA	Mercedes-Benz 412D	Crest	BC16F	1997	Skills, Nottingham, 1998

The popular Optare Solo minibus range was extended in 2004 with the introduction of a narrow version as well as Cummins-engined models. The M990 version is one of the latter, an example of which is shown with Cooks Coaches and carrying Sowton Park and Ride livery.
Tony Wilson

Cooks Coaches' livery is shown on P210JKK, a Mercedes-Benz 709 with Plaxton Beaver bodywork. The vehicle was pictured while operating Seaton town service. *Mark Bailey*

S995BTA	LDV Convoy	G&M	M16	1998	van, 1998
T788RDV	LDV Convoy	Coachsmith	M15L	1999	operated for Devon CC
T066ABF	Mercedes-Benz 412D	Onyx	BC16F	1999	Plant, Cheadle, 2003
TXI8761	Mercedes-Benz Vario 0814	Plaxton Cheetah	C29F	1999	Real Motors, South Newton, 2002
V8PCC	Mercedes-Benz Vario 0814	Autobus Classique	C25F	1999	Lawrence, Weston, 2003
V383HGG	Mercedes-Benz Vario 0814	Plaxton Beaver 2	B31F	1999	Accord Southern, Chichester, 2003
V225VAL	LDV Convoy	WJW	M16	1999	Repton, New Haw, 2003
JUI1717	Mercedes-Benz Sprinter 412	Optare/Ferqui Soroco	BC16F	2000	
Y921FDV	LDV Convoy	Coachsmith	M15L	2001	operated for Devon CC
Y334GFJ	LDV Convoy	Coachsmith	M15L	2001	operated for Devon CC
Y835HHE	Mercedes-Benz Vario 0814	Plaxton Cheetah	C33F	2001	Steels, Skipton, 2005
YF02SKO	Optare Solo M850	Optare	N27F	2002	
YF02SKV	Optare Solo M850	Optare	N27F	2002	
YF02FWK	Optare Solo M850	Optare	N27F	2002	
YN04KWN	Optare Solo M850	Optare	N29F	2004	
KX04HPN	Optare Solo M990	Optare	N35F	2004	
KX04HPP	Optare Solo M990	Optare	N35F	2004	
KX04HPU	Optare Solo M990	Optare	N35F	2004	
KX04HPV	Optare Solo M990	Optare	N35F	2004	
KX04HPY	Optare Solo M990	Optare	N35F	2004	
KX04HPZ	Optare Solo M990	Optare	N35F	2004	
SF57PVY					

Previous registrations:

BAZ7326	B29ABH, 729KTO, B29ABH	NIL7228	N172DWX
H476UYD	H476UYD, JUI1717	PIL9537	K13KCT
HAZ3346	N837YRC	SIL4465	K200SLT, K792YFV
HBZ4676	N796CVU	TXI8761	T225OWG
JUI1717	W416RYC	VIB9378	A832PPP, HSV196, A541WAV

Depots: Millfield Trading Estate, Chard; Water Lane, Exeter; Dowell Street, Honiton; Ottermere, Monkton; Blundell Road, Tiverton; Greenham Business Park, Wellington; Croftway car park, Wiveliscombe.
Special livery: Yellow and blue (Exeter Park & Ride) KX04HPN/P/U/V/Y/Z.
Web: cookscoaches-somerset.co.uk

The South West Bus Handbook

COOMBS TRAVEL

B F Coombs; BRC Enterpises Ltd, Searle Crescent, Weston-super-Mare, BS23 3YX

A158EPA	Leyland Tiger TRCTL11/3R	Plaxton Paramount 3200 E	C57F	1984	London & Country, 1997	
B289KPF	Leyland Tiger TRCTL11/3RH	Plaxton Paramount 3200 IIE	C53F	1985	London & Country, 1997	
D327TRN	Mercedes-Benz 709D	Reeve Burgess	BC19F	1987	Miles, Stratton St Margaret, 1999	
G693NUB	Renault-Dodge S56	Optare	B13FL	1990	Leeds MBC, 1998	
G699NUB	Renault-Dodge S56	Optare	B8FL	1990	Leeds MBC, 1998	
H642GRO	Leyland Tiger TRCL10/3ARZA	Plaxton Paramount 3200 III	C53F	1991	Stagecoach East London, 1995	
J271TTX	Ford Transit VE6	Ford	M8	1992	van, 1994	
J272NNC	Scania K93CRB	Plaxton Première 320	C53F	1992	Shearings, 1997	
J275NNC	Scania K93CRB	Plaxton Première 320	C53F	1992	Shearings, 1997	
J278NNC	Scania K93CRB	Plaxton Première 320	C53F	1992	Shearings, 1997	
K721HYA	Mercedes-Benz 709D	Dormobile Routemaker	C29F	1992		
K722HYA	Scania K93CRB	Plaxton Première 320	C53F	1993		
L882MWB	Mercedes-Benz 609D	Cunliffe	BC15FL	1994	Derbyshire CC, 2002	
L110UHF	Ford Transit VE6	Ford	M11	1994	Pink Elephant, Heathrow, 1996	
L691WHY	Ford Transit VE6	Ford	M14	1994	private owner, 1994	
M745ARP	Ford Transit VE6	Ford	M14	1994	Scot Hire, Exeter, 1995	
M231XWS	Dennis Javelin 12m	Wadham Stringer Vanguard II	BC70F	1995	MoD (27AY71), 2004	
M572TYB	Scania K93CRB	Van Hool Alizée HE	C57F	1995		
M573TYB	Scania K93CRB	Van Hool Alizée HE	C57F	1995		
N43ENW	LDV 400	LDV	M12L	1995	Bradford MBC, 2003	
N609DWT	LDV Convoy	Mellor	M16L	1995	Bradford MBC, 2003	
N410WJL	Mercedes-Benz 814D	Autobus Nouvelle	C29F	1995	Aztec, Bristol, 1998	
N605DOR	Ford Transit VE6	Robin Hood	M9L	1996	private owner, 1998	
N541CYA	Ford Transit VE6	Ford	M8L	1996	private owner, 2000	
N967BYD	Dennis Javelin	UVG Unistar	C57F	1996		
N970BYC	Scania K113CRB	Van Hool Alizée HE	C57F	1996		

In 2000, Coombs Travel added a new double-deck bus to its fleet. W372PHY is a Scania N113 with East Lancs Cityzen bodywork and was taking a break between school services when pictured. Clearly visible in this view are the high-back seats that were fitted to the batch of twenty bodies ordered by Scania. *Robert Edworthy*

Carrying the consecutive index mark to the double-deck, W371PHY is a Mercedes-Benz Vario with an Autobus Nouvelle 2 bus body. This, too, is fitted with high-back seating and is seen in Weston-super-Mare.
Robert Edworthy

P87JYC	Toyota Coaster HZB50R	Caetano Optimo III	C21F	1996	
P89JYC	Dennis Javelin	Plaxton Première 320	C55F	1997	
R612GHJ	Ford Transit VE6	G&M	M5L	1998	private owner, 2002
R155TNN	Ford Transit VE6	May	M16	1998	Lewis, Coventry, 2004
R879OAD	Ford Transit VE6	Ford	M6L	1998	Severn NHS Trust, 2003
V448DYB	LDV Convoy	Concept	M16	1999	
W371PHY	Mercedes-Benz Vario 0814	Autobus Nouvelle 2	BC31F	2000	
W372PHY	Scania N113DRB	East Lancs Cityzen	BC47/31F	2000	
X286DTA	Ford Transit VE6	Ford	M16	2001	private owner, 2003
Y621HHU	LDV Convoy	Concept	M16	2001	
WV02OGG	LDV Convoy	LDV	M14L	2002	
WV02OGH	Scania K114IB	Irizar InterCentury 12.32	C53F	2002	
WP52WHG	Mercedes-Benz Vario 0814	TransBus Beaver 2	BC33F	2003	
WU03FJY	Mercedes-Benz Vario 0814	TransBus Beaver 2	BC33F	2003	
WY04YCJ	Mercedes-Benz Sprinter 413CDi	Onyx	N16	2004	
WY04YCK	Mercedes-Benz Sprinter 413CDi	Onyx	N16	2004	

Previous registration:
L110UHF   L110SKB

The South West Bus Handbook

COTTRELL'S

ER Cottrell, St Michael's Close, Mill End, Mitcheldean, GL17 0HP

GBU6V	MCW Metrobus DR101/6	MCW	B43/30F	1979	GM Buses, 1986
GBU7V	MCW Metrobus DR101/6	MCW	B43/30F	1979	GM Buses, 1986
D160UGA	Leyland Lion LDTL11/1R	Alexander RH	BC49/23F	1987	Clydeside 2000, 1994
E477SON	MCW Metrobus DR102/63	MCW	B43/30F	1988	Jones, Rhos, 2002
F309RMH	Leyland Tiger TRBTL11/2RP	Duple 300	B55F	1989	Rover Bus Service, Chesham, 1993
F183UFH	Leyland Tiger TRCTL11/3ARZ	Plaxton Paramount 3200 III	C57F	1989	
H651UWR	Volvo B10M-60	Plaxton Paramount 3500 III	C53F	1991	Machin, Ashby, 1998
H932DRJ	Volvo B10M-60	Plaxton Paramount 3200 III	C53F	1991	Capital, West Drayton, 1997
M9FUG	Dennis Dart 9.8SDL3032	Wadham Stringer Portsmouth	B43F	1994	Fuggles, Benenden, 1999
P351VWR	Volvo B10M-62	Plaxton Première 350	C50FT	1997	Vale of Llangollen, 2003

Previous registration:
D160UGA   D852RDS, 705DYE

While the old established Cinderford to Gloucester service is now operated by Stagecoach, Cottrell's still provide a few market day services as well as school duties that require the double-decks. One of these, Metrobus E477SON, is seen on the Cinderford service before the transfer. *Phillip Stephenson*

COUNTRY BUS

Alansway Coaches Ltd; Alansway Taxis Ltd, King Charles BP, Old Newton Road, Heathfield, Newton Abbot, TQ12 6UT

20	D947ARE	Mercedes-Benz 609D	PMT	C27F	1987	Rays Coaches, Plymouth, 2004
	G222KWE	Mercedes-Benz 811D	Reeve Burgess Beaver	B26F	1989	Bell, Southwick, 2001
	K989TOD	Renault Master	Renault	M8	1993	private owner, 1998
17	K522EFL	Iveco Daily 49-10	Marshall C29	B25F	1993	TRS, Leicester, 2003
	L543JFS	Mercedes-Benz 609D	Crystals	BC20F	1993	Cooks Coaches, Wellington, 2005
18	L866BEA	Iveco TurboDaily 59-12	Marshall C31	B29F	1993	Speldhurst, Shefford, 2004
	M413ALU	Iveco TurboDaily 59-12	Marshall C31C	BC24FL	1994	LB Harrow, 2003
	M414ALU	Iveco TurboDaily 59-12	Marshall C31C	BC24FL	1994	LB Harrow, 2003
	M464JPA	Mercedes-Benz 709D	Reeve Burgess Beaver	B23F	1995	Arriva Cymru, 2002
2	N265VDA	LDV 400	Bedwas	BC16FL	1996	LB Harrow, 2003
1	N266VDA	LDV 400	Bedwas	BC16FL	1996	LB Harrow, 2003
4	N268VDA	LDV 400	Bedwas	BC16FL	1996	LB Harrow, 2003
6	N270VDA	LDV 400	Bedwas	BC16FL	1996	LB Harrow, 2003
19	N277VDA	LDV 400	Bedwas	BC16FL	1996	LB Harrow, 2003
7	N283VDA	LDV 400	Bedwas	BC16FL	1996	LB Harrow, 2003
8	N287VDA	LDV 400	Bedwas	BC16FL	1996	LB Harrow, 2003
5	N27YJW	Iveco TurboDaily 59-12	Marshall C31C	BC24FL	1996	LB Harrow, 2003
10	N28YJW	Iveco TurboDaily 59-12	Marshall C31C	BC24FL	1996	LB Harrow, 2003
13	N31YJW	Iveco TurboDaily 59-12	Marshall C31C	BC24FL	1996	LB Harrow, 2003
14	N34YJW	Iveco TurboDaily 59-12	Marshall C31C	BC24FL	1996	LB Harrow, 2003
11	N35YJW	Iveco TurboDaily 59-12	Marshall C31C	BC24FL	1996	LB Harrow, 2003
12	N36YJW	Iveco TurboDaily 59-12	Marshall C31C	BC24FL	1996	LB Harrow, 2003
-	N37YJW	Iveco TurboDaily 59-12	Marshall C31C	BC24FL	1996	LB Harrow, 2003
15	P974UKG	Iveco TurboDaily 59-12	UVG CitiStar	BC29F	1996	Wilkins, Cymmer, 2004
-	P481CEG	Iveco TurboDaily 59-12	Marshall C31	B27F	1996	Staines, Brentwood, 2004
-	P482CEG	Iveco TurboDaily 59-12	Marshall C31	B27F	1996	Staines, Brentwood, 2004
-	R418XFL	Iveco TurboDaily 59-12	Marshall C31	B27F	1996	Staines, Brentwood, 2004
3	R419XFL	Iveco TurboDaily 59-12	Marshall C31	B27F	1996	Staines, Brentwood, 2004

Recent arrivals with Country Bus of Newton Abbot have been several Iveco TurboDaily buses. Pictured in Chudleigh in May 2004, N35YJW illustrates the Marshall C31 design. *Mark Bailey*

CURRIAN

TJ, JT & KJ Stoneman, Currian Road Garage, Nanpean, St Austell, PL26 7YD

AAP648T	Bristol VRT/SL3/6LXB	Eastern Coach Works	B43/31F	1978	Stephensons, Rochford, 1998	
BYX239V	MCW Metrobus DR101/12	MCW	B43/28D	1979	Imperial, Rainham, 2004	
NTT575W	Volvo B58-56	Plaxton Supreme IV Express	C53F	1981	Roselyn, Par, 2005	
FIL9220	DAF MB200DKFL600	Jonckheere Jubilee	C49FT	1984	Frost, St Austell, 2002	
NIW8794	Volvo B10M-61	Plaxton Paramount 3500	C53F	1984	Kingdom, Tiverton, 1999	
C440BUV	MCW Metrobus DR101/17	MCW	BC43/28D	1985	Imperial, Rainham, 2004	
KSU454	Volvo B10M-60	Plaxton Paramount 3500 III	C49FT	1990	National Holidays, 2002	
513SRL	Bova FHD12-290	Bova Futura	C55F	1990	Bailey, Biddisham, 2002	
YUU556	Volvo B10M-62	Plaxton Excalibur	C50FT	1995	Roselyn, Par, 2005	
T936YRR	Setra S315 GT-HD	Setra	C49FT	1999	Skills, Nottingham, 2003	
WK02UHR	Bova FHD12-340	Bova Futura	C49FT	2002		
WK52VZN	Iveco EuroRider 381E.12.35	Plaxton Paragon	C49FT	2003		

Previous registrations:

513SRL	G114VDV, 28XYB, G114VDV	NIW8794	A656UGD
FIL9220	A378UNH	NTT575W	NTT575W, 647PYC
KSU454	G526LWU	YUU556	L939NWW, 244AJB

Web: www.currian-coaches.co.uk

Photographed in the north-west resort of Blackpool, Currian's 513SRL illustrates one of two Bova Futura coaches in the fleet. *Dave Heath*

D A C COACHES

DAC Coaches Ltd, Rylands Garage, St Ann's Chapel, Gunnislake, PL18 8HW

TWS914T	Bristol VRT/SL3/6LXB	Eastern Coach Works	B39/31F	1979	City Line, 2000
WSV529	Volvo B58-56	Plaxton Supreme IV	C53F	1980	Dunn Line, Nottingham, 1992
RUE300W	Bedford YMQ	Plaxton Supreme IV	C35F	1980	Dalybus, Eccles, 1995
OFV19X	Leyland Olympian ONLXB/1R	Eastern Coach Works	B45/32F	1981	Burnley & Pendle, 2004
ANA158Y	MCW Metrobus DR10/3	MCW	H43/30F	1982	Burnley & Pendle, 2002
ENF573Y	Volvo B10M-61	Duple Dominant IV	C57F	1983	West Dorset, Dorchester, 1998
D930LYC	Bedford YNV Venturer (Cum)	Duple 320	C57F	1987	Caring Coaches, St Athan, 1998
LIL7818	Volvo B10M-61	Jonckheere Jubilee	C49FT	1987	Rich, Croydon, 2003
NIL5652	Volvo B10M-60	Van Hool Alizée	C49FT	1990	Wood, Buckfastleigh, 1999
E325BVO	Volvo Citybus B10M-55	East Lancs	B47/38D	1988	City of Nottingham, 2004
H437BVU	Mercedes-Benz 709D	Cunliffe	B24FL	1990	Webber, Wheddon Cross, 1999
H914XGA	Mercedes-Benz 709D	Dormobile	B29F	1990	Fleetwing, Mayford, 2004
H534RKG	Volvo B10M-60	Plaxton Paramount 3500 III	C53F	1991	C&B Taxi, Frome, 2004
J205KTT	Mercedes-Benz 709D	Reeve Burgess	BC27F	1991	First, 2003
M345TDO	Mercedes-Benz 609D	Autobus Classique	BC23F	1994	Calne Coaches, 2001
P96GHE	Scania K113CRB	Van Hool Alizée HE	C41FT	1996	Leavens, South Mimms, 2002
R123ESG	Mercedes-Benz Vario 0814	Plaxton Cheetah	C29F	1997	Wilson, Rhu, 2002
R736EGD	Mercedes-Benz Vario 0810	Plaxton Beaver 2	B27F	1997	Dart Buses, Paisley, 2002
R880DGT	Peugeot Boxer	Peugeot	M11	1998	private owner, 2002
R16BLU	Iveco TurboDaily 59-12	Marshall C31	B26F	1998	Bluebird, Middleton, 2004
T717UOS	Volvo B10M-62	Jonckheere Mistral 50	C53F	1999	Wickson, Walsall Wood, 2004
CJZ3681	Mercedes-Benz Vario 0814	Plaxton Beaver 2	B27F	2000	Hardie, Port Glasgow, 2001
X436CDW	Mercedes-Benz Sprinter 413CDiUVG		M14L	2001	Liskeard & District, 2002
SA51PVY	Mercedes-Benz Vario 0814	Plaxton Beaver 2	B29F	2001	
FA02CJV	Mercedes-Benz Vario 0814	Plaxton Beaver 2	B32FL	2002	ITG, Anston, 2002
WJ02KDX	Bova FHD12-340	Bova Futura	C51FT	2002	
BU03SSK	Toyota Coaster BB50R	Caetano Optimo V	C26F	2003	
WA53ONL	TransBus Javelin	Transbus Prima	C53F	2002	European Training, 2003
SG04XCN	Mercedes-Benz Vito 111 cdi	Mercedes-Benz	M8	2004	

Previous registrations:

CJZ3681	V384HGG	RJI5709	G823YJF
D930LYC	D930LYC, A16BCG, PIL7046	T717UOS	HSK648
H534RKE	H904AHS, CCZ2213	WSV529	DYW169V
LIL7818	D29RKX, D30RKX		
NIL5652	H487FGL, WIA69, H487FGL		

Web: www.daccoaches.co.uk
Special livery: Yellow (School bus) E325BVO

Seen operating route 267 between Looe and Callington, DAC Coaches' M345TDO features a Autobus Classique body.
Mark Bailey

DARTLINE

Dealtop Exeter Ltd, Langdons Business Park, Old Mill Lane, Exeter, EX5 1DR

Reg	Chassis	Body	Type	Year	History
LIL7802	Volvo B10M-61	Van Hool Alizée	C51FT	1984	Leons, Stafford, 1996
D353RCY	DAF SB2305DHS585	Plaxton Paramount 3200 III	C53F	1986	Risk, Plymouth, 2003
D434OWO	DAF MB200DKFL600	Plaxton Paramount 3500 III	C53F	1986	Target, Plymouth, 2004
LIL6537	Volvo B10M-61	Plaxton Paramount 3200 III	C53F	1987	Shearings, 1993
XFJ466	Volvo B10M-61	Plaxton Paramount 3200 III	C53F	1987	Docherty's Midland Coaches, 1998
LIL8052	Volvo B10M-61	Plaxton Paramount 3500 III	C53F	1987	Phillips, Crediton, 1999
UJI3794	Van Hool T815	Van Hool Acron	C51FT	1987	Phillips, Crediton, 1999
LBZ2571	DAF SB3000DKV601	Van Hool Alizée	C53F	1987	Stagecoach Cheltenham, 1998
KIW4489	Mercedes-Benz 709D	Robin Hood	C24FL	1989	West Glamorgan CC, 1997
F484MTA	Mercedes-Benz 408D	Crystals	M15	1989	
G800PTT	Mercedes-Benz 408D	Crystals	M15	1989	
LIL6538	Volvo B10M-60	Plaxton Paramount 3500 III	C47F	1989	St Buryan Garage, St Buryan, 1994
G958VBC	DAF SB2305DHS585	Caetano Algarve II	C53F	1989	Phillips, Crediton, 1999
LIL8876	Volvo B10M-60	Plaxton Paramount 3500 III	C48FT	1990	Wray's, Harrogate, 1998
LIL9017	Volvo B10M-60	Plaxton Paramount 3500 III	C49FT	1990	Stagecoach Cheltenham, 1998
J870FGX	Mercedes-Benz 609D	Crystals	BC24F	1991	Crystals demonstrator, 1991
J824MOD	Mercedes-Benz 609D	Crystals	BC24F	1991	
J825MOD	Mercedes-Benz 609D	Crystals	BC24F	1991	
LIL9990	Volvo B10M-60	Caetano Algarve 2	C31FT	1991	Chauffeurline, Melbourne, 1995
K775UTT	Mercedes-Benz 609D	Crystals	C24F	1992	
L345ATA	Mercedes-Benz 609D	G&M	C24F	1993	
L422WHR	Mercedes-Benz 609D	Autobus Classique	C19F	1993	Shayler, Blunsden, 1994
L858COD	Mercedes-Benz 811D	Marshall C16	BC33F	1994	
YIL9895	Dennis Dart 9.8m	Northern Counties Paladin	B40F	1995	The King's Ferry, Gillingham, 2005
L479BUE	LDV 300	LDV	M8L	1994	Staffordshire CC, 2003
M646HFJ	LDV 400	LDV	M8L	1994	private owner, 1995
M158KOD	Mercedes-Benz 609D	G&M	C24F	1995	
N918WDV	LDV Convoy	LDV	M16	1996	Budget-Arrow, 2003

While minibuses dominate the rural services in the West Country, Dartline have recently added a Northern Counties single-deck to its fleet. YIL9895 shows off the clean lines of the Dartline livery. *Bill Potter*

Pictured in London, Dartline P934KYC is one of four Bova coaches operated by the Exeter-based company. In addition to local bus operations, Dartline coaches undertake a programme of excursions and tours that see the coach fleet nationwide. *Colin Lloyd*

N40TCC	Dennis Javelin GX 12m	Plaxton Première 350	C53F	1996	Stort Valley, Stansted, 2001
P429JDT	Dennis Javelin 12m	Plaxton Première 320	C53F	1996	JGS, Rotherham, 2001
P934KYC	Bova FHD12.233	Bova Futura	C51FT	1997	Phillips, Crediton, 1999
P882FMO	Dennis Javelin GX 12m	Berkhof Axial 50	C53F	1997	Voel, Dyserth, 2004
R773WOB	Volvo B10M-62	Plaxton Première 320	C53F	1997	Baker, Enstone, 2004
R774WOB	Dennis Javelin 12m	Plaxton Première 320	C53F	1997	Safeguard, Guildford, 2004
R964MDV	Mercedes-Benz Vario O810	Robin Hood	C25F	1997	
S671ETT	LDV Convoy	G&M	M16	1998	
S944WYB	Volvo B10M-62	Jonckheere Mistral 50	C51FT	1998	
S923KOD	Iveco TurboDaily 59-12	Marshall C31	B29F	1998	
S924KOD	Iveco TurboDaily 59-12	Marshall C31	B29F	1998	
S925KOD	Iveco TurboDaily 59-12	Marshall C31	B29F	1998	
S926KOD	Iveco TurboDaily 59-12	Marshall C31	B29F	1998	
W259WRV	Mercedes-Benz Vario O814	Robin Hood Millennium	C25FT	2000	
Y14DLC	Bova FHD12.370	Bova Futura	C51FT	2001	
WJ02KDZ	Bova FHD12.340	Bova Futura	C51FT	2002	
WJ02KEU	Mercedes-Benz Vario O815	Sitcar Beluga	B27F	2002	
YJ05WCX	Optare Solo M920	Optare	N33F	2005	
YJ05WCY	Optare Solo M920	Optare	N33F	2005	
YJ05WCZ	Optare Solo M920	Optare	N33F	2005	

Previous registrations:

D434OWO	D954LTX, RJI1977	LIL8052	E556UHS, UJI3792
D353RCY	D882BDF, PJI3547	LIL8876	G503LWU, A20MCW, G293PUB
KIW4489	F896BCY	LIL9017	G548LWU
LBZ2571	E341EVH	LIL9990	J304KFP, 491NFC
LIL6537	D568MVR	P882FMO	P882FMO, 8214VC
LIL6538	F23HGG	XFJ466	D573MVR, 913EWC
LIL7802	A644UGD, LOI9772, A149MFA	UJI3794	E22MMM

Special liveries: White (Majesty Holidays) LBZ2571, MIL9746, UJI3792, G958VBC, N40TCC, P429JDT, P882FMO, R77WVOB, R774WOB. (Park & Ride) S923KOD, S925KOD.
Web: www.dartline-coaches.co.uk

The South West Bus Handbook   45

DAWLISH COACHES

Dawlish Coaches Ltd, Dawlish Business Park, Exeter Road, Dawlish, EX7 0NH

E296OMG	Volvo B10M-61	Van Hool Alizée	C53F	1988	North Mymms, Potters Bar, 1992
F232DWF	Volvo B10M-61	Plaxton Paramount 3200 III	C53F	1988	Trumans, Fleet, 2003
F512LTT	Volvo B10M-60	Van Hool Alizée	C53F	1989	
F77MFJ	Volvo B10M-60	Van Hool Alizée	C53F	1989	
K922UFX	Mercedes-Benz 811D	Plaxton Beaver	C33F	1992	Amport & District, Thruxton, 1994
L193OVO	Mercedes-Benz 811D	Dormobile Routemaker	B30F	1994	City of Nottingham, 2001
L182PMX	Bova FHD.340	Bova Futura	C53F	1994	Limebourne, Battersea, 1998
L796DTT	Bova FHD12.340	Bova Futura	C53F	1994	
M587KTT	Bova FHD12.340	Bova Futura	C53F	1995	
N201DYB	Bova FHD12.340	Bova Futura	C53F	1996	
N202DYB	Bova FHD12.340	Bova Futura	C53F	1996	
P928KYC	Bova FHD12.333	Bova Futura	C49FT	1997	
P929KYC	Bova FHD12.333	Bova Futura	C49FT	1997	
P344VWR	Volvo B10M-62	Plaxton Première 350	C53F	1997	Wallace Arnold, 2002
R13OVA	Bova FHD12.300	Bova Futura	C49FT	1997	O'Donnell, Belfast, 2003
R208WYD	Bova FHD12.333	Bova Futura	C53F	1998	
R209WYD	Bova FHD12.333	Bova Futura	C53F	1998	
R2AVC	Bova FHD12.340	Bova Futura	C53F	1998	Axe Vale, Biddisham, 2002
V483XJV	Mercedes-Benz Vario O814	Autobus Nouvelle 2	C29F	2000	
W157RYB	Bova FHD12.370	Bova Futura	C53F	2000	
W562RYC	Bova FHD12.370	Bova Futura	C49FT	2000	
X584BYD	Bova FHD12.340	Bova Futura	C53F	2000	Avalon, Glastonbury, 2003
X424CFJ	Mercedes-Benz Vario O814	Plaxton Beaver 2	B27F	2000	
Y818NAY	Iveco EuroRider 391.12.35	Beulas Stergo ε	C49FT	2001	
Y835NAY	Iveco EuroRider 391.12.35	Beulas Stergo ε	C49FT	2001	
WJ02YYK	Toyota Coaster BB50R	Caetano Optimo V	C22F	2002	
WJ02KDF	Bova FHD12.340	Bova Futura	C49FT	2002	
WA04MHX	VDL Bova FHD13.340	VDL Bova Futura	C53F	2004	
BX54EBL	Mercedes-Benz 1836RL	Mercedes-Benz Touro	C41FT	2004	
	VDL Bova FHD13.340	VDL Bova Futura	C53FT	On order	

Special liveries: white (Majestic Holidays) L182PMX, M587KTT, N201DYB, N202DYB, P928/9KYC, P344VWR, R2AVC, R13OVA, R208WYD, W157RYB, W562RYC, X584BYD, WA04MHX; white and blue (Leger Holidays) WJ02KDF, BX54EBL.
Web: www.dawlishcoaches.com

Pictured in Dawlish, X424CFJ is a Mercedes-Benz Vario with Plaxton Beaver 2 bodwork. Dawlish Coaches operates the shoppers' service that connects Starcross with Coronation Drive. *Mark Bailey*

C J DOWN

CJ & JA Down, The Garage, Mary Tavy, Tavistock, PL19 9PA

Handwritten note: 415 CJD VOLVO MKIV B10M

Reg	Chassis	Body	Layout	Year	History
NIL4988	Volvo B58-56	Plaxton Supreme IV	C53F	1979	Hookways, Meeth, 2004
MIL7611	Volvo B10M-61	Van Hool Alizée H	C53F	1981	Redwoods, Henyock, 2002
241KRO	Volvo B10M-61	Van Hool Alizée H	C48FT	1981	Hussain, Walsall, 2002
JIL3967	Volvo B10M-61	Duple Dominant IV	C57F	1982	Wansbeck, Ashington, 1987
MIL7609	Volvo B10M-61	Plaxton Supreme VI	C57F	1983	Richmonds, Barley, 1999
RIL4958	Volvo B10M-61	Duple Dominant IV	C53F	1983	Friend, Harrowbarrow, 1999
RIB5086	Volvo B10M-61	Plaxton Paramount 3500	C53F	1984	Jackson, Castleford, 2001
3271CD	Volvo B10M-61	Plaxton Paramount 3500	C57F	1984	Fords, Gunnislake, 1990
3594CD	Volvo B10M-61	Plaxton Paramount 3500	C53F	1984	Kingdoms, Tiverton, 1993
9891CD	Volvo B10M-61	Plaxton Paramount 3500 III	C53F	1987	Jennings, Bude, 1989
RJI4563	Volvo B10M-61	Plaxton Paramount 3500 III	C57F	1988	Expertpoint, Stratford, 2001
NIL4987	Volvo B10M-60	Plaxton Paramount 3200 III	C53F	1989	Bee Line, Warminster, 2004
3504CD	Volvo B10M-60	Plaxton Paramount 3500 III	C53F	1990	MTL, London, 1997
8405CD	Volvo B10M-60	Plaxton Paramount 3500 III	C53F	1990	MTL, London, 1997
8515CD	Volvo B10M-60	Jonckheere Deauville 45	C53F	1995	Shearings, 2003
8933CD	Volvo B10M-60	Jonckheere Deauville 45	C53F	1995	Shearings, 2003
5448CD	Volvo B10M-60	Jonckheere Deauville 45	C53F	1996	Clarkes of London, 2003
Y7CJD	Volvo B10M-60	Jonckheere Mistral	C53F	2001	Park's of Hamilton, 2003

Previous registrations:

241KRO	NFJ380W	JIL3967	MCN238X, 8515CD
3271CD	A796TGG, 794PAF, A568YGL	MIL7609	RMH868Y, 668PTM, RMH868Y
3504CD	G43RGG, 43FJF	MIL7611	OPC122W, 712NIP, ABZ4642, USV628
3594CD	A653UGD	NIL4987	F486LHO, 1879RU, F947WFA, 6220WY
5448CD	N550SJF	NIL4988	JAB5T, ETA890T
8405CD	G86RGG, RIB5086	RIL4958	DDD311Y, PSV111, EFH295Y, UCV144Y, 3504CD, HTT225Y
9891CD	D808SGB	RJI4563	E992MHY
8515CD	M607ORJ	Y7CJD	LSK874, Y103CDS
8933CD	M606ORJ		

C J Down's fleet wholly comprises of Volvo coaches, the latest being bodied by Jonckheere. Pictured on the Embankment in London is Deauville 5448CD, an example that spent much of its early life in the capital. The fleet also features an impressive list of 'CD' index marks. *Colin Lloyd*

DUKES TRAVEL

Dukes Travel Ltd, Lakers Road Garage, Lakers Road, Five Acres, Coleford, GL16 7QT

HLZ4439	Leyland National 11351/1R	East Lancs Greenway (1994)	B52F	1974	Geoff Willetts, Pillowell, 2002
G247CLE	DAF SB220LC590	Hispano	B66F	1990	Bennetts, Gloucester, 2004
J302BVO	DAF SB220LC550	Optare Delta	B49F	1990	Trent (Barton), 2001
J303BVO	DAF SB220LC550	Optare Delta	B49F	1990	Trent (Barton), 2001
J304BVO	DAF SB220LC550	Optare Delta	B49F	1990	Trent (Barton), 2001
J305BVO	DAF SB220LC550	Optare Delta	B49F	1990	Trent (Barton), 2001
J995GCP	DAF SB220LC550	Ikarus CitiBus	B52F	1991	Travel West Midlands, 2002
J807KHD	DAF SB220LC550	Ikarus CitiBus	BC42F	1992	Capital, West Drayton, 2002
LUI1512	Dennis Dart 8.5m	Plaxton Pointer	B28F	1992	Countryman, Ibstock, 2003
H5GBD	Volvo B10M-60	Plaxton Excalibur	C49FT	1992	Shaws of Maxey, 1999
J656REY	Mercedes-Benz 811D	Wright Handybus	B29F	1992	Bromyard Omnibus, 2002
K854ODY	Mercedes-Benz 709D	Alexander Sprint	B31F	1993	EST Bus, Llandow, 2001
K859ODY	Mercedes-Benz 709D	Alexander Sprint	B25F	1993	Stagecoach South, 2001
K882UDB	Mercedes-Benz 709D	Plaxton Beaver	B27F	1993	Arriva Cymru, 2001
H8GBD	Volvo B10M-60	Berkhof Excellence 1000LD	C50FT	1993	Cantabrica, St Albans, 2001
H10GBD	Volvo B10M-60	Jonckheere Deauville 45	C50F	1993	Prindale, Castleford, 2002
H4GBD	Volvo B10M-62	Jonckheere Deauville 45	C50F	1993	Landtourers, Farnham, 1998
H6GBD	Volvo B12R	Jonckheere Deauville 65	C49FT	1994	The King's Ferry, Gillingham, 2001
H7GBD	Volvo B12R	Jonckheere Deauville 65	C49FT	1994	The King's Ferry, Gillingham, 2001
M164LNC	Mercedes-Benz 709D	Alexander Sprint	B23F	1995	Arriva North West, 2003
N347OBC	Mercedes-Benz 709D	Alexander Sprint	B27F	1995	Arriva Midlands, 2003
N348OBC	Mercedes-Benz 709D	Alexander Sprint	B27F	1995	Arriva Midlands, 2003
N349OBC	Mercedes-Benz 709D	Alexander Sprint	B27F	1995	Arriva Midlands, 2003
N157MTG	Mercedes-Benz 711D	UVG Wessex	B27F	1995	Stagecoach, 2004
N160MTG	Mercedes-Benz 711D	UVG Wessex	B27F	1995	Stagecoach, 2004
B5GBD	Mercedes-Benz 814D	Plaxton Beaver	BC33F	1996	Martin, Kettering, 2003
P939HVX	Mercedes-Benz 711D	Plaxton Beaver	BC25F	1997	Arriva Southern Counties, 2003
S781RNE	Dennis Dart SLF 11.3m	Plaxton Pointer SPD	N41F	1998	Shamrock, Pontypridd, 2003
H9GBD	Volvo B10M-62	Jonckheere Mistral 50	C53F	1999	Park's of Hamilton, 2003
Y201KMB	Dennis Dart SLF	Alexander ALX200	N38F	2000	
VX51ABF	Optare Solo M920	Optare	NC29F	2001	

Previous registrations:

676GBD	-	H8GBD	K900CCH
B5GBD	N94BHL	H9GBD	HSK645, T714UOS
B6GBD	-	H10GBD	K843HUM, UJI470, K843HUM
H4GBD	L754YGE, 676GBD	HLZ4439	GCY748N, 2464FH
H5GBD	J427HDS	LUI1512	J391GKH
H6GBD	M26HNY	T51JBA	T51JBA, 99D72546
H7GBD	M27HNY	J656REY	?

Depot: Laker's Road, Berry Hill
Special liveries: Silver (Traveland Ski Holidays) H6/7/9GBD.

Illustrating the optional low driving position on the Berkhof Excellence 1000 is Dukes Travel's H8GBD.
Dave Heath

EAGLE of BRISTOL

AJ & JA Ball, Fireclay House, Netham Road, St George, Bristol, BS5 9PJ

	Reg	Chassis	Body	Seating	Year	Notes
	WPW202S	Bristol VRT/SL3/6LXB	Eastern Coach Works	B43/31F	1977	Eurotaxis, Bristol, 1997
	VCA463W	Bristol VRT/SL3/6LXB	Eastern Coach Works	B43/31F	1980	Eastville, Bristol, 1999
	TPD112X	Leyland Olympian ONTL11/1R	Roe	B43/29F	1982	Eastville, Bristol, 2001
	TSO17X	Leyland Olympian ONLXB/1R	Eastern Coach Works	B45/32F	1982	Marchants, Cheltenham, 2003
	931DHT	DAF MB230LT615	Van Hool Alizée H	C53F	1988	
	24THU	DAF SB3000DKV601	Van Hool Alizée	C49FT	1990	Norman, Keynsham, 1999
	6130EL	DAF MB230LT615	Van Hool Alizée H	C53F	1990	Regina, Blaenau Ffestiniog, 1995
	FIL9370	DAF MB230LB615	Van Hool Alizée H	C51F	1990	Ribblesdale, Great Harwood, 1996
	2411KR	DAF MB230LB615	Van Hool Alizée H	C53F	1992	
	K518RJX	DAF MB230LTF615	Van Hool Alizée H	C57F	1993	
	M775RCP	DAF MB230LT615	Van Hool Alizée HE	C55F	1995	
	M805RCP	DAF MB230LT615	Van Hool Alizée HE	C55F	1995	First Aberdeen, 2002
	N993FWT	DAF DE33WSSB3000	Van Hool Alizée HE	C51F	1996	
	N780LHY	Mercedes-Benz 814D	Autobus Nouvelle	BC29F	1996	
w	R990EHU	Mercedes-Benz Vario O814	Plaxton Beaver 2	BC29F	1997	
	S794JTH	DAF DE33WSSB3000	Van Hool T9 Alizée	C49FT	1998	Pullman, Crofty, 2004
	T54AUA	Mercedes-Benz Vario O814	Autobus Nouvelle 2	BC29F	1999	
	V801LWT	DAF DE23RSSB2750	Smit	C36FT	1999	
	W201CDN	DAF DE33WSSB3000	Van Hool T9 Alizée	C49FT	2000	
	Y151XAE	Mercedes-Benz Vario O814	Plaxton Cheetah	C29F	2001	
	WX51YGN	Iveco 50-13	-	C16F	2002	
	YG52CKE	DAF DE40XSSB4000	Van Hool T9 Alizée	C49FT	2003	

Previous registrations:

24THU	G639LWU	2411KR	J693GTC
94SHU	-	6130EL	G999KJX
613WHT	-	FIL9370	G233NCW
863EKX	-	H731BHW	H731BHW, OO1290
931DHT	E638KCX	VWF328	-

The latest arrival with Eagle of Bristol is Van Hool-bodied DAF DE40XSSB4000. This chassis has been developed to meet the Euro 3 requirements and comes in two models, the SB4000 PF with a 9.2 litre engine and the SB4000XF with 12.6 litres. YG52CKE is seen approaching the race-course at Epsom. *Dave Heath*

EASTWOOD

Eastwood - Victory Buses

N A Eastwood, Victory Heights The Burrows, St Ives, TR26 1

JIL7714	Mercedes-Benz 609D	North West		BC24F	1988	Bromyard Omnibus, 2001
G713HOP	Mercedes-Benz 609D	Carlyle		B29F	1990	Bromyard Omnibus, 2001
G717HOP	Mercedes-Benz 609D	Carlyle		B29F	1990	Bromyard Omnibus, 2001
K186HTV	Mercedes-Benz 811D	Dormobile Routemaker		B33F	1993	City of Nottingham, 2003
L187DDW	Optare MetroRider MR15	Optare		B31F	1994	Cardiff Bus, 2001

Previous registration:
JIL7714   E900ASU

Depots: Ocean View, St Ives and former Highways depot, Trenwith Burrows.

Eastwood's minibus operation provides vehicles for the all-year *Park & Ride* service in St Ives. Pictured near the foreshore is G717HOP, a Mercedes-Benz with Carlyle bodywork. *Robert Edworthy*

EBLEY

Ebley Bus Ltd; Ebley Coaches Ltd,
27 Nailsworth Mill Est, Avening Road, Nailsworth, Stroud, GL6 0BS

Reg	Chassis	Body	Layout	Year	History
KTL25V	Bristol VRT/SL3/6LXB	Eastern Coach Works	B43/31F	1979	Marchant, Cheltenham, 2003
LBD921V	Bristol VRT/SL3/6LXB	Eastern Coach Works	B43/31F	1980	NIBS, Wickford, 2003
FDV837V	Bristol VRT/SL3/6LXB	Eastern Coach Works	B43/31F	1980	First, 2004
DBV31W	Bristol VRT/SL3/6LXB	Eastern Coach Works	B43/31F	1980	Bakers Dolphin, Weston-s-M, 2002
VCA462W	Bristol VRT/SL3/6LXB	Eastern Coach Works	B43/31F	1980	Bakers Dolphin, Weston-s-M, 2002
JEO587X	DAF MB200DKTL600	Duple Goldliner IV	C52FT	1982	Andy James, Sherston, 1993
A9ECS	DAF MB200DKFL600	Berkhof Esprite	C53F	1986	Watts, Gillingham, 1996
B21AUS	DAF MB200DKFL600	Van Hool Alizée	C50FT	1985	Stagecoach Midland Red, 1996
BUI4646	DAF SB3000DKV601	Jonckheere Deauville P599	C51FT	1988	Buddens, Romsey, 1997
F213DCC	Mercedes-Benz 709D	Robin Hood	BC25F	1989	Bailey Group, Blackburn, 2003
G230FJC	Mercedes-Benz 709D	Robin Hood	BC25F	1988	Bailey Group, Blackburn, 2003
G115TNL	Mercedes-Benz 814D	Reeve Burgess Beaver	BC33F	1989	Andy James, Tetbury, 2002
G896TGG	Mercedes-Benz 811D	Reeve Burgess Beaver	B33F	1989	Western Greyhound, Newquay, 2003
G451XJH	Ford Transit VE6	Ford	M8	1988	private owner, 2000
H24GRE	Ford Transit VE6	Ford	M11	1990	Rover, Horsley, 2001
H886LOX	Dennis Dart 8.5m	Carlyle Dartline	B35F	1991	Warrington Transport, 2004
H888LOX	Dennis Dart 8.5m	Carlyle Dartline	B35F	1991	Warrington Transport, 2003
H889LOX	Dennis Dart 8.5m	Carlyle Dartline	B35F	1991	Warrington Transport, 2004
H843NOC	Dennis Dart 8.5m	Carlyle Dartline	B35F	1991	Warrington Transport, 2003
H104CHG	Dennis Dart 9m	Reeve Burgess Pointer	B35F	1991	Rossendale, 2004
H105CHG	Dennis Dart 9m	Reeve Burgess Pointer	B35F	1991	Rossendale, 2004
H23JMJ	Leyland Tiger TRCL10/3ARZA	Plaxton Paramount 3200 III	C53F	1992	Clunes, Edinburgh, 2001
J229JJR	Renault S75	Plaxton Beaver	B28F	1991	Green Triangle, Atherton, 2000
K345PJR	Renault S75	Plaxton Beaver	B31F	1992	Andy James, Tetbury, 2003
A6ECS	DAF SB3000DKV601	Van Hool Alizée	C51FT	1992	Hallmark, Luton, 2000
M608RCP	EOS E180Z	EOS 90	C51FT	1995	Ardcavan, Castlebridge, 2001
R816LFV	Mercedes-Benz Vario 0810	Plaxton Beaver 2	B27F	1997	Andybus, Dauntsey, 2005
R629YOM	Mercedes-Benz Vario 0814	Plaxton Beaver 2	B31F	1998	Hatts, Foxham, 2005
R630YOM	Mercedes-Benz Vario 0814	Plaxton Beaver 2	B31F	1998	Hatts, Foxham, 2005

Ancillary vehicle:

Reg	Chassis	Body		Layout	Year	History
IIB8903	Leyland Leopard PSU3F/5R	Duple Dominant II		RV	1981	Boulton, Cardington, 1999

Previous registrations:

A6ECS	J63GCX, HC6422, J63GCX	IIB8903	TUM980W
A9ECS	C588KTW	JEO587X	PFR835X, 2428WW
BUI4646	F955RNV	M608RCP	M608RCP, 95WX3711
G896TGG	G896TGG, UWR498		

Named vehicles: A9ECS *Tiger*; BUI4646 *Lion*; G451XJH *Kitten*; IIB8903 *Leopard*; H23JMJ *Cheetah*.

Robin Hood bodywork on the Mercedes minibus features the rounded roofline as seen on G230FJC seen here. The bus was new to Crosville Wales.
Robert Edworthy

EUROTAXIS

Eurotaxis (Bristol) Ltd, 16 Highfields Close, Harry Stoke, Bristol, BS34 8YA

Reg	Chassis	Body	Type	Year	History
HAZ3540	Leyland Tiger TRCTL11/3RZ	Wadham Stringer Vanguard	BC70F	1986	Ulsterbus, 2004
D215JHY	Leyland Tiger TRCTL11/3RZ	Plaxton Derwent 2	BC54F	1987	MoD (87KF49), 1999
E660XND	Mercedes-Benz 507D	Cunliffe	M8L	1988	Manchester Social Services, 1997
G524YAE	Leyland Tiger TRCTL11/3LZM	Plaxton Derwent 2	BC68F	1989	MoD (03KJ47), 1999
G525YAE	Leyland Tiger TRCTL11/3LZM	Plaxton Derwent 2	BC68F	1989	MoD (03KJ40), 1999
G629XWS	Leyland Tiger TRCTL11/3LZM	Plaxton Derwent 2	BC68F	1989	MoD (03KJ33), 1997
G783XWS	Leyland Tiger TRCTL11/3LZM	Plaxton Derwent 2	BC68F	1990	MoD (03KJ21), 1998
G828XWS	Leyland Tiger TRCTL11/3LZM	Plaxton Derwent 2	BC68F	1990	MoD (03KJ30), 1998
K496SUS	Dennis Javelin 10m	Wadham Stringer Vanguard II	BC40F	1993	Stonehouse Coaches, 2003
K714PHU	Dennis Javelin 10m	Wadham Stringer Vanguard II	BC40F	1993	MoD (74KK31), 2002
K271BRJ	Dennis Javelin 10m	Wadham Stringer Vanguard II	BC40F	1993	MoD (74KK39), 2003
L703JSC	Mercedes-Benz 410D	Devon Conversions	M16L	1994	Ferguson, East Whitburn, 2000
L3RDC	Mercedes-Benz 814D	Autobus Classique	C33F	1994	Reynolds Diplomat, Bushey, 1998
L404BBC	Mercedes-Benz 811D	Wadham Stringer Wessex	B31FL	1994	LB Hammersmith & Fulham, 2002
L405BBC	Mercedes-Benz 811D	Wadham Stringer Wessex	B31FL	1994	LB Hammersmith & Fulham, 2002
L407BBC	Mercedes-Benz 811D	Wadham Stringer Wessex	B31FL	1994	LB Hammersmith & Fulham, 2002
M45GRY	Mercedes-Benz 811D	Mellor	BC33F	1994	
M46GRY	Mercedes-Benz 811D	Mellor	BC33F	1994	
M47GRY	Mercedes-Benz 811D	Mellor	BC33F	1994	
M48GRY	Mercedes-Benz 811D	Mellor	BC33F	1994	
M301TSF	Mercedes-Benz 308D	Aitken	M8L	1995	Ferguson, East Whitburn, 2000
M646OOM	Mercedes-Benz 410D	TBP	M12L	1995	West Midlands Special Needs, 2001
M935XKA	Mercedes-Benz 609D	Devon Conversions	BC16F	1995	Greater Manchester Access, 2003
N542BFY	Mercedes-Benz 409D	Concept	M15	1995	
N586OAE	Dennis Javelin 10m	Wadham Stringer Vanguard II	BC40F	1995	MoD (ES18AA), 2002
N990AEF	Mercedes-Benz 814L	Buscraft	C31F	1995	Fairley, Tudhoe, 2001
N482BFY	Mercedes-Benz 208D	Olympus	M11	1995	private owner, 1999
N627BWG	Mercedes-Benz 811D	Mellor	B31F	1995	JP Travel, Middleton, 2001
N312HUM	Mercedes-Benz 609D	Devon Conversions	BC13F	1995	Leeds MBC, 2001
N933CJA	Mercedes-Benz 609D	Crystals	B16FL	1996	Greater Manchester Access, 2003
N814NHS	Volvo B10M-62	Jonckheere Deauville 50	C53F	1996	Castell, Caerphilly, 2001
P311GTO	Renault Trafic	Renault	M8L	1996	Nottinghamshire CC, 2001
P314GTO	Renault Trafic	Renault	M8L	1996	Nottinghamshire CC, 2001
P317GTO	Renault Trafic	Renault	M8	1996	Nottinghamshire CC, 2001

Pictured in the coastal resort of Brean, XIL8505 is the latest arrival with Brean and Berrow *(see page 27)* a Setra S210. This shorter model of the Setra 200 series lacks nothing of the larger coaches, and features a roomy toilet and refreshment area as well as twenty-eight seats. The company is most prominent in the summer when it operate the open-top Atlantean to the Northam Holiday Centre. *Bill Potter*

The sale of many Ministry of Defence buses has seen them transformed into school transport for several smaller operators across the country. Some have been fitted with 3+2 seating with capacities for around 70 students. Pictured with Eurotaxis, Leyland Tiger D215JHY is typical. This vehicle features a Plaxton Derwent 2 body and, as can be seen here, lacks destination equipment. *Robert Edworthy*

P655EAU	Mercedes-Benz Vito 308D	Traveliner	M12	1996	private owner, 2001
P183RSC	Mercedes-Benz Sprinter 614D	Aitken	C24F	1997	Haggis B'packers, Edinburgh, 1999
P473MNA	Mercedes-Benz Vito 312D	Traveliner	M12	1997	Sky Park, Manchester, 2000
P474MNA	Mercedes-Benz Vito 312D	Traveliner	M12	1997	Sky Park, Manchester, 2000
R991HNS	Mercedes-Benz Vito 208D	Traveliner	M11	1998	private owner, 2000
R625GFS	Mercedes-Benz Vario 0814	Cymric	BC24F	1998	van, 2000
R6LON	Dennis Javelin GX 12m	Neoplan Euroliner	C53F	1998	The Londoners, 2002
C1EGO	Mercedes-Benz Vario 0814D	Autobus Classique	C33F	1998	BT, 1998
R583DYG	Mercedes-Benz Sprinter 614D	Crest	C24F	1998	Haggis B'packers, Edinburgh, 2001
S234FGD	Mercedes-Benz Sprinter 614D	Crest	C24F	1998	Haggis B'packers, Edinburgh, 1999
V798EWF	Mercedes-Benz Vito 310	Traveliner	M16	1999	private owner, 2003
W985WDB	Mercedes-Benz Vario 0814	Plaxton Cheetah	C24FL	1999	Patterson, Birmingham, 2003
W953WDS	Mercedes-Benz Sprinter 412	Scott	M16	2000	Stonehouse Coaches, 2001
W764ABV	Volkswagen LT46	Olympus	M15	2000	Morestyle, East Didsbury, 2003
X314HOU	Mercedes-Benz Vario 0814	Eurocoach	BC24F	2001	McGinn, Ballycastle, 2001
X346AVJ	Mercedes-Benz Vario 0814	Autobus Nouvelle	BC31F	2001	Bromyard Omnibus, 2004
Y502BSF	Mercedes-Benz Vario 0614	Onyx	C24F	2001	Airpark, Linwood, 2004
Y503BSF	Mercedes-Benz Vario 0614	Onyx	C24F	2001	Airpark, Linwood, 2004
Y36HBT	Optare Solo M850	Optare	N29F	2001	First Group, 2004
Y37HBT	Optare Solo M850	Optare	N29F	2001	First Group, 2004
RO51UWD	Mercedes-Benz Vito 311	Traveliner	M16	2001	van, 2003
RO51UVL	Mercedes-Benz Vito 311	Traveliner	M16	2001	van, 2003
WV51RDY	Mercedes-Benz Vito 311	Traveliner	M16	2001	
VU51AXR	Optare Solo M850	Optare	N27F	2001	Bromyard Omnibus, 2004
MP51BUS	Optare Solo M850	Optare	N27F	2001	Bromyard Omnibus, 2004
SG02VXH	Mercedes-Benz Vito 310	Traveliner	M16	2001	

Previous registrations:
C1EGO   R35WDA   X314HOU   ANZ7007
K271BRJ 15KL46   K496SUS   74KK39

Depot: Jorricks Estate, Westerleigh Road, Bristol.

The South West Bus Handbook

EXCELSIOR COACHES

Excelsior Coaches Ltd, Central Business Park, Bournemouth, BH1 3SJ

353	XEL158	Volvo B10M-62	Plaxton Première 320	C53F	1999	
437	A3XCL	Volvo B10M-62	Plaxton Excalibur	C36FT	1998	
601	A2XEL	Volvo B10M-62	Plaxton Panther	C43FT	2000	
602	A3XEL	Volvo B10M-62	Plaxton Panther	C43FT	2000	
603	A4XEL	Volvo B10M-62	Plaxton Panther	C43FT	2000	
604	A5XEL	Volvo B10M-62	Plaxton Panther	C45FT	2000	
605	A6XEL	Volvo B10M-62	Plaxton Panther	C45FT	2000	
606	A7XEL	Volvo B10M-62	Plaxton Panther	C45FT	2000	
607	XEL24	Volvo B10M-62	Plaxton Panther	C49FT	2000	
608	XEL31	Volvo B10M-62	Plaxton Panther	C49FT	2000	
609	FN03DXY	Volvo B12B	Sunsundegui Sideral	C49FT	2003	
610	FN03DXZ	Volvo B12B	Sunsundegui Sideral	C49FT	2003	
805	A9XCL	Volvo B10M-62	Plaxton Paragon	C44FT	2000	
901	A2XCL	Volvo B10M-62	Plaxton Excalibur	C49FT	1998	
905	A7XCL	Volvo B10M-62	Plaxton Paragon	C44FT	2000	
906	A8XCL	Volvo B10M-62	Plaxton Paragon	C44FT	2000	
907	FN03DYA	Volvo B12B	Jonckheere Mistral 50	C44FT	2003	
908	FN03DYB	Volvo B12B	Jonckheere Mistral 50	C44FT	2003	
M15	A18EXC	Ford Transit VE6	Ford	M8	1995	private owner, 2002
M16	A8EXC	Mercedes-Benz Sprinter 308CDi	Crest	M8	2002	
M17	A9EXC	Mercedes-Benz Sprinter 308CDi	Crest	M8	2002	
M18	A12EXC	Mercedes-Benz Sprinter 308CDi	Crest	M8	2002	
M19	A13EXC	Mercedes-Benz Sprinter 308CDi	Crest	M8	2002	

Previous registrations:
A2XCL	XEL4, R423LCG, A2XEL	A7XCL	A7XCL, X852XLJ
A3XCL	XEL31, S809ORU	A18EXC	M812LPR
A4XCL	XEL24, T992FRU	XEL24	A8XEL, W98RRU
A4XEL	A4XEL, W609RRU	XEL31	A9XEL, W102RRU

Depot: Southcote Road, Bournemouth
Web: www.excelsior-coaches.com

The 2003 intake of vehicles for Excelsior Coaches included a pair of Volvo B12s with Sunsundegui Sideral bodies. Number 610, FN03DXZ, is seen in London's Victoria district. *Tony Wilson*

FARESAVER

J V Pickford, 10 Bumpers Enterprise Centre, Vincients Road, Chippenham, SN14 6QA

XIL9631	Mercedes-Benz 709D	Whittaker Europa	BC25F	1990	Arriva The Shires, 2000
GJZ6083	Mercedes-Benz 811D	Carlyle C19	B29F	1990	GHA, New Broughton, 2001
IDZ8561	Mercedes-Benz 811D	Wright Nimbus	B26F	1990	Arriva Midlands, 2003
WCZ4815	Mercedes-Benz 811D	Wright Nimbus	BC33F	1991	Stagecoach Midland Red, 2002
YIL4529	Mercedes-Benz 811D	Carlyle C19	B23F	1991	Stagecoach Bluebird, 2002
H781GTA	Mercedes-Benz 811D	Carlyle C19	B25F	1991	Stagecoach Bluebird, 2002
K365TJF	Mercedes-Benz 811D	Dormobile Routemaker	B33F	1992	Shamrock, Pontypridd, 2003
K878UDB	Mercedes-Benz 709D	Plaxton Beaver	B27F	1993	Arriva Midlands, 2003
L422CPB	Mercedes-Benz 709D	Dormobile Routemaker	B25F	1993	Arriva Fox County, 2001
L423CPB	Mercedes-Benz 709D	Dormobile Routemaker	B25F	1993	Arriva Cymru, 2001
FNZ5636	Mercedes-Benz 709D	Alexander Sprint	BC16F	1993	Stagecoach South, 2002
L151FRJ	Mercedes-Benz 709D	Alexander Sprint	B23F	1993	Paul Chivers, Radstock, 2004
L228HRF	Mercedes-Benz 709D	Dormobile Routemaker	B27F	1993	Arriva Fox County, 2002
L231HRF	Mercedes-Benz 709D	Dormobile Routemaker	B27F	1993	Arriva Fox County, 2002
L233HRF	Mercedes-Benz 709D	Dormobile Routemaker	B27F	1993	Arriva Fox County, 2003
FNZ7649	Mercedes-Benz 709D	Alexander Sprint	BC19F	1994	Arriva Midlands, 2004
L316AUT	Mercedes-Benz 709D	Alexander Sprint	BC19F	1994	Arriva Midlands, 2004
L318AUT	Mercedes-Benz 709D	Alexander Sprint	B25F	1994	Arriva Fox County, 2002

The Faresaver fleet exclusively comprises Mercedes-Benz minibuses, though a variety of bodywork has been taken into stock. Showing the simple livery of white and mauve, is J408PRW, a Wright Nimbus-bodied example that has been re-registered WCZ4815. *Robert Edworthy*

One of the older examples of Mercedes-Benz 609 that has recently been sold by Faresaver is F378UCP. This minibus has Reeve Burgess Beaver bodywork and is seen at the company base in Chippenham.
Robert Edworthy

M459EDH	Mercedes-Benz 709D	Marshall C16	B31F	1994	Arriva Midlands, 2003
M454HPG	Mercedes-Benz 709D	Alexander Sprint	B23F	1994	Arriva North West & Wales, 2004
M457HPG	Mercedes-Benz 709D	Alexander Sprint	B23F	1994	Arriva North West & Wales, 2004
M122YCM	Mercedes-Benz 709D	Alexander Sprint	B27F	1995	Arriva Cymru, 2002
M236KNR	Mercedes-Benz 709D	Alexander Sprint	B29F	1995	Arriva Fox County, 2002
M411BEY	Mercedes-Benz 811D	Alexander Sprint	B25F	1995	Arriva North West & Wales, 2004
M412BEY	Mercedes-Benz 811D	Alexander Sprint	B29F	1995	Arriva North West, 2004
M998XRF	Mercedes-Benz 811D	Marshall C16	B31F	1995	Arriva North West & Wales, 2004
M276FNS	Mercedes-Benz 811D	Wadham Stringer Wessex	B33F	1995	Arriva Scotland, 2004
M799EUS	Mercedes-Benz 811D	Wadham Stringer Wessex	B33F	1995	Arriva Scotland, 2004
M193TMG	Mercedes-Benz 709D	Plaxton Beaver	BC20FL	1995	LB Barking & Dagenham, 2003
M39WUR	Mercedes-Benz 811D	Plaxton Beaver	BC31F	1995	Arriva The Shires, 2004
M41WUR	Mercedes-Benz 709D	Plaxton Beaver	B27F	1995	Arriva The Shires, 2004
M42WUR	Mercedes-Benz 811D	Plaxton Beaver	BC31F	1995	Arriva The Shires, 2004
N195EMJ	Mercedes-Benz 709D	Plaxton Beaver	B27F	1995	Arriva The Shires, 2004
N918ETM	Mercedes-Benz 709D	Plaxton Beaver	B27F	1995	Arriva The Shires, 2004
N346OBC	Mercedes-Benz 709D	Alexander Sprint	B27F	1995	Arriva Midlands, 2004
N352OBC	Mercedes-Benz 709D	Alexander Sprint	B27F	1995	Arriva Midlands, 2004
N602JGP	Mercedes-Benz 709D	Crystals	B25F	1995	Crystals, Dartford, 2004
N603JGP	Mercedes-Benz 709D	Crystals	B25F	1995	Crystals, Dartford, 2004
N780EUA	Mercedes-Benz 811D	Plaxton Beaver	B31F	1995	Arriva The Shires, 2004
N253PGD	Mercedes-Benz 711D	UVG CitiStar	B33F	1996	Arriva Scotland, 2004
P490TGA	Mercedes-Benz 711D	UVG CitiStar	B29F	1996	Arriva Scotland, 2004

Previous registrations:

FNZ5636	K865ODY	WCZ4815	J408PRW
FNZ7649	L316AUT	XIL9631	H523SWE
GJZ6083	G844UDV	YIL4529	H110HDV

TRAVEL FILER'S

R J & I H Filer, Slade Lodge, Slade Road, Ilfracombe, EX34 8LB

Reg	Chassis	Body	Type	Year	History
MIL9751	Volvo B10M-56	Plaxton Paramount 3200 E	C53F	1983	Hardings, Bagborough, 1995
RJI8606	Volvo B10M-60	Plaxton Paramount 3200 III	C53F	1989	Bakers Dolphin, Weston-s-M, 1999
K537CWN	DAF SB3000DKVF601	Caetano Algarve II	C53F	1993	Weavaway, Newbury, 2002
K539CWN	DAF SB3000DKVF601	Caetano Algarve II	C53F	1993	Girlings, Plymouth, 2002
L336DTG	Bova FHD 12.290	Bova Futura	C53FT	1994	Thomas-Rhondda, 1999
M823HNS	Volvo B10M-62	Van Hool Alizée HE	C53F	1995	Armchair, Brentford, 2001
M825HNS	Volvo B10M-62	Van Hool Alizée HE	C53F	1995	Armchair, Brentford, 2001
N751DAK	Bova FHD12.340	Bova Futura	C49FT	1996	Dunn-Line, 2001
S139ATA	Volkswagen Transporter LT55	G&M		M11	1998
T825OBL	Volkswagen Transporter LT55	Onyx		M16	1999	van, 2001
T406OWA	Scania L94IB	Irizar Century 12.35	C49FT	1999	Bus Eireann, 2004
V957EOD	Mercedes-Benz 614D	G&M	C24F	1999	
W445CFR	Bova FHD12.370	Bova Futura	C49FT	2000	Rossendale, 2004
WJ52MTU	Bova FHD12.340	Bova Futura	C49FT	2003	
WJ52MTV	Mercedes-Benz Vario O815	Sitcar Beluga	C29F	2002	
WA03SYV	LDV Convoy	LDV	M16	2003	

Previous registrations:

K537CWN	K537CWN, B10MTT, B10MSE	MIL9751	JYD877Y
M823HNS	LSK497	RJI8606	G261JCY
M825HNS	LSK498	T406OWA	99D55045

Much of Filer's bus work is now undertaken by First Devon and Cornwall allowing the Filer family to concentrate on coaching work and school contracts under the Travel Filer's name. Illustrating one of the 1995 Van Hool Alizée coaches is M822HNS. *Robert Edworthy*

GEOFF WILLETTS

FR Willetts & Co (Yorkley) Ltd, Main Road, Pillowell, Lydney, GL15 4QY

E169XWF	Mercedes-Benz L307D	Whittaker	M14	1988	Rover, Horsley, 2002
G290XFH	Leyland Tiger TRCL10/3ARZA	Plaxton Paramount 3200 III	C57F	1989	
H937DRJ	Volvo B10M-60	Plaxton Paramount 3200 III	C53F	1991	Shearings, 1995
890CVJ	Setra S250	Setra Special	C53FT	1996	Travellers, Hounslow, 1998
T896LBF	Dennis Javelin GX 12m	Plaxton Première 350	C53F	1999	Bassetts, Tittensor, 2003
X904ADF	Mercedes-Benz Vario O814	Plaxton Cheetah	C33F	2000	

Previous registrations:
890CVJ   N200TCC   E169XWF   W169XWF, B7AND

When coach operator Bassetts of Tittensor in Staffordshire closed during 2003 many modern coaches were placed on the market. From that fleet Geoff Willetts has acquired Dennis Javelin T896LBF. The coach has a Plaxton Première 350 body. *Robert Edworthy*

GLENVIC

Glenvic of Bristol Ltd, The Old Colliery, Pensford, Bristol, BS39 4BZ

NIL8255	Leyland Olympian ONLXB/1R	Eastern Coach Works	B45/32F	1981	Stagecoach East Midlands, 2001
NIL8259	Leyland Olympian ONLXB/1R	Eastern Coach Works	B45/32F	1981	Stagecoach East Midlands, 2001
SND489X	Leyland Atlantean AN68A/1R	Northern Counties	B43/32F	1982	Maynes of Manchester, 1999
OHV783Y	Leyland Titan TNLXB/2RR	Leyland	B43/30F	1983	Gwyn Williams, Lower Tumble, 2004
TIL4679	Leyland Tiger TRCTL11/3R	Plaxton Paramount 3200 III	C53F	1983	Blagdon Lioness, Blagdon, 2001
SCZ9765	Volvo B10M-61	Plaxton Paramount 3500 III	C51FT	1984	Millner, Tunley, 2004
E181AUJ	Scania K112CRS	Jonckheere Jubilee	C51FT	1988	Paragon, Stamshall, 2004
A17GVC	Mercedes-Benz 709D	Wadham Stringer Wessex	BC24FL	1994	HAD, Shotts, 2004
A18GVC	Mercedes-Benz 709D	Wadham Stringer Wessex	BC24FL	1994	HAD, Shotts, 2004
A16GVC	Dennis Javelin 10m	Wadham Stringer Vanguard II	BC47F	1995	MoD (ES14AA), 2003
M272POS	Volvo B10M-62	Jonckheere Deauville	C51FT	1995	MCT Group, Motherwell, 2002
S49JFV	LDV Convoy	LDV	M16	1999	North Bristol Project, Horfield, 2003
YR52MBU	Volvo B7R	TransBus Prima	C55F	2002	

Previous registrations:

A16GVC	N122BSL, N819OAE	M272POS	M272POS, M1MCT
A17GVC	L854WDS	NIL8255	NHL301X
A18GVC	L144XDS	NIL8259	NHL304X
A529LPP	A529LPP, TSV617	SCZ9765	A677WEV, LIL5072, XSV839, A400WGH
E181AUJ	E444LNP, DSK515, E967MWP, PAG366A	SND489X	SND489X, NIL8255
		TIL4679	A443RYC

In 2002 Glenvic added a rear-engined Volvo B7R to the fleet, a chassis seen as Volvo's response to the Dennis Javelin. Pictured at the depot preparing for an early school run, YR02MBU illustrates the TransBus Prima body styling, a version of the Première designed for Javelin/B7R. *Bill Potter*

GREY CARS

Millmans Coaches Ltd, 6 Daneheath Business Park, Wentworth Road, Heathfield, Newton Abbot, TQ12 6TL

Reg	Chassis	Body	Seating	Year	Previous owner
GIL3113	Volvo B10M-61	Plaxton Paramount 3200 III	C53FT	1985	
PJI2804	Volvo B10M-61	Plaxton Paramount 3200 III	C53F	1985	Frames Rickards, Brentford, 1991
PJI2805	Volvo B10M-61	Plaxton Paramount 3200 III	C53F	1985	Frames Rickards, Brentford, 1991
MIL3010	Volvo B10M-61	Plaxton Paramount 3500 III	C49FT	1987	Park's of Hamilton, 1988
SIL4460	Leyland Tiger TRCTL11/3RZ	Plaxton Paramount 3200 III	C53F	1987	Hedingham, 1999
D603MVR	Volvo B10M-61	Van Hool T9 Alizée	C53F	1987	Mills, Gornalwood, 2003
2091MX	Volvo B10M-61	Van Hool T9 Alizée	C53F	1988	Mills, Gornalwood, 2003
E906UNW	Volvo B10M-61	Plaxton Paramount 3500 III	C53F	1988	Price, Wolverhampton, 2002
E907UNW	Volvo B10M-61	Plaxton Paramount 3500 III	C53F	1988	Price, Wolverhampton, 2002
F909UPR	Volvo B10M-60	Plaxton Paramount 3500 III	C51F	1988	Holmeswood Coaches, 2002
MIL2066	Neoplan Skyliner N122/3	Neoplan	C57/18CT	1988	Rothwells Super Travel, 1999
MIL2088	Neoplan Skyliner N122/3	Neoplan	C57/18CT	1988	Airport Coaches Ltd, 1999
PJI2803	Volvo B10M-60	Jonckheere Deauville P599	C51FT	1989	Marbill, Beith, 1991
F105SSE	Volvo B10M-60	Plaxton Paramount 3500 III	C57F	1988	First Midland Scottish, 2002
MOD642	Volvo B10M-60	Plaxton Paramount 3500 III	C49FT	1989	Price, Wolverhampton, 2002
MIL3012	Volvo B10M-62	Van Hool Alizée HE	C49FT	1994	Park's of Hamilton, 1996
K3BUS	Toyota Coaster HDB30R	Caetano Optimo III	C21F	1995	First Western National, 1999
SIL4470	Volvo B10M-62	Van Hool Alizée HE	C51FT	1996	
SIL3066	Dennis Javelin GX	Berkhof Axial 50	C53F	1997	Limebourne, Battersea, 1998
KUB97	Volvo B10M-62	Van Hool T9 Alizée	C51FT	1998	

Previous registrations:

2091MX	E642UNE, 101RTD, E890FRS	MIL3010	D819SGB, 944JTT, D922UOD, PJI2807
E506CTT	E506CTT, MIL3012, MIL1942	MIL3012	LSK483, L629AYS
E906UNW	E906UNW, HIL6245	MOD642	F405DUG, 3267HX, F560LEO, SIB3934, F295GNT
E907UNW	E907UNW, LJI8160	PJI2803	G842GNV
F105SSE	F105SSE, ESK958	PJI2804	B534BML
F909UPR	F909UPR, SIW1909	PJI2805	B535BML
GIL3113	B230RRU	SIL3066	P889FMO
K3BUS	M582DAF	SIL4460	D584MVR
KUB97	S748XYA	SIL4460	D584MVR
MIL2066	E482YWJ, KFK172, E706CHS, HGR150, MIL2066	SIL4466	D600MVR
MIL2088	E473YWJ	SIL4470	N25EYD

Web: www.greycars.com

Plaxton Paramount-bodied Volvo B10M MIL3010 was photographed in June 2004 in Plymouth carrying vinyls for *90 years of Grey Cars operations.* During that time, however, the Grey Cars name has had several owners.
Mark Bailey

HAMBLYS OF KERNOW

P A & A F Hambly, The Garage, Jubilee Hill, Pelynt, Looe, PL13 2JZ

539WCV	Volvo B58-61	Plaxton Supreme IV	C53F	1981	Travel Filer's, Ilfracombe, 1996
URM141X	Volvo B10M-61	Van Hool Alizée	C48F	1982	Stagecoach Cumberland, 1999
710VCV	Volvo B10M-61	Plaxton Paramount 3500	C53F	1983	Prout, Port Isaac, 1995
YCV500	Volvo B10M-61	Van Hool Alizée	C53F	1985	Taunton Coaches, 1998
H362BDV	Mercedes-Benz 709D	Wadham Stringer Wessex	B25F	1990	Plymouth Citybus, 1998
WAF156	Mercedes-Benz Vario 0814	TransBus Beaver 2	BC33F	2004	

Previous registrations:
539WCV	PFH5W, 29DRH, SFH694W, PJI2417	GAF167V	YCV500
645UCV	CEB135V, WUF955	URM141X	LJC800, URM141X, WAF156
710VCV	LTR444Y, 800GTR, 710VCV, BYJ967Y	YCV500	B319UNB, XFJ379

Comparison with the Plaxton Paramount 3500 on the previous page illustrates the detailed changes in style between the early and Mark 3 versions. 710VCV is seen arriving in Plymouth from Lanreath while operating route 273. The service includes a link from Looe into the regional centre. *Mark Bailey*

HATTS EUROPA

Hatts Europa Ltd; Messrs Hillier, The Coach House, Foxham, Chippenham, SN15 4NB

Reg	Chassis	Body	Seats	Year	History
PJI6909	Leyland Tiger TRCTL11/3R	Plaxton Paramount 3200	C57F	1982	Cyril Evans, Senghenydd, 1989
LIL3060	Leyland Tiger TRCTL11/3RZ	Plaxton Paramount 3500 II	C57F	1984	Hawker, South Shields, 1994
D272BJB	Leyland Tiger TRCTL11/3RZ	Plaxton Paramount 3200 II	C53F	1987	Weavaway, Newbury, 2002
ACZ1133	Volvo B10M-61	Van Hool Alizée	C49DTL	1987	Sovereign, Stevenage, 1999
BAZ6170	Volvo B10M-60	Van Hool Alizée	C53F	1990	Shearings, 1997
BAZ6516	Volvo B10M-60	Van Hool Alizée	C53F	1990	Shearings, 1997
J853KHD	DAF SB2305DHTD585	Van Hool Alizée	C53F	1992	Kent CC, 2002
K505RJX	DAF SB2700DHTD585	Van Hool Alizée	C53F	1992	Reading Buses, 2001
JIL3959	DAF SB3000DKS601	Van Hool Alizée	C52FT	1993	Murray, St Helens, 1996
K727UTT	Iveco TurboDaily 59-12	Mellor	B29F	1993	Andy James, Tetbury, 2003
L524BDH	Iveco Daily 49-10	Mellor	B16FL	1994	Coventry MBC, 2001
M657COR	Volvo B10M-62	Van Hool Alizée HE	C46FT	1995	Coliseum, Southampton, 2002
M6HAT	EOS E180Z	EOS 90	C51FT	1995	
M8HAT	EOS E180Z	EOS 90	C51FT	1995	
M153XHW	Dennis Javelin 12m	UVG	BC70F	1995	MoD (CX68AA), 2002
N722DKJ	Iveco Daily 45-10	Euromotive	B16F	1996	Kent CC, 2003
P321ARU	Volvo B10M-62	Berkhof Axial 50	C49FT	1997	Yellow Buses, Bournemouth, 2002
P534PLB	Mercedes-Benz Vario O814	Autobus Classique	BC15F	1997	Central Parking, Heathrow, 2002
P74VWO	Mercedes-Benz 814D	Autobus Nouvelle	BC33F	1997	Bebb, Llantwit Fardre, 1999
R450YDT	MAN 11.220	Irizar MidiCentury 12.32	C35F	1998	Steventon Coaches, 2003
R873BKW	Scania L94IB	Irizar InterCentury 12.32	C57F	1998	Cedar, Bedford, 1998
R9HAT	Scania L94IB	Irizar Century 12.35	C49FT	1998	APT Coaches, Rayleigh, 2003

Illustrating the graphic livery applied by Hatts Europa is W554SJM, a Volvo B10M with Berkhof Axial 50 bodwork, pictured while on a trip to Ascot. At 3.55 metres, this is the lower of the two heights for this model, the other being 3.7 metres. *Dave Heath*

Hatts Europa took delivery of an Iveco EuroRider in 2000 and this carries a Beulas Stergo ε body. Beulas bodies are constructed in Spain and are available in Britain and Ireland exclusively on Iveco's Spanish-built EuroRider chassis and have primarily become popular with small family operations. A dark red version of the livery is applied to W818AAY. *Robert Edworthy*

T623KFH	Mercedes-Benz Vario 0814	Autobus Nouvelle 2	BC33F	1999	Northern, Martletwy, 2003	
T436TEU	Mercedes-Benz Vario 0814	Autobus Nouvelle 2	BC29F	1999	Andy James. Tetbury, 2003	
CNZ3829	Volvo B7R	Plaxton Prima	C57F	1999	Chambers, Moneymore, 2003	
T892LKJ	Renault Master	Rohill	B12F	1999	*Operated for Wiltshire CC*	
T893LKJ	Renault Master	Rohill	B12F	1999	*Operated for Wiltshire CC*	
T894LKJ	Renault Master	Rohill	B12F	1999	*Operated for Wiltshire CC*	
T905LKE	Scania L94IB	Irizar Century 12.35	C49FT	1999	The King's Ferry, Gillingham, 2003	
W818AAY	Iveco EuroRider 391E.12.35	Beulas Stergo ε	C49FT	2000		
W415HOB	Mercedes-Benz Vario 0814	Cymric	BC33F	2000		
W416HOB	Mercedes-Benz Vario 0814	Cymric	BC33F	2000		
W554SJM	Volvo B10M-62	Berkhof Axial 50	C49FT	2000		
X751VWR	Volvo B10M-62	Van Hool T9 Alizée	C51FT	2001	Freestones, Beetley, 2004	
Y736OBE	Mercedes-Benz Vario 0814	Autobus Nouvelle 2	B33F	2001		
YP52BRF	Optare Alero AL3	Optare	N14F	2002		
AJ03LXD	Ayats Atlantis A18-12/AT	Ayats	C53FT	2003		
BW03ZVA	Mercedes-Benz Sprinter 411CDi	Traveliner	M16	2003		
BW03ZUB	Mercedes-Benz Sprinter 411CDi	Traveliner	M16	2003		
BW03ZUC	Mercedes-Benz Sprinter 411CDi	Traveliner	M16	2003		
VU03ZPT	Mercedes-Benz Vario 0814	Mellor	BC33F	2003		
VX53AVJ	Mercedes-Benz Vario 0814	TransBus Beaver 2	BC33F	2004		
VX04KTK	Mercedes-Benz Vario 0814	TransBus Beaver 2	BC33F	2004		

Special event vehicle:

LTA755	Bedford OB	Duple Vista	C29F	1950	Mid Devon, Bow, 2003

Previous registrations:

ACZ1133	D350KVE		M153XHW	CX68AA
BAZ6170	G850RNC		M657COR	MIB650
BAX6516	G846RNC		MIL5237	F35CWY
CNZ3829	S88CCH		PJI6909	SAX998Y, EEU359, UDW385Y
D272BJB	D602MVR, SIB9043, B10MLT		R9HAT	R476YDT, 98D41119, APT42S
JIL3939	K104TCP		R873BKW	R9CCC
LIL3060	B511UNB, A6WEH, B452JVK		T436TEU	T436TEU, T30ARJ

HOOKWAYS

Hookways-Pleasureways - Greenslades - Jennings

Hookways Ltd, The Garage, Meeth, Okehampton, EX20 3EP

CSU938	Leyland Leopard PSU3E/4R	Plaxton Paramount 3200 (1977)	C45F	1977	Thomas Bros, Llangadog, 2002
990XYA	Volvo B58-56	Plaxton Supreme IV	C51C	1980	Greenslades, Exeter, 1996
NIW8290	Volvo B58-56	Plaxton Supreme IV	C51C	1981	Greenslades, Exeter, 1996
OBO631X	Leyland Tiger TRCTL11/2R	Plaxton Supreme V	C51F	1982	Summerdale Cs, Letterston, 1999
UIL4705	Volvo B10M-61	Jonckheere Jubilee	C51FT	1983	Watson, Yeovil, 2003
SGL498Y	Volvo B10M-61	Plaxton Paramount 3200	C57F	1983	Jennings, Bude, 1998
6185RU	DAF MB200DKFL600	Plaxton Paramount 3200	C35FL	1983	Reynolds Diplomat, Perivale, 1993
MIL4680	Leyland Tiger TRCTL11/3RZ	Plaxton Paramount 3200	C57F	1986	Inland Travel, Flimwell, 2001
GOU908	Volvo B10M-61	Plaxton Paramount 3200 II	C53F	1986	Dorset Queen, East Chaldon, 2004
WXI3860	Volvo B10M-61	Plaxton Paramount 3200 II	C53F	1986	Dorset Queen, East Chaldon, 2004
2603HP	DAF SB2300DHTD685	Plaxton Paramount 3200 III	C57F	1987	Seward, Dalwood, 1999
B726OBC	Bova EL28-581	Duple Calypso	C51F	1987	Wreake Valley, Syston, 1987
789FAY	Volvo B10M-61	Duple 340	C57F	1987	Jennings, Bude, 1998
6740HP	Volvo B10M-61	Plaxton Paramount 3500 III	C53F	1987	Bysiau Ffoshelig, 1999
9743HP	Volvo B10M-61	Plaxton Paramount 3200 III	C57F	1987	Jennings, Bude, 1998
3315HP	Volvo B10M-61	Plaxton Paramount 3500 III	C49FT	1987	Jennings, Bude, 1998
VJI8687	Volvo B10M-61	Plaxton Paramount 3500 III	C57F	1987	New Bharat, Southall, 2003
D778NYG	Volvo B10M-61	Plaxton Paramount 3500 III	C49FT	1987	Crawley Luxury Coaches, 2003
E716CPC	Mercedes-Benz 811D	Robin Hood	BC24F	1988	Altonian, Alton, 2000
F215DCC	Mercedes-Benz 709D	Robin Hood	B29F	1988	Arriva Cymru, 2001
F221DCC	Mercedes-Benz 709D	Robin Hood	B29F	1988	Arriva Cymru, 2001

In recent years, Hookways had expanded eastwards with the acquisition of the Dorset Queen operation. However, a restructuring in 2005 has seen a withdrawal of this fringe business. The Greenslades name continues as shown on the front of J42VWO, a Volvo B10M with Plaxton Paramount bodywork, which was pictured near Cardiff.   *Chris Newsome*

A suitable vehicle for Hookways' stage operations is Autobus Classique-bodied Mercedes 814 K729GBE. Pictured at Holsworthy in June 2004, it was allocated to route 649 which operates through to Bude. *Mark Bailey*

	PIL6581	Volvo B10M-61	Plaxton Paramount 3200 III	C48FT	1988	Chiltern Queens, Woodcote, 2001
	9878HP	Volvo B10M-61	Plaxton Paramount 3200 III	C57F	1988	Jennings, Bude, 1998
	4846HP	LAG Panoramic G355Z	LAG	C49FT	1988	Mid Wales Motorways, 1998
	SJI8117	Volvo B10M-61	Plaxton Paramount 3500 III	C51FT	1989	Buddens, Romsey, 1997
	7346HP	Volvo B10M-61	Plaxton Paramount 3500 III	C49FT	1989	Stevens, Bristol, 1999
	KAZ6911	Volvo B10M-61	Plaxton Paramount 3500 III	C53F	1989	New Bharat, Southall, 2003
w	F714EUG	Toyota Coaster HB31R	Caetano Optimo	C21F	1989	Redhill & Singh, Thornbury, 2000
w	748JTA	Toyota Coaster HB31R	Caetano Optimo	C21F	1989	Gale, Haslemere, 1999
w	G105APC	Toyota Coaster HB31R	Caetano Optimo	C21F	1990	Chariots, Stanford-le-Hope, 2000
	5351HP	LAG Panoramic G355Z	LAG	C49FT	1990	Cumfilux Travel, Hillingdon, 1997
	H346JFX	Volvo B10M-60	Plaxton Expressliner	C46FT	1990	Rest & Ride, Smethwick, 2001
	4415HP	Volvo B10M-61	Plaxton Paramount 3500 III	C51FT	1991	Hill, Hanwell, 2001
	3785HP	Volvo B10M-61	Plaxton Paramount 3500 III	C51FT	1991	Leon's of Stafford, 2001
	7876HP	Volvo B10M-61	Plaxton Paramount 3500 III	C51FT	1991	Leon's of Stafford, 2001
	223TUO	Toyota Coaster HDB30R	Caetano Optimo II	C18F	1991	Richmond, Barley, 2001
	J42VWO	Volvo B10M-60	Plaxton Paramount 3500 III	C49FT	1992	Ferris, Nantgarw, 2001
	J511LRY	Volvo B10M-60	Caetano Algarve II	C55F	1992	Dorset Queen, East Chaldon, 2003
	K729GBE	Mercedes-Benz 814D	Autobus Classique	BC25F	1993	MacLeod, Rogart, 2003
	K227WNH	MAN 16.290	Jonckheere Deauville	C57F	1993	Alec Head, Lutton, 2003
	3427HP	Volvo B10M-60	Plaxton Première 350	C53F	1993	Goode, West Bromwich, 2002
	M681HGG	Volkswagen Caravelle	Volkswagen	M7	1995	Meet & Greet, Wemyss Bay, 2003
	M533BLU	Volkswagen Caravelle	Volkswagen	M7	1995	Abbey, Hitchin, 2003
	1434HP	Volvo B10M-62	Plaxton Excalibur	C53F	1995	Dodsworth, Boroughbridge, 2001
	9880HP	Volvo B10M-62	Plaxton Excalibur	C53F	1997	Dodsworth, Boroughbridge, 2001
	4691HP	Volvo B10M-62	Plaxton Excalibur	C49FT	1997	Dorset Queen, East Chaldon, 2003
	R252EMV	MAN 18.310	Noge Catalan 350	C49FT	1998	Alec Head, Lutton, 2003
	R253EMV	MAN 18.310	Noge Catalan 350	C49FT	1998	Alec Head, Lutton, 2003
	R254EMV	MAN 18.310	Noge Catalan 350	C49FT	1998	Alec Head, Lutton, 2003
	W161CWR	Volkswagen Caravelle	Volkswagen	M7	2000	Wallace Arnold, 2003
	Y814HUB	Volkswagen Transporter	Volkswagen	M8	2001	Wallace Arnold, 2003
	Y223NYA	Mercedes-Benz Vario O815	Sitcar Beluga	C27F	2001	Dorset Queen, East Chaldon, 2003

The South West Bus Handbook

Cherished index numbers are keenly used by coach operators, many of whom have their own sets of marks. Hookways has built a collection of 'HP' plates, with 4415HP and 7346HP illustrated here. When not in use, plates may be placed on retention for a while, as is the case at present with 6230HP. Current changes in business have seen the withdrawal and storage of a number of vehicles for immediate sale. These have been omitted from the list although many were still on the company's premises as we went to press. *Mark Bailey*

Previous registrations:

223TUO	J135LLK, 577HTX, J135LLK	9880HP	P741YUM
409FRH	URU651X	B726OBC	B726OBC, 5781HP
748JTA	-	C942DHT	C942DHT, 244SYA
789FAY	D36LRL	CSU938	WUG128S
990XYA	DYW170V	D778NYG	D887EEH, BVA300, BIW6496, LBZ2577
1434HP	M740YNW	E716CPC	E480JLK, WET590, E81LLO, KXI599
2603HP	D490RUS	GOU908	C195CYO
3315HP	D809SGB	H346JFX	H346JFX, XYN670
3427HP	A11GOO, L160EOG	K227WNH	K227WNH, A111OAV
3785HP	H891JVR, 972SYD, H168ETU	KAZ6911	F104CCL
3692HP	-	MIL3727	-
4415HP	H660UWR, GSU382, H660UWR	MIL4680	C331PEW, AEF315A, B542HAM, AEF315A
4691HP	P8RJH	NIW8290	HYR175W
4846HP	F774PFF	PIL6581	E533PRU
5351HP	G487KBD	R252EMV	R252EMV, 4388WX
6185RU	ANA447Y	R253EMV	R253EMV, A8EAD
6230HP	-	R254EMV	R254EMV, 8098NK
6740HP	E565UHS, FSU375, DSU772, E857WEP	RJI5701	-
7105HP	-	SJI8117	F308URU
7346HP	H834AHS	TJI9141	-
7876HP	H912JVR, 588EH, H169ETU	UIL4705	TJR500Y
9743HP	D275MCV	VJI8687	D882FYL, 917DBO
9878HP	E561RRL	WXI3860	D280JNE
		XYN670	-

Depots: Lansdown Road, Bude; Pinhoe Trading Estate, Exeter; Littleham, Exmouth and The Garage, Meeth
Web: www.hookways.com

HOPLEY'S COACHES

DR & NA Hopley, Sunic, Rope Walk, Mount Hawke, Truro, TR4 8DW

KVF248V	Bristol VRT/SL/6LXB	Eastern Coach Works	B43/31F	1980	Stagecoach Red & White, 1999
IAZ2314	Leyland Olympian ONLXB/1R	Eastern Coach Works	B45/32F	1982	Arriva The Shires, 2002
508AHU	Volvo B10M-56	Plaxton Supreme V Express	C53F	1982	Tillingbourne, Cranleigh, 1994
TSV302	Volvo B10M-61	Jonckheere Jubilee	C49FT	1983	Rover, Horsley, 1998
640UAF	Volvo B10M-60	Jonckheere Deauville P599	C51FT	1992	Vale of Llangollen, 2001
N536SJF	Volvo B10M-62	Jonckheere Deauville P599	C49FT	1996	Clarke's of London, 2003
Y922DCY	Mercedes-Benz Sprinter 614D	Cymric	C24F	2001	
WK03BTE	Optare Solo M920	Optare	N31F	2003	
WK03BTF	Optare Solo M920	Optare	N31F	2003	
WK03ENM	Optare Solo M920	Optare	N33F	2003	

Previous registrations:
508AHU	NUH262X		IAZ2314	MUH288X
640UAF	J986GLG, VLT149, VLT293, VLT280		TSV302	ONV653Y

To operate tendered services around Truro three of the longer Optare Solo buses are operated by Hopley's Coaches. Seen arriving in Truro on route 304 from Porthtowan is WK03BTF. *Mark Bailey*

JAMES BEVAN

James Bevan (Lydney) Ltd, Bus Station, Hams Road, Lydney, GL15 5PE

GBU2V	MCW Metrobus DR101/6	MCW	B43/30F	1979	Cottrells, Mitcheldean, 2004	
K216SUY	Dennis Javelin 10m	Wadham Stringer Vanguard II	BC53F	1992	MoD (74KF74), 2001	
K237SUY	Dennis Javelin 10m	Wadham Stringer Vanguard II	B53F	1992	MoD (74KK72), 2001	
N653THO	Volvo B10M-62	Plaxton Première 350	C49F	1995	Excelsior, Bournemouth, 1999	
N967OAE	Dennis Javelin 8.5m	Wadham Stringer Vanguard III	B37F	1996	MoD, 2004	
P590CFH	MAN 11.220 HOCL-R	Caetano Algarve II	C53F	1997	Eirebus, Dublin, 2002	
P347VWR	Volvo B10M-62	Plaxton Première 350	C50F	1997	Wallace Arnold, 2002	
R170SUT	Volvo B7R	Plaxton Prima	C53F	1998		
W678DDN	Optare Solo M850	Optare	N30F	2000		
FP53JYB	Volvo B7R	Sunsundegui Sideral	C53F	2004		

Previous registrations:
N653THO XEL254   P590CFH   97D23704

The sole double-deck operating with James Bevan is Metrobus GBU2V which was new to Greater Manchester. As shown here the vehicle carries an all-over grey colour scheme. *Robert Edworthy*

MARCHANTS

Marchants Coaches Ltd, 61 Clarence Street, Cheltenham, GL50 3LB

RUA452W	Bristol VRT/SL3/6LXB	Eastern Coach Works	B43/31F	1980	Bennett, Gloucester, 2000
RUA457W	Bristol VRT/SL3/6LXB	Eastern Coach Works	B43/31F	1980	Bennett, Gloucester, 2001
CWR512Y	Leyland Olympian ONLXB/1R	Eastern Coach Works	BC43/29F	1982	UK North, Manchester, 2003
EEH902Y	Leyland Olympian ONLXB/1R	Eastern Coach Works	B45/32F	1983	Bennett, Gloucester, 2004
JEY124Y	Volvo B10M-61	Plaxton P'mount 3200 (1990)	C57F	1983	Arvonia, Llanrug, 1990
LIL9843	Neoplan Skyliner N112/3	Neoplan	C57/20CT	1988	Lambert's, Beccles, 1998
E322PMD	Volvo B9M	Plaxton Derwent II	B40F	1988	Capital, West Drayton, 1999
E323PMD	Volvo B9M	Plaxton Derwent II	B40F	1988	Capital, West Drayton, 1999
E324PMD	Volvo B9M	Plaxton Derwent II	B40F	1988	Capital, West Drayton, 1999
F312JTY	Leyland Olympian ONLXB/1R	Alexander RH	BC43/30F	1988	Arriva North East, 2003
G50ONN	Volvo B10M-60	Plaxton Paramount 3500 III	C57F	1989	Skills, Nottingham, 1997
L543YUS	Volvo B10M-60	Van Hool Alizée HE	C49FT	1993	National Holidays, 1998
M756XET	Volvo B10M-62	Plaxton Première 350	C53F	1995	-, 2003
N101HGO	Volvo B6BLE	Wright Crusader	N36F	1995	Travel West Midlands, 2004
P10TCC	Neoplan Skyliner N122/3	Neoplan	C57/20DT	1996	The King's Ferry, Gillingham, 2002
P6WRS	Volvo B10M-62	Plaxton Première 350	C51F	1997	Spring, Evesham, 2003
R360OWO	Volvo B7R	Plaxton Première 320	C55F	1998	2 Travel, Swansea, 2005
R370OWO	Volvo B7R	Plaxton Première 320	C55F	1998	2 Travel, Swansea, 2005
R380OWO	Volvo B7R	Plaxton Première 320	C55F	1998	2 Travel, Swansea, 2005
R431FWT	Volvo B10M-62	Plaxton Excalibur	C48FT	1998	Wallace Arnold, 2000
R432FWT	Volvo B10M-62	Plaxton Excalibur	C48FT	1998	Wallace Arnold, 2000
R452FWT	Volvo B10M-62	Plaxton Première 320	C53F	1998	Wallace Arnold, 2000
R48WUY	Mercedes-Benz Sprinter 312	Mercedes-Benz	M14	1998	-, 2005
VX51AWO	Mercedes-Benz Vario O814	Plaxton Cheetah	C25F	2001	
FJ54ZCV	Volvo B12B	VDL Jonckheere Mistral	C51FT	2005	
FJ54ZCX	Volvo B12B	VDL Jonckheere Mistral	C51FT	2005	
	Volvo B12B	VDL Jonckheere Mistral	C49FT	On order	
	Volvo B12B	VDL Jonckheere Mistral	C49FT	On order	

Previous registrations:

		LIL9843	E214BOD
JEY124Y	MSU593Y, VYB704	P6WRS	P332VWR
L543YUS	XIA257, KSK954	P10TCC	P981HWF

Depot: Prestbury Road, Cheltenham
Web: www.marchants-coaches.com

Marchants operates three Volvo B9M buses which spent their early days operating hotel shuttles into Heathrow Aiport. Showing off the Plaxton Derwent body is E324PMD, which has been rebuilt to forward entrance.
Robert Edworthy

69

MICHAELS TRAVEL

Forest Hopper - The Forest of Dean Tour - Michaels Travel

M Davies, 2 Colchester Close, Mitcheldean, GL17

DCA528X	Bristol VRT/SL3/6LXB	Eastern Coach Works	O43/31F	1981	Arriva North West and Wales, 2004
MIL2175	DAF MB230LT615	Van Hool Alizée	C49FT	1990	Odgen, St Helens, 2004
JAZ9910	Toyota Coaster HDB30R	Caetano Optimo II	C21F	1991	Ryder, West Bromwich, 1998
P785KRV	Mercedes-Benz 311D	Mercedes-Benz	M16	1997	
FX51AXP	LDV Convoy	Excel	M16	2001	van, 2001

Previous registrations:
JAZ9910   J2JBT, J113CWJ   MIL2175   G232NCW

Depot: Gloucester Road, Mitcheldean

Michaels Travel has been operating The Forest of Dean Tour using open-top Bristol VR DCA528X which was latterly at Rhyl with Arriva Cymru. It is seen on August Bank Holiday Saturday 2004 at the Beechenhurst Lodge picnic area and timing point. However, a partial open-top bus is being sought for the 2005 season. *Tom Johnson*

MID DEVON COACHES

K J Wills, Midco, Station Road, Bow, Crediton, EX17 6JD

MIL5579	Bedford YMT	Plaxton Paramount 3200	C53F	1982	Wainfleet, Nuneaton, 1986
MIL5991	Ford R1114	Duple Dominant II	C53F	1982	Bryants, Williton, 1996
MIL5578	Leyland Tiger TRCTL11/2R	Plaxton Paramount 3200	C53F	1983	
WAW354Y	Ford R1114	Plaxton Supreme IV Express	C53F	1983	Pratt, Moreton Valence, 2002
MIL6682	Ford R1115	Plaxton Paramount 3200	C53F	1983	Andrews, Marshfield, 1998
SJI8285	Leyland Tiger TRCTL11/3R	Plaxton Paramount 3200 Exp	C53F	1983	Heritage, Sturminster Marshall, 2003
MIL5992	Leyland Tiger TRCTL11/2RH	Plaxton Paramount 3200 Exp	C53F	1983	Lock, Surrey Docks, 2003
WFV530	Bova FHD12.280	Bova Futura	C53F	1984	Hills Services, Stibb Cross, 2000
A35AWA	Ford R1115 8.5m	Plaxton Paramount 3200	C35F	1984	C J Down, Mary Tavy, 2002
NSU205	Scania K112CRF	Jonckheere Jubilee P599	C53F	1984	Harris, Wombwell, 1999
LIL4348	Leyland Tiger TRCTL11/3R	Plaxton Paramount 3500	C55F	1984	Newton, Guildford, 2002
TIL2812	Leyland Tiger TRCTL11/3R	Plaxton Paramount 3500	C57F	1984	Newton, Guildford, 2002
MIL5577	Leyland Tiger TRCTL11/3R	Plaxton Paramount 3400	C49FT	1984	Arlington demonstrator, 1986
LIL9174	Bova FLD12.250	Bova Futura	C53F	1986	Chivers, Midsomer Norton, 2001
TSU649	Scania K112CRF	Jonckheere Jubilee P599	C53FT	1986	Flintham, Metheringham, 1999
MIL6684	Scania K112CRB	Plaxton Paramount 3500 III	C49FT	1988	Blakes Coaches, East Anstey, 2002
F198JKL	Ford Transit VE6	Ford	M16	1988	-, 2000
OIW1319	Volvo B10M-60	Plaxton Paramount 3500 III	C49FT	1989	Wallace Arnold, 2002
MIL5993	Volvo B10M-60	Plaxton Paramount 3500 III	C53F	1989	South Dorset, Swanage, 2003
G167XJF	Toyota Coaster HB31R	Caetano Optimo	C21F	1990	Swallow, Bristol, 2000
SIL5960	Scania K113CRB	Irizar Century 12.35	C49FT	1990	Coachstyle, Nettleton, 2004
WIL3621	Volvo B10M-60	Plaxton Paramount 3500 III	C49FT	1991	Roberts Coaches, Maerdy, 2004
K926TTA	Toyota Coaster HDB30R	Caetano Optimo II	C21F	1992	Seward Dalwood, 2000
L589BFJ	Ford Transit VE6	Ford	M8	1993	private owner, 2001
M965LDV	Ford Transit VE6	Ford	M8	1994	private owner, 2004
N844DKU	Scania K113TRB	Irizar Century 12.37	C49FT	1996	Chanel Coachways, Bow, 2003

Special event vehicles:

MJH280L	Seddon-Pennine IV	Plaxton Panorama Elite	C44F	1973	Laing, Greenford, 1978
OTG44R	AEC Reliance 6MU4R	Duple Dominant	C41F	1977	Central, Ripponden, 1980

Previous registrations:

A35AWA	A35AWA, USV620, NIL4987	MIL6682	EFK148Y
FIL5960	N11HDC	MIL6684	E584OEF, 24PAE, E667MWP
G167XJF	G167XJF, 253DAF	NSU205	A57JLW
LIL4348	A150RMJ	OIW1319	F35HGG
LIL9174	C126AHP, 2086PP, C160XRT	SJI8285	FKK838Y, TSU638, RIL9731
MIL5577	A198RUR	TIL2812	A281GEC, BIB2994, A242SCW
MIL5578	FTA850Y	TSU649	C412LRP
MIL5579	YUT637Y	WAW354Y	WAW354Y, TIL5933
MIL5991	HYC642Y	WIL3621	H607UWR, CCZ2212
MIL5992	A114EPA, YSU895	WSV530	A660EMY
MIL5993	F474WFX		

Seen in central London, Plaxton Paramount-bodied OIW1319 leads coach bound for Exeter.
Dave Heath

71

MIKE'S TRAVEL

B Cainey, 50 Castle Street, Thornbury, Bristol, BS35 1HB

4	SRY759X	AEC Reliance	Plaxton Supreme	C53F	1977	Pugh, Chipping Sodbury, 1991
14	DAD600Y	Leyland Tiger TRCTL11/3R	Plaxton Paramount 3500	C57F	1983	Pulham, Bourton-on-the-Water, 1998
7	A707GPR	Leyland Tiger TRCTL11/3R	Duple Dominant IV	C53F	1984	Martin, West End, 2003
	CHZ9055	Leyland Tiger TRCTL11/3RH	Duple Lazer	C57F	1983	Cotswold Green, Whitminster, 2004
16	E458CGM	Mercedes-Benz 609D	Robin Hood	B20F	1987	Bugler, Bristol, 1999
17	E995KJF	Mercedes-Benz O303/15R	Mercedes-Benz	C53F	1988	Talbott, Moreton-in-Marsh, 2000
20	M569SRE	Mercedes-Benz 709D	Plaxton Beaver	BC25F	1994	First Potteries, 2002

Special event vehicle:
| 624 | 338EDV | Bristol SUL4A | Eastern Coach Works | B34F | 1960 | Weaverbus, Weymouth, 2000 |

Previous registrations:
| CHZ9055 | A601HVT, PF2045, A243YGF | | DAD600Y | DAD600Y, VDF365 |

Depot: Bryndeir Farm, The Naite, Olbury-on Severn.
Named vehicles: SRY Supreme Reliance; DAD Tigger; CGM Robbie; KJF Otto; SRE The Reiver.

Mike's Travel operates Leyland Tiger DAD600Y, seen here in Mike's Travel fleet livery though it was new to Pulhams of Bourton-on-the-Water. *Robert Edworthy*

PETER CAROL

P F Collis, Bamfield House, Bamfield, Whitchurch, Bristol BS14 0XD

ROI1229	MAN 11.190 HOCL-R	Caetano Algarve II	C15FT	1996	
ROI2929	Scania K113CRB	Berkhof Axial 50	C30FT	1998	Shamrock, Pontypridd, 1999
800XPC	Neoplan Cityliner N316	Neoplan	C27FT	1998	
ROI7435	Neoplan Skyliner N122/3	Neoplan	C57/20DT	1999	
ROI6774	Toyota Coaster BB50R	Caetano Optimo V	C12FT	2001	
ROI8235	Scania K124IB4	Van Hool T9 Alizée	C53F	2001	
ROI8358	Bova FHD10-340	Bova Futura	C32FT	2001	
ROI1417	MAN 18.350	Noge Catalan Star 350	C49FT	2002	
WA53SFY	Bova FHD10-340	Bova Futura	C27FT	2004	
BX54ECA	Mercedes-Benz 1836RL	Mercedes-Benz Touro	C49FT	2004	
BX54ECE	Mercedes-Benz 1836RL	Mercedes-Benz Touro	C49FT	2004	
BX54ECT	Mercedes-Benz 1836RL	Mercedes-Benz Touro	C49FT	2004	

Previous registrations:

800XPC	R275THL		ROI6774	FJ51JXX
ROI1229	N790ORY		ROI7435	S150SET
ROI1417	YR52ZKC		ROI8235	Y989HET
ROI2929	R83RBY		ROI8358	Y218NYA

Web: www.luxurycoach.co.uk

Illustrating the Peter Carol fleet is one of two Neoplan Skyliners currently operated. Shown here as S150SET, the coach has subsequently been re-registered with one of the fleet's ROI plates, ROI7435. *Robert Edworthy*

PLYMOUTH CITYBUS

Plymouth Citybus - Plymouth Citycoach

Plymouth Citybus Ltd, Milehouse, Plymouth, Devon, PL3 4AA

1-12			Dennis Dart SLF		Plaxton Pointer		N39F	1996		
1	N101UTT	3	N103UTT	5	N105UTT	8	N108UTT	10	N110UTT
2	N102UTT	4	N104UTT	7	N107UTT	9	N109UTT	12	N112UTT

13-27			Dennis Dart SLF		Plaxton Pointer 2		N39F	1998-99		
13	R113OFJ	16	R116OFJ	19	R119OFJ	22	R122OFJ	25	R125OFJ
14	R114OFJ	17	R117OFJ	20	R120OFJ	23	R123OFJ	26	R126OFJ
15	R115OFJ	18	R118OFJ	21	R121OFJ	24	R124OFJ	27	S127FTA

28-40			Dennis Dart SLF		Plaxton Pointer SPD		N43F	1999		
28	T128EFJ	31	T131EFJ	34	T134EFJ	37	T137EFJ	39	T139EFJ
29	T129EFJ	32	T132EFJ	35	T135EFJ	38	T138EFJ	40	T140EFJ
30	T130EFJ	33	T133EFJ	36	T136EFJ				

41-48			Dennis Dart SLF		Plaxton Pointer SPD		N41F	2000-01		
41	X141CDV	43	X143CFJ	45	Y645NYD	47	Y647NYD	48	Y648NYD
42	X142CDV	44	Y644NYD	46	Y646NYD				

51	M51HOD	Volvo B6-9.9M	Plaxton Pointer	B40F	1994
52	M52HOD	Volvo B6-9.9M	Plaxton Pointer	B40F	1994
53	M53HOD	Volvo B6-9.9M	Plaxton Pointer	B40F	1994

In 2000, Plymouth Citybus added a pair of East Lancs-bodied Volvo Citybuses to the fleet. These were similar to some already operated, and came from Arriva. Seen in the city, 173, G643CHF, is seen on school duties.
Mark Bailey

Park & Ride livery is carried by Plymouth Citybus Dart 69, WA03BHY. It is one of a batch of the longer Super Pointer Darts supplied by TransBus. *Mark Bailey*

55-59   Dennis Dart SLF 11.3m   Plaxton Pointer SPD   N41F   2001

| 55 | WA51ACO | 56 | WA51ACU | 57 | WA51ACV | 58 | WA51ACX | 59 | WA51ACY |

60-71   TransBus Dart 11.3m   TransBus Super Pointer   N41F   2002-03

60	WJ52GNY	63	WJ52GOC	66	WJ52GOK	68	WA03BHX	70	WA03BHZ
61	WJ52GNZ	64	WJ52GOE	67	WA03BHW	69	WA03BHY	71	WA03BJE
62	WJ52GOA	65	WJ52GOH						

72-79   Alexander-Dennis Dart 10.7m   Alexander-Dennis Pointer   N37F   2004

72	WA54JVV	74	WA54JVX	76	WA54JVZ	78	WA54JWD	79	WA54JWE
73	WA54JVW	75	WA54JVY	77	WA54JWC			80	WJ55HLG
								81	WJ55HLH

101-110   Dennis Dart 9.8SDL3017   Plaxton Pointer   B40F   1992

101	K101SFJ	103	K103SFJ	105	K105SFJ	108	K108SFJ	83	WJ55HLM
102	K102SFJ	104	K104SFJ	107	K107SFJ	109	K109SFJ	110	K110SFJ
								86	WJ55HLP
								87	WJ55HLR

112-126   Dennis Dart 9.8SDL3035   Plaxton Pointer   B40F   1993

112	L112YOD	115	L115YOD	118	L118YOD	121	L121YOD	124	L124YOD
113	L113YOD	116	L116YOD	119	L119YOD	122	L122YOD	125	L125YOD
114	L114YOD	117	L117YOD	120	L120YOD	123	L123YOD	126	L126YOD

127-132   Dennis Dart 9.8SDL3040   Plaxton Pointer   B40F   1994

| 127 | M127HOD | 129 | M129HOD | 130 | M130HOD | 131 | M131HOD | 132 | M132HOD |
| 128 | M128HOD | | | | | | | | |

162	TTT162W	Leyland Atlantean AN68C/1R	East L'ancs	B43/31F	1981	
170	TTT170W	Leyland Atlantean AN68C/1R	East Lancs	B43/31F	1981	
171	TTT171W	Leyland Atlantean AN68C/1R	East Lancs	B43/31F	1981	
173	G643CHF	Volvo Citybus B10M-50	East Lancs	B49/39F	1989	Arriva Southern Counties, 2000
174	G640CHF	Volvo Citybus B10M-50	East Lancs	B49/39F	1989	Arriva Southern Counties, 2000
175	B175VDV	Volvo Citybus B10M-50	East Lancs	B42/35F	1984	

The South West Bus Handbook   75

Plymouth Citybus acquired twelve Alexander-bodied Volvo Citybuses, previously operated by Trent, that displaced older double-decks. Seen in the city while operating to the Derriford Hospital is 180, G614OTV, *Richard Godfrey*

176	B176VDV	Volvo Citybus B10M-50		East Lancs		B42/35F	1984		
177	H177GTT	Volvo Citybus B10M-50		East Lancs		BC48/30F	1991		
178	H178GTT	Volvo Citybus B10M-50		East Lancs		BC48/30F	1991		

179-190 Volvo Citybus B10M-50 Alexander RV B47/37F 1988-89 Trent Buses, 1999-2000

179	G612OTV	182	G621OTV	185	F602GVO	187	F604GVO	189	F606GVO
180	G614OTV	183	F600GVO	186	F603GVO	188	F605GVO	190	F607GVO
181	G615OTV	184	F601GVO						

195	F50ACL	Volvo Citybus B10M-50	Alexander RV		B45/37F	1989	Chambers, Bures, 2000
196	F51ACL	Volvo Citybus B10M-50	Alexander RV		B45/37F	1989	Chambers, Bures, 2000
197	G623OTV	Volvo Citybus B10M-50	Alexander RV		B47/37F	1989	Chambers, Bures, 2000
201	X201CDV	Dennis Dart SLF	Plaxton Pointer MPD		N29F	2000	
202	X202CDV	Dennis Dart SLF	Plaxton Pointer MPD		N29F	2000	
203	X203CDV	Dennis Dart SLF	Plaxton Pointer MPD		N29F	2000	
204	X204CDV	Dennis Dart SLF	Plaxton Pointer MPD		N29F	2000	
205	WA03BJF	TransBus Dart 8.8m	TransBus Mini Pointer		N29F	2003	

257-289 Mercedes-Benz 709D Plaxton Beaver B25F 1992-95

257	L257YOD	266	M266HOD	272	M272HOD	278	N278PDV	284	N284PDV
258	L258YOD	267	M267HOD	273	M273HOD	279	N279PDV		
261	M261HOD	268	M268HOD	274	M274HOD	280	N280PDV	286	N286PDV
262	M262HOD	269	M269HOD	275	N275PDV	281	N281PDV	287	N287PDV
263	M263HOD	270	M270HOD	276	N276PDV	282	N282PDV	288	N288PDV
264	M264HOD	271	M271HOD	277	N277PDV	283	N283PDV	289	N289PDV
265	M265HOD								

301	K301WTA	Volvo B10M-60	Plaxton Première 350	C51F	1993	
302	L302YOD	Volvo B10M-60	Plaxton Première 350	C51F	1993	
304	M304KOD	Volvo B10M-62	Plaxton Première 350	C49FT	1995	
305	M305KOD	Volvo B10M-62	Plaxton Première 350	C49FT	1995	
307	N307UTT	Volvo B10M-62	Plaxton Première 350	C49FT	1996	
308	P308CTT	Volvo B10M-62	Plaxton Première 350	C49FT	1997	
309	R309STA	Volvo B10M-62	Plaxton Première 350	C49FT	1998	

311	W311SDV	Volvo B10M-62	Plaxton Première 350	C49FT	2000		
312	W312STA	Volvo B10M-62	Plaxton Première 350	C53F	2000		
313	Y313NYD	Volvo B10M-62	Plaxton Paragon	C49FT	2001		
314	Y314NYD	Volvo B10M-62	Plaxton Paragon	C49FT	2001		
315	WA03MGE	Volvo B12M	TransBus Paragon	C49FT	2003		
316	WA03MGJ	Volvo B12M	TransBus Paragon	C49FT	2003		
340	JSK261	Volvo B10M-60	Plaxton Paramount 3500 III	C53F	1989	Fishwick, Leyland, 1992	
341	JSK262	Volvo B10M-60	Plaxton Paramount 3500 III	C53F	1989	Park's of Hamilton, 1992	
346	JSK264	Volvo B10M-60	Plaxton Paramount 3500 III	C53F	1990	Park's of Hamilton, 1990	
350	JSK265	Volvo B10M-61	Van Hool Alizée	C53F	1984	Park's of Hamilton, 1988	

Special event vehicle:
358	MCO658	Leyland Titan PD2/12	Metro-Cammell	O30/26R	1956	

Ancillary vehicle:
251	L251YOD	Mercedes-Benz 709D	Plaxton Beaver	TV	1992	

Previous registrations:
JSK261	F973HGE		JSK265	J602UGD, MCO658, UJY932
JSK262	F968HGE		MCO658	MCO658, ADV935A
JSK264	F988HGE			

Livery: Red, white and grey; yellow and green (Park and Ride) 69-71, 205

POLPERRO TRAM Co

AP, KM and PD Wright, 63 Carey Park, Killigarth, Polperro, PL13 2JPW

JDR661F	Morrison Electricars	Wright, St Austell	M14	1968	milk float conversion, 1994	
REO207L	Morrison Electricars	Wright, St Austell	M14	1972	milk float conversion, 1994	
BEO731V	Morrison Electricars	Wright, St Austell	M16	1979	milk float conversion, 1994	

Named vehicles: JDR661F *Maud*; REO207L *Lizzie*; BEO731V *Dotty*
Depot: Polperro Road, Looe

The most unusual bus service included this Handbook is provided by the Polperro Tram Company which uses Morrison Electricars - more normally associated with milk floats - to connect the village car park with the harbour. Illustrating this intriguing vehicle is REO207L. During the summer season this route is closed to normal traffic.
Tony Wilson

PULHAM'S

Pulham & Sons (Coaches) Ltd, Station Road Garage, Bourton-on-the-Water, GL54 2EN

Reg	Chassis	Body	Type	Year	History
NDD672	Volvo B10M-56	Plaxton Paramount 3200	C53F	1984	Marchants, Cheltenham, 1997
VAD141	Volvo B10M-56	Plaxton Paramount 3200	C53F	1983	Smith's of Tring, 1995
UDF936	Volvo B10M-61	Plaxton Paramount 3500 III	C53F	1989	
G680YLP	Ford Transit VE6	Dormobile	M16L	1990	LB Harrow, 1996
HDF661	Volvo B10M-60	Plaxton Paramount 3200 III	C53F	1991	Supreme, Coventry, 1993
H156HAC	Volvo B10M-60	Plaxton Paramount 3200 III	C53F	1991	Supreme, Coventry, 1993
VDF365	Leyland Tiger TR2R62C18Z5/8	Plaxton Paramount 3200 III	C53F	1991	Metropolitan Police, 1997
ODF561	Leyland Tiger TRCL10/3ARZA	Plaxton Paramount 3200 III	C53F	1992	Metropolitan Police, 1997
L202MHL	Leyland DAF 400	Ace	M16	1993	private owner, 1998
XDG614	Volvo B10M-62	Plaxton Première 350	C53F	1994	Truemans, Fleet, 2001
M943JBO	Dennis Javelin 11m	Plaxton Interurban	BC60F	1994	Burnley & Pendle, 2003
M944JBO	Dennis Javelin 11m	Plaxton Interurban	BC60F	1994	Burnley & Pendle, 2003
LDD488	Volvo B9M	Van Hool Alizée HE	C38F	1996	Cheyne, Daviot, 1999
WDD194	Volvo B10M-62	Van Hool Alizée HE	C49FT	1996	
FDF965	Volvo B10M-62	Plaxton Première 350	C53F	1997	Southern Vectis, 2000
WDF946	Volvo B10M-62	Van Hool T9 Alizée	C49FT	1998	Bassetts, Tittensor, 2003
Y852SDD	Mercedes-Benz Vario 0814	Plaxton Cheetah	C33F	2001	
PDF567	Volvo B10M-62	Plaxton Première 320	C57F	2002	
GL52PUL	Volvo B7R	Plaxton Prima	BC57F	2002	
GL03PUL	Mercedes-Benz Vario 0814	TransBus Cheetah	C29F	2003	
GL53PUL	Mercedes-Benz Vario 0814	TransBus Beaver	BC29F	2003	
VO03MWW	Volvo B7R	TransBus Profile	BC57F	2003	

Previous registrations:

FDF965	P618FTV, 473CDL, P618FTV	UDF936	F401UAD
HDF661	H155HAC	VAD141	A22NRO
H156HAC	H156HAC, PDF567	VDF365	J933CYK
LDD488	P9WAC	WDD194	N680RDD
NDD672	A733JAY, 6349D, A899YOV, A4DOF, A233NDD	WDF946	S893BRE
ODF561	J935CYK	XDG614	L671OHL
PDF567	VU51FGN		

Plaxton produces two bodies for the Mercedes-Benz Vario, the Beaver 2 which is a bus shell and the Cheetah for coach duties. Pictured is GL03PUL, a Cheetah produced during the time of TransBus ownership. The Scarborough plant has since been bought from the TransBus receivers to re-emerge as Plaxton. *Mark Bailey*

QUANTOCK MOTOR SERVICES

Quantock Motor Services Ltd, Rosebank, Langley Marsh, Wiveliscombe, Taunton, TA4 2UJ

Special event vehicles - *original operators shown*

JG9938	Leyland Tiger TS8	Park Royal	C32R	1937	East Kent Road Car
AJA132	Bristol L5G	Burlingham (1950)	B35R	1938	North Western Road Car
HKL819	AEC Regal I 0662	Beadle	OB35F	1946	Maidstone & District MS
EMW893	Daimler CVD6SD	Park Royal	B35C	1947	Swindon Corporation
JUO992	Leyland PD1A	Eastern Coach Works	L27/26R	1947	Southern National OC
HUO510	AEC Regal I 0662	Weymann	B35F	1948	Devon General OC
JFM575	AEC Regal III	Strachans	B35F	1948	Crosville Motor Services
JTE546	AEC Regent III 6811A	Park Royal	B33/26R	1949	Morecambe & Heysham Corporation
KTF594	AEC Regent III 9621E	Park Royal	O33/26R	1949	Morecambe & Heysham Corporation
JLJ402	Leyland Tiger PS2/3	Burlingham	C31F	1949	Bournemouth Corporation
CFN121	Dennis Lancet III	Park Royal	B35R	1949	East Kent Road Car
LJH665	Dennis Lancet III	Duple A	C35F	1949	Lee, Barnet
GWN432	Dennis Lancet III	Thurgood (1960)	FC37F	1950	Modern Super Coaches, Tottenham
CHL772	Daimler CVD6SD	Willowbrook	B35F	1950	Bullock, Featherstone
JFJ875	Daimler CVD650	Weyman	B35F	1950	Exeter Corporation
KFM767	Bristol L5G	Eastern Coach Works	B35R	1950	Crosville Motor Services
KFM893	Bristol L5G	Eastern Coach Works	B35R	1950	Crosville Motor Services
LFM717	Bristol L5G	Eastern Coach Works	B35R	1950	Crosville Motor Services
LFM734	Bristol LL5G	Eastern Coach Works	B39R	1950	Crosville Motor Services
FMO949	Bristol LL6B	Eastern Coach Works	B39F	1951	South Midland
DCK219	Leyland Titan PD2/3	East Lancs	BC27/26R	1951	Ribble Motor Services
LFM302	Leyland Tiger PS1	Weymann	BC35F	1951	Crosville Motor Services
ADV854A	Leyland Titan PD2/12	Leyland	B30/26R	1953	Plymouth Corporation
NLJ271	Leyland Royal Tiger PSU1/13	Burlingham	B42F	1954	Bournemouth Corporation
CHG545	Leyland Tiger PS2/14	East Lancashire	B39F	1954	BCN Joint Transport
JVH378	AEC Regent I 9613E	East Lancashire	B33/28R	1955	Huddersfield JOC
BAS562	Bristol LD6G	Eastern Coach Works	O33/27R	1956	Southern Vectis
BAS563	Bristol LD6G	Eastern Coach Works	O33/27R	1956	Southern Vectis
BAS564	Bristol LD6G	Eastern Coach Works	O33/27R	1956	Southern Vectis
838AFM	Bristol LD6G	Eastern Coach Works	B33/27R	1957	Crosville Motor Services
466DHN	Guy Arab IV	Roe	H33/28R	1957	Darlington Corporation
GSU678	Leyland Titan PD2/40	Metro Cammell	RV	1957	Portsmouth Corporation

Quantock Motor Services has been formed to operate tendered services and private hire in north west Somerset. The origins of this business were in the operation of vintage buses in connection with the North Somerset Railway. One of many vehicles restored is former Crosville KFM893, a Bristol L5G with Eastern Coach Works body. *Robert Edworthy*

For use on tendered services, coaches carry Quantock MS livery. Here, NUB93V shows its Plaxton Supreme bodywork as it emerges from the depot. Several vehicles previously used on tendered work have reverted to special event status after contract changes, including this AEC Reliance. Many of the special event vehicles listed are still to be restored completely and are not yet in service. *Robert Edworthy*

NDB356	Leyland Tiger Cub PSUC1/13	Crossley	B44F	1958	Stockport Corporation
890ADV	AEC Reliance 2MU3RV	Willowbrook	C41F	1959	Grey Cars, Torquay
120JRB	Daimler Freeline D650HS	Burlingham Seagull	C37F	1959	Blue Bus, Willington
501BTA	Bristol Lodekka LD6G	Eastern Coach Works	B33/27R	1959	Western National OC
503BTA	Bristol Lodekka LD6G	Eastern Coach Works	B33/27R	1959	Western National OC
LDB756	Leyland Tiger Cub PSUC1/2	Willowbrook	BC43F	1960	North Western Road Car
VDV752	Bristol Lodekka LD6G	Eastern Coach Works	O33/33R	1961	Western National OC
VDV753	Bristol Lodekka LD6G	Eastern Coach Works	O33/33R	1961	Western National OC
572CNW	Daimler CVG6LX	Roe	B39/31F	1962	Leeds Corporation
3655NE	Leyland Tiger Cub PSUC1/12	Park Royal	BC38D	1962	Manchester City Transport
569EFJ	AEC Reliance 2MU4RA	Harrington Cavalier 315	C40F	1962	Devon General (Greenslades)
AFE719A	AEC Reliance 2MU3RV	Harrington	OB40F	1962	Maidstone & District MS
AHN455B	Daimler CCG5DD	Roe	B33/28R	1964	Darlington Corporation
JJD511D	AEC Routemaster RH2H/1	Park Royal	B42/33R	1965	London Transport
DPV65D	AEC Regent V	Neepsend	B37/28R	1966	Ipswich Corporation
HJA965E	Leyland Titan PD2/40	Neepsend	B36/28R	1967	Stockport Corporation
CYA181J	AEC Reliance 6MU4R	Plaxton Derwent	B53F	1971	Hutchings and Cornelius
TDK686J	AEC Reliance 6U3ZR	Plaxton Panorama Elite II Exp	C53F	1971	Yelloway, Rochdale
CRO671K	AEC Reliance 6U3ZR	Plaxton Panorama Elite II Exp	B60F	1972	London Country Bus Services
MUR217L	AEC Reliance 6U3ZR	Plaxton Panorama Elite III	C57F	1973	Derek Randall, Acton
HVU247N	AEC Reliance 6U3ZR	Plaxton Panorama Elite III	C53F	1975	Yelloway, Rochdale
NFX134P	Daimler Fleetline CRL6	Alexander AL	CO43/31F	1976	Bournemouth Corporation
NNN9P	AEC Reliance 6U2R	Plaxton Supreme III	C53F	1976	Derby City Transport
NNC854P	AEC Reliance 6U3ZR	Plaxton Supreme III	C49F	1976	London Country Bus Services
RCV283R	AEC Reliance 6U3ZR	Plaxton Supreme III	C55F	1977	Wheal Briton Bus Services
TPT6R	AEC Reliance 6U3ZR	Plaxton Supreme III	C53F	1976	Venture, Consett
APT834S	AEC Reliance 6U3ZR	Plaxton Supreme III	C53F	1977	Gardiner, Spennymoor
TPD28S	AEC Reliance 6U2R	Duple Dominant II Express	C53F	1977	London Country Bus Services
VPH53S	AEC Reliance 6U2R	Duple Dominant II Express	C49F	1978	London Country Bus Services
BUR438T	AEC Reliance 6U2R	Plaxton Supreme III	C53F	1978	Best, London
APM114T	AEC Reliance 6U2R	Plaxton Supreme III	C49F	1979	London Country Bus Services
ANA5T	AEC Reliance 6U3ZR	Plaxton Supreme III	C53F	1978	Greater Manchester (Godfrey Abbott)
EBM448T	AEC Reliance 6U3ZR	Plaxton Supreme IV	C57F	1978	Derek Randels, North Acton
YPL78T	AEC Reliance 6U2R	Duple Dominant II Express	C49F	1979	London Country Bus Services

The South West Bus Handbook

Taking a rest in the depot is one of the short Bristol LHS coaches, JTL150T carries a Plaxton Supreme IV body and is fitted with a set of thirty-three seats. *Robert Edworthy*

YPL92T	AEC Reliance 6U2R	Duple Dominant II Express	C53F	1979	London Country Bus Services
YPL105T	AEC Reliance 6U2R	Duple Dominant II Express	B53F	1979	London Country Bus Services
WDK562T	AEC Reliance 6U3ZR	Plaxton Supreme IV	C53F	1979	Yelloway, Rochdale
JTL150T	Bristol LHS6L	Plaxton Supreme IV Express	C33F	1979	Lincolnshire Road Car
FDV417V	Leyland Leopard PSU3E/4R	Plaxton Supreme IV Express	B53F	1979	Western National OC
KTA986V	Leyland Leopard PSU3E/4R	Plaxton Supreme IV Express	C53F	1979	Western National OC
NUB93V	AEC Reliance 6U3ZR	Plaxton Supreme IV	C53F	1980	Compass, Wakefield
OIL2947	Van Hool T815	Van Hool Acron	C51F	1984	MM Coachlines, Walderslade, 2004
A462ODY	Bedford YNT	Plaxton Paramount 3200	C53F	1984	Annetts, Innersdown, 2002
GSU372	DAF MB3000DKVL600	Van Hool Alizée	C48FT	1987	Taunton Coaches, 2004
TYR95	Van Hool T815	Van Hool Acron	C53F	1987	Nottinghamshire CC, 2004
CAZ2749	Hestair-Duple SDA1512	Duple 425	C53F	1989	Birmingham International, 2004
TCZ6123	Leyland Tiger TRCL10/3ARZM	Plaxton Paramount 3200 III	C53F	1989	Lothian Buses, 2004
TCZ6122	Leyland Tiger TRCL10/3ARZM	Plaxton Paramount 3200 III	C53F	1991	Lothian Buses, 2004
VYD333	DAF SB3000KV601	Van Hool Alizée	C51FT	1993	Eavesway, Ashton-in-Makerfield, '04
L549EHD	DAF SB3000KV601	Van Hool Alizée	C55F	1993	Weaverway, Newbury, 2004
H226TCP	DAF SB2305DHS585	Duple Caribbean 2	C51FT	1993	Bus Na Comhairle, 2004
W224CDN	EOS E180Z	EOS 90	C49FT	1995	Fishwick, Leyland, 2004
X574BYD	Volvo B10M-62	Van Hool T9 Alizée	C53F	2000	Avalon, Glastonbury, 2004

Previous registrations:

A462ODY	A637YWF, ODY395		KTA986V	FDV803V, 925GTA
ADV854A	HJY297		L549EHD	L549EHD, B10MBT
AEF719A	325NKT			
BAS952	MDL953		OIL2947	
BAS953	MDL952		RCV283R	OKY64R, 176XYD
BAS954	MDL955		TCZ6122	H72NFS
CAZ2749	F32KHS		TCZ6123	G67DFS
GSU372	D864EFS, 87KK1315, OIW1451		TYR95	D731WCH
GSU678	ORV991		VYD333	K105TCP
HVU247N	HVU247N, 146FLD		YPL105T	YPL105T, IUI7210
JTL150T	FTW133T, 10OOX, ATH108T, NBZ1671			

Livery: Original schemes for special event buses, red and gold remainder. **Web:** www.heritagebus.co.uk
Depots: Taunton Industrial Estate, Norton Fitzwarren, Taunton and Langley Green, Wiveliscombe.

REDWOODS

B J & P J Redwood, 3 Station Road Ind Est, Hemyock, Cullompton, EX15 3SE

Reg	Chassis	Body	Seating	Year	History
USV556	Volvo B10M-61	Plaxton Paramount 3500	C53F	1984	J&B, Horsforth, 2002
USV625	Bova EL26-581	Bova Europa	C53F	1985	
USV620	Bova FHD12-280	Bova Futura	C53F	1986	Baker, Duloe, 2001
USV331	DAF MB200DKFL600	Plaxton Paramount 3500 II	C53F	1986	Filer, Ilfracombe, 2002
USV474	Mercedes-Benz 811D	Optare StarRider	BC29F	1989	Tedd, Old Sarum, 2003
USV676	DAF MB230LB615	Plaxton Paramount 3200 III	C49F	1989	Cropper, Kirkstall, 2000
USV630	Volvo B10M-60	Plaxton Paramount 3500 III	C49FT	1990	Seward, Dalwood, 2003
USV462	Volvo B10M-60	Duple 340	C53FT	1990	Skills, Nottingham, 2001
USV330	DAF MB230LB615	Caetano Algarve II	C49FT	1992	Boorman, Henlow, 2001
N2RED	Volvo B10M-62	Van Hool Alizée HE	C53F	1995	National Holidays, 2002
S400RED	Iveco EuroRider 391E.12.29	Beulas Stergo ε	C53F	1998	Excalibur, Battersea, 2003
R60RED	Scania K113TRB	Irizar Century 12.37	C49FT	1998	Mayne, Buckie, 2003
T2RED	Scania K113TRB	Irizar Century 12.37	C49FT	1999	
S639UUG	LDV Convoy	LDV	M16	1999	Birmingham Air Park, 2003
T3RED	Volvo B10M-61	Plaxton Première 350	C49FT	1999	Wallace Arnold, 2001
X499AHE	Scania L94IB	Irizar Century 12.37	C53F	2000	Bus Eireann, 2004
YN04AKU	Scania K114IB4	Irizar Century 12.35	C49FT	2004	
YN04AWR	MAN 18.350 HOCL-R	Noge Catalan Star 350	C51FT	2004	

Special event vehicle:

Reg	Chassis	Body	Seating	Year	History
108GYC	Bedford SB5	Duple Embassy	C41F	1960	Bowerman, Taunton, 1964

Previous registrations:

N2RED	N314BYA, N262PYS		
R60RED	7MCB, R836MSA	USV556	A517NCL, A11WEH
S400RED	S104KJF	USV605	-
T3RED	T531EUB	USV620	C33VJF
USV330	J299KFP	USV625	B901YYC
USV331	C770MVH, TJL800, C307VMX, MIL9751	USV630	G92RGG
USV462	G56RTO	USV676	F639OHD, HIL7670
USV474	G122KUB	X499AHE	00D83735

Named vehicles: USV 330, *Butch Cassidy*; USV331 *Hondo*; USV474, *My Little Pony*; USV620, *Sundance Kid*; USV625 *Smudge*; USV628 *Crazy Horse*; USV630 *Virginian*; USV676 *Lone Wolf*; USV859 *Red Cloud*; R60RED *Flipper*; N2RED *Maverick*; T2RED *Gentle Giant*; T3RED *Buffalo Bill*; YN04AKU *Gentle Giant*; YN04AWR *Geronimo*.
Special livery: white (Majestic Holidays) S400RED, X499AHE. **Web:** www.redwoodstravel.com

Redwood's striking livery is applied to this Irizar Century, T2RED, one of four Scania coaches currently operated.
Bill Potter

RIVER LINK

Dart Pleasure Craft Ltd, 5 Lower Street, Dartmouth, TQ6 9AJ

1	UWV614S	Bristol VRT/SL3/6LXB	Eastern Coach Works	CO43/31F	1977	Stagecoach Devon, 2000
2	UWV604S	Bristol VRT/SL3/6LXB	Eastern Coach Works	CO43/31F	1977	Stagecoach Devon, 2000
3	WTU467W	Bristol VRT/SL3/6LXB	Eastern Coach Works	O43/31F	1981	Arriva Cymru, 2002
4	F301RUT	Mercedes-Benz 709D	Robin Hood	B26F	1989	APT Coaches, Rayleigh, 2002
5	TTT165X	Leyland Atlantean AN68C/1R	East Lancs	B43/31F	1981	Citybus, Plymouth, 2003

Depot: Baltic Wharf, St Peter's Quay, Totnes
Web: www.riverlink.co.uk

Representing the River Link fleet is open-top Bristol VR WTU467W which was latterly used by Arriva on its sea-front service at Rhyl. The River Link operation is associated with the Paignton to Kingswear Steam Railway and the ferry boats that ply between Kingswear and Dartmouth providing a unique, tri-modal circular service which is increasingly popular in this tourist-rich area. *Robert Edworthy*

ROSELYN COACHES

Roselyn Coaches Ltd, Middleway Garage, St Blazey Road, Par, PL24 2JA

TMW997S	AEC Reliance 6UZR	Duple Dominant II Express	C49F	1978	MC Travel, Melksham, 1991
AFH390T	Bedford YMT	Duple Dominant II	C53F	1978	Prout, Port Isaac, 1995
XAN48T	Bristol VRT/SL3/6LXB	Eastern Coach Works	B43/34F	1978	Berrys, Taunton, 1999
BKH983T	Bristol VRT/SL3/501	Eastern Coach Works	B43/31F	1978	East Yorkshire, 1996
AJH854T	Bristol VRT/SL3/6LXB	Eastern Coach Works	B43/31F	1979	Berrys, Taunton, 2001
HUD495W	Bristol VRT/SL3/6LXB	Eastern Coach Works	B43/27D	1980	Arriva Cymru, 1998
HUD501W	Bristol VRT/SL3/6LXB	Eastern Coach Works	B43/27D	1980	Arriva Cymru, 1998
ATK153W	Leyland Atlantean AN68B/1R	East Lancs	B45/28D	1980	Plymouth Citybus, 2001
ATK156W	Leyland Atlantean AN68B/1R	East Lancs	B45/28D	1980	Plymouth Citybus, 2000
ATK157W	Leyland Atlantean AN68B/1R	East Lancs	B45/28D	1980	Plymouth Citybus, 2000
TTT163X	Leyland Atlantean AN68C/1R	East Lancs	B45/31F	1981	Plymouth Citybus, 2003
TTT164X	Leyland Atlantean AN68C/1R	East Lancs	B45/31F	1981	Plymouth Citybus, 2003
239AJB	Volvo B58-56	Plaxton Supreme IV Express	C53F	1981	
LWS116Y	DAF MB200DKTL600	Plaxton Supreme V	C57F	1982	Ford's Coaches, Gunnislake, 1995
A168PAE	Volvo B10M-61	Duple Laser	C53F	1984	Girlings, Plymouth, 2004
237AJB	Volvo B10M-61	Van Hool Alizée	C53F	1988	
241AJB	Volvo B10M-61	Plaxton Paramount 3500 III	C53F	1988	Bakers, Biddulph, 1995
G170XJF	Toyota Coaster HB31R	Caetano Optimo	C18F	1990	Group Taxibus, Chelmsford, 2003
TIL6878	Volvo B10M-60	Van Hool Alizée	C48FT	1993	Helmore, Paignton, 2003
L920NWW	Volvo B10M-60	Van Hool Alizée HE	C49FT	1994	Berrys, Taunton, 2004
M325KRY	Volvo B10M-62	Jonckheere Deauville	C51FT	1995	Clarkes of London, 2001
M42HSU	Volvo B10M-62	Van Hool Alizée	C53F	1995	Pride of the Clyde, 2004
M981HNS	Volvo B10M-62	Van Hool Alizée HE	C53F	1995	Pride of the Clyde, 2004
728FDV	Volvo B10M-62	Plaxton Première 350	C49FT	1995	Skills, Nottingham, 2002
647PYC	Volvo B10M-62	Plaxton Première 350	C53F	1995	Procter, Leeming Bar, 2004
V205EAL	Iveco EuroRider 391E.12.29	Beulas Stergo ε	C49FT	1999	TWH, New Cross, 2003
WB03EDE	Volvo B12M	Van Hool T9 Alizée	C49FT	2003	

Previous registrations:

237AJB	E44SAF		LWS116Y	LWS116Y, 6139EL, YOR456
239AJB	KAF129W		M42HSU	LSK513
241AJB	E803NVT, 9995RU		M981HNS	LSK507
244AJB	-		N754BKW	N754BKW, DSU313
647PYC	N754BKW		TIL6878	K810HUM
728FDV	M34TRR		TMW997S	VPH57S, 701CGA
A168PAE	A879UHY, 3138DP		YOR456	-

Special livery: White (Leger) WB03EDE
Web: www.roselyncoaches.co.uk

Roselyn Coaches operates five Bristol VRs on school transport work, one of which is this dual-doored example that was new to City of Oxford.
Mark Bailey

ROVER

D R Hand, The Garage, Horsley, Stroud, GL6 0PU

29DRH	Bedford YNT	Plaxton Paramount 3200	C53F	1983	Brooks, Ryarsh, 1999	
H853OWN	Mercedes-Benz 811D	Reeve Burgess Beaver	B31F	1990	First Cymru, 2002	
K945OPX	Dennis Javelin 10m	Wadham Stringer Vanguard Ii	BC45F	1993	LB Lewishan, 2005	
N873XMO	Dennis Javelin 12m	Berkhof Excellence 1000	C53F	1996	Taw & Torridge, Merton, 2004	
P50AND	Bova FHD12-340	Bova Futura	C49FT	1997		
74DRH	Bova FHD12-340	Bova Futura	C49FT	1997	Ellison, St Helens, 2000	
X534JOV	Toyota Coaster BB50R	Caetano Optimi IV	C21F	2000	Allenby Coach Hire, 2005	
K18AND	Bova FHD12-370	Bova Futura	C51FT	2001		
DH02DRH	Bova FHD12-340	Bova Futura	C55F	2002		
FH53DRH	Bova FHD12-340	Bova Futura	C49FT	2004		
904DRH	Bova FHD12-340	Bova Futura	C49FT	2004		

Previous registrations:
29DRH	APP617Y		904DRH	WA04EWN
74DRH	P100VWX			

Depots: Spring Mills Ind Est, Nailsworth and The Garage, Horsley

Six Bova Futura coaches are operated by Stroud-based Rover. DH02DRH carries an example of the latest type of DVLA Select index marks that includes personally chosen letters either side of the year number.
Robert Edworthy

SAFEWAY SERVICES

V L Gunn, North Street, South Petherton, TA13 5PA

ASV900	Dennis Lance III	Reading	C33F	1949	
GIB5970	Leyland Leopard PSU3E/4R	Willowbrook Warrior (1992)	B48F	1977	Border, Burnley, 1992
HIL7772	Leyland Leopard PSU3E/4R	Willowbrook Warrior (1991)	B48F	1980	Alexcars, Cirencester, 2000
NPA228W	Leyland Leopard PSU3E/4R	Plaxton Supreme IV Express	C49F	1981	London & Country, 1986
YYA122X	Leyland Leopard PSU3F/5R	Plaxton Supreme IV Express	C53F	1982	
OWO235Y	Leyland Leopard PSU3G/5R	Duple Dominant	B53F	1982	Smith, Pylle, 2003
A983NYC	Leyland Tiger TRCTL11/2R	Plaxton Paramount 3200 E	C53F	1983	
RJI3046	Volvo B10M-61	Duple Laser	C51F	1984	Kingdom, Tiverton, 2001
A710SDV	DAF SB2300DHS585	Plaxton Paramount 3200	C53F	1984	Redwood, Hemyock, 2003
E565YYA	Leyland Tiger TRCTL11/3RZ	Duple 320	C55F	1988	
F202HSO	Leyland Tiger TRCTL11/3ARZ	Plaxton Paramount 3200 III	C55F	1988	Park's of Hamilton, 1993
NIB8459	Volvo B10M-61	East Lancs EL2000 (1991)	B55F	1988	Buffalo, Flitwick, 2002
YXI9528	Volvo B10M-61	Van Hool Alizée	C53F	1989	Skills, Nottingham, 2002
ELZ2062	DAF SB2300	Jonckheere Deauville P599	C51FT	1990	Isaac, Barnstaple, 2003
H533YCX	DAF SB220LT550	Ikarus CitiBus	B50F	1991	Eastbourne Buses, 2005
J601KCU	Dennis Dart 9.8m	Wright Handybus	B40F	1991	Go-Coastline, 2001
K835HUM	Volvo B10M-60	Jonckheere Deauville 45	C50F	1993	Burton, Haverhill, 2000

Previous registrations:

A710SDV	A546RVH, PIL6501, USV630	HIL7772	TPD25V
ASV900	ETP184	NIB8459	E637NEL
ELZ2062	G975LRP	RJI3046	RMU967Y
GIB5970	XCW153R	YXI9528	F751ENE

Initially built with a coach body, Safeway Services' NIB8459 was re-bodied by East Lancs with their EL2000 model in 1991. The resulting bus has now joined the South Petherton operation and is seen on the principal service to Yeovil. *Phillip Stephenson*

SEWARDS

IA & RM Seward, Glendale, Dalwood, Axminster, EX13 7EJ

D759UTA	Leyland Tiger TRCTL11/3RZ	Plaxton Derwent	B54F	1986	MoD (82KF06), 1996
D86VDV	Leyland Tiger TRCTL11/3RZ	Plaxton Derwent	B54F	1987	MoD (82KF11), 1999
E325CTT	Dennis Javelin 12m	Plaxton Paramount 3200 III	B54F	1987	
G276WFU	Leyland-DAF 200	Leyland-DAF	M8	1990	private owner, 1997
J127DGC	Mercedes-Benz 811D	PMT Ami	BC25F	1992	Crystal Palace FC, 1996
K744RBX	Renault Master	Cymric	M16	1992	
K562YFJ	Dennis Javelin 10m	Wadham Stringer Vanguard II	B48F	1992	MoD (74KK28), 2002
K458YPK	Dennis Javelin 12m	Plaxton Première 320	C53F	1993	LB Lewisham, 2000
L486HKN	Bova FHD 12.340	Bova Futura	C55F	1994	The King's Ferry, Gillingham, 1999
N770VTT	Dennis Javelin 12m	Berkhof Excellence 1000L	C53F	1996	
R608OTA	Dennis Javelin 12m	Caetano Porto	C57F	1998	
R609OTA	MAN 11.220	Berkhof Axial 30	C35F	1998	
T953RTA	MAN 11.220	Caetano Algarve II	C35F	1999	
W346VOD	Mercedes-Benz O404-15R	Hispano Vita	C53F	2000	
W347VOD	MAN 13.220	Berkhof Axial 30	C41F	2000	
X149BTA	Iveco Daily 49-10	G&M	M16	2001	
Y166GTT	Dennis R	Plaxton Paragon	C53F	2001	
WA03JXY	Toyota Coaster BB50R	Caetano Optimo V	C21F	2003	
WA03HRJ	Bova FHD12-340	Bova Futura	C53F	2003	
WA04HNC	BMC 850 Club	BMC	BC35F	2004	
WA54JYX	MAN 14-280	Caetano Enigma	C39F	2004	

Previous registrations:
K562YFJ   K152KAB   L486HKN   L8KFC

Special livery: yellow (school bus) D86VDV, K562VFJ

One of two vehicles dedicated to school bus duties, K562YFJ is a 10 metre Dennis Javelin now demobbed from military service. Like many coaches supplied to the British Army, it carries Wadham Stringer Vanguard bodywork and features twin rear doors for stretcher access, in its original dual role as an ambulance.
Robert Edworthy

SHAFTESBURY & DISTRICT

Shaftesbury & District MS Ltd, 2 Melbury Motors, Cann Common, Shaftesbury, SP7 0EB

MXX398	AEC Regal IV	Metro-Cammell	B30F	1953	preservation, 2004
OLD564	AEC Regent III 0961	Park Royal	B30/26R	1954	Bragg, Lower Dean, 2002
KGJ603D	AEC Routemaster R2RH/2	Park Royal	B40/32F	1966	Western Scottish, 1992
RIL6390	Bristol LH6L	Plaxton Supreme III Express	C41F	1979	Grey Cars, Newton Abbot, 1999
AFJ734T	Bristol LH6L	Plaxton Supreme III Express	C41F	1979	Grey Cars, Newton Abbot, 1999
YAZ6393	AEC Reliance 6U2R	Plaxton Supreme III Express	C53F	1980	Barrys, Weymouth, 1998
NUW557Y	Leyland Titan TNLXB2RR	Leyland	B44/27F	1982	Carter, Ipswich, 2004
YAZ6391	Leyland Tiger TRCTL11/2R	Duple Dominant IV Express	C53F	1983	Dorset CC, 1999
YAZ6394	Leyland Tiger TRCTL11/3RH	Alexander TC	C49F	1985	Stagecoach Fife, 2000
POI4905	DAF SB2300DHS585	Berkhof Esprite 340	C57F	1985	Edwards, High Wycombe, 1998
HIL8518	Leyland Tiger TRCTL11/3ARZ	Plaxton Paramount 3200 III	C57F	1988	Hearn, Harrow Weald, 2002
G221VDX	Optare MetroRider MR01	Optare	B33F	1989	Coachmasters, Rochdale, 2001
H913FTT	Volvo B10M-60	Ikarus Blue Danube 350	C49FT	1991	G&A, Caerphilly, 2001
P165ANR	Toyota Coaster HZB50R	Caetano Optimo IV	C21F	1996	Steventon Transport, 2004

Previous registrations:

		YAZ6391	YPD138Y
HIL8518	E318OMG	YAZ6392	
POI4905	B690BTW, 7947RU	YAZ6393	FCX576W
RIL6390	AFJ734T	YAZ6394	B207FFS, GSU341, B207FFS

E-mail: rogerroutemaster@aol.com
Depot: Mayo Farm, Higher Blandford Road, Shaftesbury

One of the interesting buses operated by Shaftesbury & District is forward-entrance Routemaster KGJ603D which was new to London for the BEA services that plied between the London check-in centre at Cromwell Road and London Heathrow airport. At that time checked-in luggage was accommodated in trailers with many services directly linked with specific flights. As shown it now carries a red livery. *Bill Potter*

SHAMROCK BUSES

Dorset Heritage Transport Services, 11 Evering Avenue, Poole, BH12 4JF

101	B863XYR	Volvo Citybus B10M-61	East Lancs (1992)	B44/30D	1985	2Travel, Swansea, 2005
102	B865XYR	Volvo Citybus B10M-61	East Lancs (1992)	B44/30D	1985	2Travel, Swansea, 2005
103	B866XYR	Volvo Citybus B10M-61	East Lancs (1992)	B44/30D	1985	2Travel, Swansea, 2005
143	AJT143T	Leyland Fleetline FE30ALR	Alexander AL	B43/31F	1978	On loan to Bournemouth TM
182	TJT182X	Leyland Olympian ONLXB/1R	Marshall	B47/31F	1982	Wheelers Travel, N Baddesley, 2004
192	TJT192X	Leyland Olympian ONLXB/1R	Marshall	B47/31F	1982	Wheelers Travel, N Baddesley, 2004
201	UIB3987	Leyland AT68M/2RFT	Northern Counties Paladin (1992)	BC42F	1971	MacEwan, Amisfield, 2002
300	JFR10W	Leyland Olympian ONLXB/1R	Eastern Coach Works	B45/32F	1981	Lancashire United, 2003
301	JFR11W	Leyland Olympian ONLXB/1R	Eastern Coach Works	B45/32F	1981	Lancashire United, 2003
302	DBV132Y	Leyland Olympian ONLXB/1R	Eastern Coach Works	B45/32F	1983	Burnley & Pendle, 2004
303	JFR3W	Leyland Olympian ONLXB/1R	Eastern Coach Works	B45/32F	1981	Lancashire United, 2003
304	OFV14X	Leyland Olympian ONLXB/1R	Eastern Coach Works	B45/32F	1981	Lancashire United, 2003
305	OFV15X	Leyland Olympian ONLXB/1R	Eastern Coach Works	B45/32F	1981	Burnley & Pendle, 2003
306	OFV23X	Leyland Olympian ONLXB/1R	Eastern Coach Works	B45/32F	1981	Burnley & Pendle, 2004
307	B152TRN	Leyland Olympian ONLXB/1R	Eastern Coach Works	B45/32F	1984	Lancashire United, 2004
308	C178ECK	Leyland Olympian ONLXB/1R	Eastern Coach Works	BC42/30F	1984	Lancashire United, 2004
311	C481YWY	Leyland Olympian ONLXB/1R	Eastern Coach Works	BC42/29F	1985	Burnley & Pendle, 2004
313	JFR13W	Leyland Olympian ONLXB/1R	Eastern Coach Works	B45/32F	1981	Burnley & Pendle, 2004

Previous registration:
UIB3987   TKU469K, WNT294

Depot: 31 Newtown Business Park, Poole

One of the interesting heritage buses maintained by Quantock Motor Services (page 79) **is Ribble 1248, DCK219, a Leyland Titan PD2 with coach-seated East Lancs bodywork. For 1951 the coach-seated double-decks were an innovation by Ribble that continued once the Atlantean models arrived.** *Mark Lyons*

SOMERBUS

Somerbus Ltd, 64 Brookside, Paulton, Bristol, BS39 7TR

D615ASG	Leyland Tiger TRCTL11/3R	Alexander P	B61F	1987	Stonehouse Coaches, 2002	
J129GMP	Dennis Dart 9m	Plaxton Pointer	BC35F	1992	Andybus, Dauntsey, 2004	
816SHW	Mercedes-Benz 811D	Marshall C16	B33F	1996	Johnsons, Henley-in-Arden, 2003	
704BYL	Optare Solo M850	Optare	N30F	2001		
MX04DSV	Mercedes-Benz Vario 0814	Onyx	BC24F	2004	Hutchinson, York, 2005	
NHG541	Optare Solo M850SL	Optare	NC27F	2004		
ER05BUS	Optare Solo M850SL	Optare	NC27F	2005		

Previous registration:
816SHW   N815CDA

Web: www.somerbus.co.uk
Depot: Stanton Wick, Pensford

SOUTH GLOUCESTERSHIRE

South Gloucestershire - Durbin

J G Durbin, Coach Depot Pegasus Park, Gypsy Patch Lane, Patchway, Bristol, BS34 6LR

GYE261W	Leyland Titan TNLXB2RR	Leyland	B43/34F	1982	Autocar, Five Oak Green, 2000	
TPD120X	Leyland Olympian ONTL11/1R	Roe	B43/29F	1982	Eastville, Bristol, 2004	
MIL8328	Leyland Titan TNLXB2RR	Leyland	B44/32F	1983	Dunn-Line, Nottingham, 2002	
OHV766Y	Leyland Titan TNLXB2RR	Leyland	B44/29D	1983	London Central, 2000	
OHV798Y	Leyland Titan TNLXB2RR	Leyland	B44/29D	1983	Trustline, Potters Bar, 2000	
OFS668Y	Leyland Olympian ONTL11/2R	Eastern Coach Works	B50/31D	1983	Lothian Buses, 2000	
A887SYE	Leyland Titan TNLXB2RR	Leyland	B44/26D	1983	A2B, Prenton, 2002	
A892SYE	Leyland Titan TNLXB2RR	Leyland	B44/26D	1983	Hawker, Little Stoke, 2002	
A898SYE	Leyland Titan TNLXB2RR	Leyland	B44/26D	1983	A2B, Prenton, 2002	
A943SYE	Leyland Titan TNLXB2RR	Leyland	B44/26D	1984	London Central, 2000	
A649THV	Leyland Titan TNLXB2RR	Leyland	B44/32F	1984	Dunn-Line, Nottingham, 2003	
B883YTC	Leyland Tiger TRCTL11/3LZ	Wadham Stringer Vanguard	BC68F	1985	MoD (37KC05), 1999	
C681EHU	Leyland Tiger TRCTL11/3LZ	Wadham Stringer Vanguard	BC54F	1985	MoD (37KC45), 1998	
C822EHU	Leyland Tiger TRCTL11/3LZ	Wadham Stringer Vanguard	BC68F	1985	MoD (37KC22), 1998	
C28EUH	Leyland Olympian ONTL11/2R	East Lancs	C47/31F	1985	First Bristol, 2001	
C29EUH	Leyland Olympian ONTL11/2R	East Lancs	C47/31F	1985	First Bristol, 2001	
C30EUH	Leyland Olympian ONTL11/2R	East Lancs	C47/31F	1985	Eastville, Bristol, 2004	
HIL3188	Leyland Olympian ONTL11/2RH	East Lancs	C47/31F	1985	Eastville, Bristol, 2003	
ESK812	Volvo B10M-61	Van Hool Alizée HE	C48FT	1987	First Bristol, 2001	
PSU527	Volvo B10M-61	Van Hool Alizée HE	C49FT	1987	First Bristol, 2001	
E461CGM	Mercedes-Benz 609D	Robin Hood	B20F	1987	Ensignbus (Bath Bus), 2004	
D706YHK	Leyland Olympian ONLXB/1RH	Eastern Coach Works	B42/30F	1987	LMS Buses, Aintree, 2003	
E156OMD	Leyland Olympian ONLXB1/RH	Optare	B47/29F	1988	LMS Buses, Aintree, 2003	
YYD699	Volvo B10M-60	Plaxton Paramount 3500 III	C51F	1988	Eastville, Bristol, 2000	
OIL9262	Leyland Tiger TRCTL11/3ARAZ	Plaxton Paramount 3200 III E	C53F	1988	First Bristol, 2001	
OIL9263	Leyland Tiger TRCTL11/3ARAZ	Plaxton Paramount 3200 III E	C53F	1988	First Bristol, 2001	
OIL9264	Leyland Tiger TRCTL11/3ARAZ	Plaxton Paramount 3200 III E	C53F	1988	First Bristol, 2001	
E219WBG	Leyland Olympian ONCL10/1RZ	Northern Counties	B45/30F	1988	LMS Buses, Aintree, 2004	
F306JTY	Leyland Olympian ONCL10/2RZ	Alexander RH	B47/33F	1988	LMS Buses, Aintree, 2004	
F309JTY	Leyland Olympian ONCL10/2RZ	Alexander RH	B47/33F	1988	LMS Buses, Aintree, 2004	
F310JTY	Leyland Olympian ONCL10/2RZ	Alexander RH	BC43/33F	1988	LMS Buses, Aintree, 2004	
F311JTY	Leyland Olympian ONCL10/2RZ	Alexander RH	BC43/33F	1988	LMS Buses, Aintree, 2004	
F538LUF	Leyland Lynx LX112L10ZR1R	Leyland	B47F	1989	Brighton & Hove, 2000	
F544LUF	Leyland Lynx LX112L10ZR1R	Leyland	B47F	1989	Brighton & Hove, 2000	

The largest bus in the five-vehicle Somerbus operation is Leyland Tiger D615ASG which carries an Alexander P-type body. This rather angular frontal design was changed for a large order for Singapore BS and that design was adopted for all subsequent P-types, the Singapore version then being known as the PS model. The Somerbus vehicle is seen in Gloucester bus station having worked from Trowbridge. *Phillip Stephenson*

South Gloucestershire has gathered together several of the East Lancs coach-bodied Olympians supplied new to the municipal fleets. Carrying Durbin's names, C28EUH was new to Rhymney Valley, and is now used primarily on school contract duties. *Robert Edworthy*

A major supplier of school buses, South Gloucestershire Bus and Coach uses three former Leyland Tiger army buses fitted with Wadham Stringer Vanguard bodies. These have been refurbished with high-capacity high-back seating as illustrated by B883YTC. *Robert Edworthy*

BHZ6986	Leyland Lynx LX112L10ZR1R	Leyland	B47F	1989	Brighton & Hove, 2000
BHZ6987	Leyland Lynx LX112L10ZR1R	Leyland	B47F	1989	Brighton & Hove, 2000
F249YTJ	Leyland Olympian ONCL10/1RZ	Alexander RH	B45/30F	1989	LMS Buses, Aintree, 2004
G104EOG	Leyland Lynx LX2R11C15Z4R	Leyland	B49F	1989	Travel West Midlands, 2002
G159EOG	Leyland Lynx LX2R11C15Z4R	Leyland	B49F	1989	Rapsons, Inverness, 2004
G174EOG	Leyland Lynx LX2R11C15Z4R	Leyland	B49F	1989	Travel West Midlands, 2002
G177EOG	Leyland Lynx LX2R11C15Z4R	Leyland	B49F	1989	Travel West Midlands, 2002
G296EOG	Leyland Lynx LX2R11C15Z4R	Leyland	B49F	1989	Travel West Midlands, 2002
PJI5013	Volvo B10M-60	Van Hool Alizée	C57F	1989	Eastville, Bristol, 2003
PJI5016	Volvo B10M-60	Van Hool Alizée	C57F	1989	Eastville, Bristol, 2003
G823KWF	Mercedes-Benz 811D	Reeve Burgess Beaver	B31F	1989	Stagecoach East Midlands, 2001
G840UDV	Mercedes-Benz 811D	Carlyle C17	B33F	1990	Stagecoach Oxford, 2000
G128TJA	Mercedes-Benz 811D	Carlyle C17	B33F	1990	Arriva Midlands North, 2002
G900TJA	Mercedes-Benz 811D	Mellor	B32F	1990	Arriva Midlands North, 2000
G992VWV	Leyland Lynx LX112L10ZR1R	Leyland	B47F	1990	Brighton & Hove, 2000
G993VWV	Leyland Lynx LX112L10ZR1R	Leyland	B47F	1990	Brighton & Hove, 2000
H544FVN	Leyland Lynx LX2R11C15Z4R	Leyland	B51F	1990	Halton Transport, 2000
H980PTW	Leyland Olympian ON2R50C13Z4	Alexander RH	B47/31F	1990	Dublin Bus, 2003
H986PTW	Leyland Olympian ON2R50C13Z4	Alexander RH	B47/31F	1990	Dublin Bus, 2003
H337TYG	Leyland Lynx LX2R11C15Z4R	Leyland	B51F	1990	Arriva Yorkshire, 2005
H341UWT	Leyland Lynx LX2R11C15Z4R	Leyland	B51F	1991	Arriva Yorkshire, 2005
H342UWT	Leyland Lynx LX2R11C15Z4R	Leyland	B51F	1991	Arriva Yorkshire, 2005
H343UWX	Leyland Lynx LX2R11C15Z4R	Leyland	B51F	1991	Arriva Yorkshire, 2005
H344UWX	Leyland Lynx LX2R11C15Z4R	Leyland	B51F	1991	Arriva Yorkshire, 2005
H345UWX	Leyland Lynx LX2R11C15Z4R	Leyland	B51F	1991	Arriva Yorkshire, 2005
H346UWX	Leyland Lynx LX2R11C15Z4R	Leyland	B51F	1991	Arriva Yorkshire, 2005
H347UWX	Leyland Lynx LX2R11C15Z4R	Leyland	B51F	1991	Arriva Yorkshire, 2005
H356WWX	Leyland Lynx LX2R11C15Z4R	Leyland	B51F	1991	Arriva Yorkshire, 2005
H357WWX	Leyland Lynx LX2R11C15Z4R	Leyland	B51F	1991	Arriva Yorkshire, 2005
H460WWY	Leyland Lynx LX2R11C15Z4R	Leyland	B51F	1991	Arriva Yorkshire, 2005
H756WWW	Leyland Lynx LX2R11C15Z4R	Leyland	B51F	1991	Arriva Yorkshire, 2005
H757WWW	Leyland Lynx LX2R11C15Z4R	Leyland	B51F	1991	Arriva Yorkshire, 2005
H34HBG	Leyland Lynx LX2R11C15Z4R	Leyland	B51F	1991	Halton Transport, 2000
H422GPM	Mercedes-Benz 709D	Phoenix	B27F	1991	Tillingbourne, Cranleigh, 2000

Volvo PJI5016, one of only eighteen coaches in the fleet, arrived with the Eastville coach business. Eastville's former owner has restarted operations resurrecting that name. *Mark Bailey*

J430PPF	Mercedes-Benz 709D	Dormobile Routemaker	B29F	1991	Tillingbourne, Cranleigh, 2000	
J297NNB	Mercedes-Benz 709D	Plaxton Beaver	B27F	1992	Arriva Cymru, 2001	
J601WHJ	Mercedes-Benz 811D	Plaxton Beaver	B28F	1991	Ensignbus (Bath Bus), 2004	
J606WHJ	Mercedes-Benz 709D	Plaxton Beaver	B28F	1991	Arriva London, 2001	
J988TVU	Mercedes-Benz 709D	Plaxton Beaver	B23F	1992	Crichton, Low Fell, 2002	
J369YWX	Leyland Lynx LX2R11C15Z4R	Leyland	B51F	1992	Arriva Yorkshire, 2005	
J120SPF	Dennis Lance 11m	Northern Counties Paladin	B48F	1992	Travel Dundee, 2001	
J215OCW	Dennis Lance 11m	Plaxton Verde	B47F	1992	Travel Dundee, 2001	
BHZ6984	Dennis Lance 11m	Plaxton Verde	B47F	1992	Travel Dundee, 2001	
BHZ6985	Dennis Lance 11m	Plaxton Verde	B47F	1992	Travel Dundee, 2001	
K622YVN	Leyland Lynx LX2R11V1824S	Leyland Lynx 2	B49F	1992	Stagecoach, 2005	
K623YVN	Leyland Lynx LX2R11V1824S	Leyland Lynx 2	B49F	1992	Stagecoach, 2005	
K624YVN	Leyland Lynx LX2R11V1824S	Leyland Lynx 2	B49F	1992	Stagecoach, 2005	
K625YVN	Leyland Lynx LX2R11V1824S	Leyland Lynx 2	B49F	1992	Stagecoach, 2005	
K628YVN	Leyland Lynx LX2R11V1824S	Leyland Lynx 2	B49F	1992	Stagecoach, 2005	
K326PHT	Dennis Javelin 12m	Wadham Stringer Vanguard II	BC54F	1993	MoD (75KK33), 2000	
K327PHT	Dennis Javelin 12m	Wadham Stringer Vanguard II	BC70F	1993	MoD (75KK34), 2000	
K239FAW	Mercedes-Benz 811D	Plaxton Beaver	B31F	1993	Arriva North West, 2001	
K879UDB	Mercedes-Benz 709D	Plaxton Beaver	B27F	1989	Arriva Cymru, 2001	
K695RNR	Toyota Coaster HDB30R	Caetano Optimo II	C21F	1993	First Badgerline, 2001	
K371RTY	Dennis Dart 9.8m	Wright Handybus	B40F	1993	Go-North East, 2002	
L657MFL	Volvo B6-9.9m	Marshall C37	B32F	1993	WG Services, Harlow, 2003	
L84CNY	Volvo B6-9.9m	Marshall C37	BC32F	1993	Redby, Sunderland, 2003	
BHZ6988	Dennis Dart 9.8m	Marshall C37	B40F	1994	Halton Transport, 2000	
L433CPJ	Mercedes-Benz 811D	Plaxton Beaver	B31F	1994	Arriva Southern Counties, 2002	
L776RWW	Mercedes-Benz 811D	Plaxton Beaver	B31F	1994	Arriva The Shires, 2003	
L778RWW	Mercedes-Benz 811D	Plaxton Beaver	B31F	1994	Arriva North West, 2002	
L779RWW	Mercedes-Benz 811D	Plaxton Beaver	B31F	1994	Arriva North West, 2002	
M102BLE	Dennis Dart 9.8m	Plaxton Pointer	B39F	1994	Metroline, Harrow, 2005	
M107BLE	Dennis Dart 9.8m	Plaxton Pointer	B39F	1994	Metroline, Harrow, 2005	
M108BLE	Dennis Dart 9.8m	Plaxton Pointer	B39F	1994	Metroline, Harrow, 2005	
M503ALP	Dennis Dart 9.8m	Plaxton Pointer	B40F	1994	Metroline, Harrow, 2005	
M504ALP	Dennis Dart 9.8m	Plaxton Pointer	B40F	1994	Metroline, Harrow, 2005	
M505ALP	Dennis Dart 9.8m	Plaxton Pointer	B40F	1994	Metroline, Harrow, 2005	
M485VST	Toyota Coaster HZB50R	Caetano Optimo III	C21F	1995	Burdett, Haywards Heath, 2003	
M46POL	Mercedes-Benz 811D	Plaxton Beaver	B31F	1995	Chambers, Bures, 2002	
M862TYC	Volvo B10M-62	Van Hool Alizée HE	C53F	1995	Chalfont, Southall, 2001	
M861TYC	Volvo B10M-62	Van Hool Alizée HE	C53F	1995	Chalfont, Southall, 1998	
M419VYD	Volvo B10M-62	Van Hool Alizée HE	C53F	1995	Eastville, Bristol, 2003	
N754CYA	Volvo B12T	Van Hool Astrobel	C57/14CT	1996	Eagle Line, Andoversford, 2004	
N24EYB	Volvo B10M-62	Van Hool Alizée HE	C53F	1996	Eastville, Bristol, 2004	
P298MLD	Dennis Dart 9.8m	Plaxton Pointer	B39F	1996	Metroline, Harrow, 2005	

The South West Bus Handbook

Following on from the disposal of Leyland Tigers, in 2000 the Ministry sold many Dennis Javelins too. These mainly carried Wadham Stringer Vanguard 2 bodies, with two of this model joining the South Gloucestershire Bus and Coach fleet. Illustrating the type is K326PHT. *Robert Edworthy*

P299MLD	Dennis Dart 9.8m	Plaxton Pointer	B39F	1996	Metroline, Harrow, 2005
R843GRN	Iveco TurboDaily 59-12	Leicester Carriage	B18FL	1997	Lune Valley, Lancaster, 2004
S583VOB	Volvo B6LE	Wright Crusader	N40F	1998	Dunn-Line, Nottingham, 2004
S584VOB	Volvo B6LE	Wright Crusader	N40F	1998	Dunn-Line, Nottingham, 2004
S627ETV	Volvo B10M-62	Plaxton Première 350	C53F	1998	Bus Eireann, 2004
T118UCH	Volvo B10M-62	Plaxton Première 350	C53F	1999	Bus Eireann, 2004
T213UCH	Volvo B10M-62	Plaxton Première 350	C53F	1999	Bus Eireann, 2004
T215UCH	Volvo B10M-62	Plaxton Première 350	C53F	1999	Bus Eireann, 2004
T323UCH	Volvo B10M-62	Plaxton Première 350	C53F	1999	Bus Eireann, 2004
T463UCH	Volvo B10M-62	Plaxton Première 350	C53F	1999	Bus Eireann, 2004
T134AST	Volvo B6BLE	Wright Crusader 2	N37F	1999	Rapsons, Inverness, 2003
Y263KNB	Dennis Dart SLF 8.8m	Alexander ALX200	N29F	2001	Pete's Travel, West Bromwich, 2003
MW52PZP	TransBus Dart 9.5m	TransBus Pointer	N31F	2003	
MW52PZR	TransBus Dart 9.5m	TransBus Pointer	N31F	2003	

Previous registrations:

BHZ6984	J215OCW	MIL8328	KYV479X
BHZ6985	J120SPF	N754CYA	N754CYA, SIL4458
BHZ6986	F546LUF	OIL9262	F615XWY
BHZ6987	F545LUF	OIL9263	F617XWY
BHZ6988	M87DEW	OIL9264	F620XWY
D706YHK	D260FYM, VLT20	PJI5013	F533WGL
ESK812	D502GHY	PJI5016	G965UHU
H544FVM	H544FVM, BHZ5987	PSU527	D510HHW
H980PTW	90D1034	S627ETV	?
H986PTW	90D1090	T118UCH	99D41294
HIL3188	D888YHG	T213UCH	?
J988TVU	J58MHF, J7SLT	T215UCH	99D41291
K695RNR	K695RNR, SSU437	T323UCH	99D41307
		T463UCH	99D41301
M485VST	M485VST, A11CWR	YYD699	E576UHS

Special liveries: Black and orange (Orange Communications) - shown orange in fleet; black, white and red (Bristol University) - shown pink in the fleet; red and blue - shown in blue. **Web:** www.southglos.pwp.blueyonder.co.uk

SOUTH WEST COACHES

South West Coaches Ltd, Southgate Road, Wincanton, BA9 9EB

No	Reg	Chassis	Body	Seats	Year	Previous owner
01	A109EPA	Leyland Tiger TRCTL11/2R	Plaxton Paramount 3200 E	BC53F	1984	The Bee Line, 1996
02w	A130EPA	Leyland Tiger TRCTL11/2R	Plaxton Paramount 3200 E	BC53F	1984	Scarlet Coaches, Minehead, 1995
03	A799REO	Leyland Tiger TRCTL11/3R	Marshall Campaigner	B56F	1983	Holmeswood Coaches, 1994
04	LUI2527	Leyland Tiger TRCTL11/3R	Plaxton Paramount 3200	C57F	1984	Armchair, Brentford, 1986
05	A256VYC	Leyland Tiger TRCTL11/3R	Wadham Stringer Vanguard	B59F	1984	MoD (CK5669), 1999
06	ANZ4372	DAF SB3000DKV301	Van Hool Alizée DH	C51FT	1992	Aztecbird, Guiseley, 2001
07	ANZ4373	Volvo B10M-62	Plaxton Première 320	C53F	1995	Excelsior, Bournemouth, 1997
08	ANZ4374	Dennis Javelin 8.5m	Plaxton Paramount 3200 III	C35F	1989	Hulberts Coaches, Yeovil, 2000
09	DKZ4602	Leyland Tiger TRCTL11/3RZ	Plaxton Paramount 3200 II Exp	C57F	1985	
10	BYD795X	Leyland Leopard PSU3F/5R	Duple Dominant IV Express	BC53F	1982	
11	EGV695Y	Leyland Tiger TRCTL11/2R	Plaxton Paramount 3200E	BC53F	1983	Leiston Motor Hire, 1996
13	GLZ7465	Volvo B10M-61	Plaxton Paramount 3200 III	C53F	1989	Hulberts Coaches, Yeovil, 2000
14	LUI2528	Leyland Tiger TRCTL11/2R	Plaxton Paramount 3200	C53F	1983	Lodge's, High Easter, 1989
15	TIL9685	Volvo B10M-60	Plaxton Paramount 3500 III	C53F	1990	
16	UIL1335	Volvo B10M-60	Plaxton Paramount 3200 III	C57F	1990	Excelsior, Bournemouth, 1993
17	JIL8319	Leyland Tiger TRCTL11/2R	Plaxton Paramount 3200E	BC53F	1983	Torr's Coaches, Gedling, 1995
18	KYA284Y	Leyland Tiger TRCTL11/3R	Plaxton Paramount 3200	C57F	1983	
19	LIL2167	Leyland Tiger TRCTL11/2R	Plaxton Paramount 3200E	BC53F	1983	Torr's Coaches, Gedling, 1995
20	LYA315V	Bedford YMT	Duple Dominant II Express	B53F	1979	
21	R41EDW	Setra S250 Special	Setra	C48FT	1997	Streamline, Maidstone, 2004
24	VIL9482	Volvo B10M-61	Van Hool Alizée	C53F	1984	Kingsbury Episcopi, 2003
25	RIL1475	Leyland Tiger TRCTL11/3R	Plaxton Paramount 3200 II	BC53F	1984	Edwards Bros, Tiers Cross, 1999
26	UYD950W	Bedford YMT	Duple Dominant	B57F	1981	Osmond, Curry Rivel, 1988
27	WSV323	Leyland Leopard PSU5C/4R	Plaxton P'mount 3200 III (1992)	C57F	1980	Ebdon's, Sidcup, 1983
28	WSV868	Leyland Tiger TRCTL11/3R	East Lancs EL2000 (1995)	B59F	1983	Northern Bus, Anston, 1994
29w	WYD103W	Leyland Leopard PSU3F/5R	Duple Dominant IV	C53F	1981	
30	WYD104W	Leyland Leopard PSU3F/5R	Duple Dominant IV	C53F	1981	
31	XBJ860	Bedford YMQS	Plaxton Supreme IV	C35F	1981	Armchair, Brentford
32w	XYC248W	Bedford YMT	Duple Dominant II Express	BC53F	1980	
33	M103CYR	Iveco TurboDaily 59.12	Marshall C31	B25F	1994	-, 2005
34	ECZ4634	Setra S250 Special	Setra	C48FT	1997	Chenery, Dickleburgh, 2004
	R614AAU	Setra S250 Special	Setra	C53F	1997	Skills, Nottingham, 2005
	R616AAU	Setra S250 Special	Setra	C52F	1997	Skills, Nottingham, 2005
39	KLZ3240	Setra S250 Special	Setra	C49FT	1997	Clarkes of London, 2002
40	LAZ5826	Volvo B10M-60	Plaxton Expressliner	C49FT	1990	Tally Ho!, Kingsbridge, 2002
41	LUI2529	Mercedes-Benz 811D	LHE Commuter	B29F	1990	Arriva North Midlands, 2001
42	TDZ8157	Mercedes-Benz 709D	Marshall C16	B25F	1993	Arriva North West, 2004
43	L55BUS	Mercedes-Benz 709D	Plaxton Beaver	B27F	1994	Nightingale, Maidenhead, 2004
44	L807ORD	Mercedes-Benz 709D	Plaxton Beaver	B33F	1994	Nightingale, Maidenhead, 2004

Pictured in central London, ECZ4634 is one of five Setra S250 Specials operated by South West Coaches.
Dave Heath

South West Coaches operates tendered services in the Bridport area using a fleet of minibuses. Seen in the town in June 2004, 42, TDZ8157, is a Mercedes-Benz with Marshall C16 bodywork. *Tony Wilson*

45	MAZ6792	Volvo B10M-60	Plaxton Expressliner	C51FT	1990	Tally Ho!, Kingsbridge, 2002
46	SAZ2511	Volvo B10M-60	Plaxton Expressliner	C51FT	1990	Tally Ho!, Kingsbridge, 2002
47	RAZ8598	Volvo B10M-60	Plaxton Expressliner	C49FT	1990	Tally Ho!, Kingsbridge, 2002
48	HIL5697	Optare Excel L1150	Optare	N42F	1997	East Yorkshire, 2002
49	XIL8531	Mercedes-Benz 811D	Marshall C16	B33F	1993	Stagecoach, 2004
50	NUI5167	Mercedes-Benz 811D	Marshall C16	B31F	1994	Arriva Midlands, 2004
51	F997KCU	Mercedes-Benz 609D	Devon Conversion	BC23F	1988	Hulberts Coaches, Yeovil, 2000
52	F734USF	Mercedes-Benz 609D	Alexander Sprint	BC24F	1988	Hulberts Coaches, Yeovil, 2000
53	L210OYC	Mercedes-Benz 410D	Deansgate	M16	1994	Hulberts Coaches, Yeovil, 2000
54	L211OYC	Mercedes-Benz 410D	Deansgate	M16	1994	Hulberts Coaches, Yeovil, 2000
55	H484BND	Ford Transit VE6	Made-to-Measure	M16	1990	Hulberts Coaches, Yeovil, 2000
56	V852DYB	Mercedes-Benz Vario 0814	Onyx	C24F	1999	
57	R652TYA	Mercedes-Benz 412D	G&M	M16	1997	
58	H538ETT	Ford Transit VE6	Ford	M14	1991	Stoford Van Hire, 1992
59	G444NYC	Ford Transit VE6	Ford	M14	1990	Stoford Van Hire, 1992
60	F134JHO	Ford Transit VE6	Ford	M14	1989	Stoford Van Hire, 1992
61	F578SHT	Ford Transit VE6	Ford	M14	1989	Stoford Van Hire, 1992
62	F449XFX	Ford Transit VE6	Bristol Street Motors	M12	1989	Hulberts Coaches, Yeovil, 2000
63	F450XFX	Ford Transit VE6	Bristol Street Motors	M12	1989	Hulberts Coaches, Yeovil, 2000
64	F387FYC	Ford Transit VE6	Ford	M7L	1989	Hulberts Coaches, Yeovil, 2000
65	W453CRN	Ford Transit VE6	Ford	M16	2000	Hulberts Coaches, Yeovil, 2000
66	D649NYC	Volkswagen LT28	Devon Conversion	M8	1987	Hulberts Coaches, Yeovil, 2000
67	E758XYB	Volkswagen LT28	Devon Conversion	M8	1988	Hulberts Coaches, Yeovil, 2000
68	E845YYA	Volkswagen LT28	Devon Conversion	M8	1988	Hulberts Coaches, Yeovil, 2000
69	H170SAB	Ford Transit VE6	Ford	M8	1991	Hulberts Coaches, Yeovil, 2000
70	D65RMW	Ford Transit VE6	Chassis Developments	M12	1987	Hulberts Coaches, Yeovil, 2000
71	W454CRN	Ford Transit VE6	Ford	M16	2000	Hulberts Coaches, Yeovil, 2000
72	F693GYD	Volkswagen LT28	Devon	M14	1989	Hulberts Coaches, Yeovil, 2000
-	E416YYB	Volkswagen LT28	Devon Conversions	M8	1988	Hulberts Coaches, Yeovil, 2000
-	F329GYA	Volkswagen LT28	Devon Conversions	M8	1989	Hulberts Coaches, Yeovil, 2000
74	M104SWG	Ford Transit VE6	Ford	M8	1995	van, 1999
75	M103SWG	Ford Transit VE6	Ford	M8	1995	van, 1999
76	M102SWG	Ford Transit VE6	Ford	M8	1995	van, 1999
77	M101SWG	Ford Transit VE6	Ford	M8	1995	van, 1999
-	L687PYD	Volkswagen LT35D	Devon Conversions	M14	1994	Vincent, Yeovil, 2001
-	L688PYD	Volkswagen LT35D	Devon Conversions	M14	1994	Vincent, Yeovil, 2001
80	L865TFB	Ford Transit	Ford	M14	1994	Vincent, Yeovil, 2002

Seen while on a school trip to London, TIL9685, Volvo B10M with a Plaxton Paramount 3500 III body complete with central off-side continental exit. *Dave Heath*

Previous Registrations:

A799REO	20KB46	LUI2529	G166YRE
ANZ4372	J823KHD	MAZ6792	G542FFX
ANZ4373	A17EXC, M375MRU	NUI5467	M454EDH
ANZ4374	F990FYB	P643TMV	P100TCC
DKZ4602	B155AYD	RIL1475	B268KPF, WJB490
ECZ4634	R34AWO	SAZ8598	G543FFX
EGV695Y	EVH240Y, 448HWT	TDZ8157	L716WCC
GLZ7465	F555FYD	TIL9685	G183OYC
HIL5697	P447SWX	UIL1335	G520EFX, G518EFX
JIL8319	GNW121Y	VIL9482	A193MNE, PJI8326, A193MNE
KLZ3240	P643TMV	WSV323	LVS421V
LAZ5826	G329PEW	WSV868	BDF205Y
LIL2167	GNW122Y	XBJ860	UUR341W
LUI2527	A831PPP	XIL8531	L320CHB
LUI2528	FNM862Y	XYC248W	SYD1W

Depots: Southgate Road, Wincanton and Oak Way, Yeovil

ST IVES MINI BUS CO

J Stevens, Treva Croft, Alexander Road, St Ives, TR26

C680KFM	Mercedes-Benz L608D	PMT		BC25F	1987	Hill, Congleton, 1992
FIL6783	Mercedes-Benz 609D	North West		BC24F	1988	Friend, Harrowbarrow, 2003
F193UGL	Mercedes-Benz 609D	G&M		BC24F	1988	Thomas, Hayle, 1996
L226JFA	Mercedes-Benz 709D	Dormobile Routemaker		B29F	1993	Arriva Midlands North, 2003

Previous registration:
FIL6783   E104WFY

The South West Bus Handbook

SURELINE

Mabberley Ltd, 4 The Courtyard, Southwell Business Park, Portland, DT5 2NS

NFX133P	Daimler Fleetline CRL6-30	Alexander AL	CO43/31F	1976	Yellow Buses, Bournemouth, 2004
NFX135P	Daimler Fleetline CRL6-30	Alexander AL	CO43/31F	1976	Yellow Buses, Bournemouth, 2004
NFX136P	Daimler Fleetline CRL6-30	Alexander AL	CO43/31F	1976	Yellow Buses, Bournemouth, 2004
NFX137P	Daimler Fleetline CRL6-30	Alexander AL	CO43/31F	1976	Yellow Buses, Bournemouth, 2004
C407VVN	Mercedes-Benz L608D	Reeve Burgess	O20F	1986	East Yorkshire, 2003
C516DND	Volvo B10M-61	Plaxton Paramount 3500 II	C53F	1986	Taylors, Tintinhull, 2004
F275AWW	Leyland Lynx LX112L10ZR1R	Leyland	B49F	1988	Prentice, Haddington, 2004
J112DUV	Dennis Dart 8.5m	Plaxton Pointer	B24F	1992	Askew, Dringhouses, 2004
J114DUV	Dennis Dart 8.5m	Plaxton Pointer	B24F	1992	Askew, Dringhouses, 2004
K105OMW	Dennis Dart 8.5m	Plaxton Pointer	B33F	1993	Thamesdown, 2004
K109OMW	Dennis Dart 8.5m	Plaxton Pointer	B33F	1993	Thamesdown, 2004
L303AUT	Mercedes-Benz 709D	Alexander Sprint	B25F	1994	Arriva Fox County, 2002
L306AUT	Mercedes-Benz 709D	Alexander Sprint	B25F	1994	Arriva Fox County, 2002
L307AUT	Mercedes-Benz 709D	Alexander Sprint	B25F	1994	Arriva Fox County, 2002
L312AUT	Mercedes-Benz 709D	Alexander Sprint	B25F	1994	Arriva Fox County, 2002
L317AUT	Mercedes-Benz 709D	Alexander Sprint	B25F	1994	Arriva Fox County, 2002
M166WTJ	Mercedes-Benz 709D	Alexander Sprint	B25F	1994	Arriva Fox County, 2002
M454JPA	Mercedes-Benz 709D	Alexander Sprint	B23F	1994	Arriva Fox County, 2002
M459JPA	Mercedes-Benz 709D	Alexander Sprint	B23F	1994	Arriva Fox County, 2002
M460JPA	Mercedes-Benz 709D	Alexander Sprint	B23F	1994	Arriva Fox County, 2002
N350OBC	Mercedes-Benz 709D	Alexander Sprint	B27F	1996	Arriva Fox County, 2002
N351OBC	Mercedes-Benz 709D	Alexander Sprint	B27F	1996	Arriva Fox County, 2002
X844MBM	LDV Convoy	LDV	M16	2001	private owner, 2004

Previous registration:
F275AWW   F275AWW, JSU550

Depot: 17 Tradecroft Industrial Estate, Portland
Web: www.surelinebuses.co.uk

Sureline was established in 2002 and currently operates commercial services between Portland, Weymouth and Dorchester. Increased from Easter 2003, these services now operate every 20 minutes for most of the day. The fleet includes the open-top Mercedes-Benz L608 latterly used by East Yorkshire and pictured in the *Yorkshire Bus Handbook*. Illustrating the fleet is M166WTJ, one of many Alexander Sprints acquired from Arriva. *Tony Wilson*

SWANBROOK

Swanbrook Coaches Ltd, Thomas House, St Margaret's Road, Cheltenham, GL50 4DZ

Reg	Chassis	Body	Type	Year	History
BYX186V	MCW Metrobus DR101/9	MCW	B43/28D	1979	London United, 1998
A900SUL	MCW Metrobus DR101/16	MCW	B43/32F	1984	London General, 2000
A926SUL	MCW Metrobus DR101/16	MCW	B43/32F	1984	London General, 2000
A958SYF	MCW Metrobus DR101/17	MCW	B43/28D	1984	London United, 1998
A703THV	MCW Metrobus DR101/18	MCW	B43/28D	1984	London United, 1998
B149WUL	MCW Metrobus DR101/17	MCW	B43/32F	1985	Metroline, London, 2001
B221WUL	MCW Metrobus DR101/17	MCW	B43/32F	1985	Arriva London, 2001
B120UUD	Leyland Tiger TRCTL11/3RH	Plaxton Paramount 3500 IIE	C51F	1985	Oxford Bus Company, 1996
C142SPB	Leyland Tiger TRCTL11/3RH	Berkhof Everest 370	C53F	1986	Coombs, Weston-super-Mare, 1999
E325PMD	Volvo B10M-46	Plaxton Derwent II	B42F	1988	Marchants, Cheltenham, 2003
H423GPM	Mercedes-Benz 709D	Phoenix	B27F	1990	Magpie, Wooburn Moor, 2001
H683NEF	Iveco Daily 49-10	Dormobile Routemaker	B25F	1991	Dinorwic Power Station, 2000
H97PVW	Leyland Olympian ON2R50C13Z4	Alexander RH	B47/33F	1991	Dublin Bus, 2004
H119PVW	Leyland Olympian ON2R50C13Z4	Alexander RH	B47/33F	1991	Dublin Bus, 2004
H137PVW	Leyland Olympian ON2R50C13Z4	Alexander RH	B47/33F	1991	Dublin Bus, 2004
UJI1761	Volvo B10M-60	Plaxton Paramount 3500 III	C51F	1991	Oxford Bus Company, 2000
UJI1762	Volvo B10M-60	Plaxton Paramount 3500 III	C51F	1991	Oxford Bus Company, 2000
UJI1763	Volvo B10M-60	Plaxton Paramount 3500 III	C51F	1991	Oxford Bus Company, 2000
L194OVO	Mercedes-Benz 811D	Plaxton Beaver	B33F	1994	City of Nottingham, 2001
L195OVO	Mercedes-Benz 811D	Plaxton Beaver	B33F	1994	City of Nottingham, 2001
R100PAR	Optare Excel L1150	Optare	N40F	1997	
R200PAR	Optare Excel L1150	Optare	N40F	1997	
R300PAR	Optare Excel L1150	Optare	N40F	1997	
T12SBK	Dennis Dart SLF	Marshall Capital	B43F	1999	
T35CNN	Scania L94IB	Irizar InterCentury 12.32	C57F	1999	Dunn-Line, Nottingham, 2003
V844OOF	Optare Solo M850	Optare	B28F	2000	Zak's, Birmingham, 2004
V845OOF	Optare Solo M850	Optare	B28F	2000	Zak's, Birmingham, 2004
X469XUT	Volvo B6LE	East Lancs Spryte	B36F	2001	Kent Coach Tours, Ashford, 2002
SK51SBK	Dennis Dart SLF	Marshall Capital	B40F	2002	

Previous registrations:

H97PVW	91D1097		UJI1761	H957DRJ
H119PVW	91D1096		UJI1762	H960DRJ
H137PVW	91D1095		UJI1763	H958DRJ

Depot: Pheasant Lane, Golden Valley, Staverton
Web: www.swanbrook.co.uk

Three low-floor Optare Excel buses were used by Swanbrook on the Arle Court *Park & Ride* service in Cheltenham now operated by Bennetts. Illustrating the livery then used on these vehicles is R300PAR. The normal Swanbrook livery is illustrated on the rear cover. *Phillip Stephenson*

TALLY HO!

SJ & S Wellington, Station Yard, Kingsbridge, TQ7 1ES

Reg	Chassis	Body	Config	Year	History
LUB512P	Volvo B58-56	East Lancs EL2000 (1991)	BC51F	1976	Yellow Bus, Stoke Mandeville, 2003
KJD410P	Bristol LH6L	Eastern Coach Works	B43F	1976	London Buses, 1986
KJD413P	Bristol LH6L	Eastern Coach Works	B43F	1976	London Transport, 1982
OJD51R	Bristol LH6L	Eastern Coach Works	B43F	1976	London Transport, 1982
DCZ2307	Volvo B58-61	Plaxton Supreme IV	C53F	1979	Dartington & Totnes DC, 1999
NIL4842	Leyland Leopard PSU5C/4R	Plaxton Supreme IV	C51F	1979	Peacock, Bromley, 2002
DAD200T	Leyland Leopard PSU3E/4R	Plaxton Supreme IV	C53F	1979	Clarke, Tredegar, 2003
DNT717T	Leyland Leopard PSU3E/4R	Plaxton Supreme IV	C53F	1979	Cudlipp, Henstridge, 2003
KHL460W	Volvo B58-61	Plaxton Supreme IV	C53F	1981	Taylor, Tintinhull, 2003
VWX293X	Leyland Tiger TRCTL11/3R	Plaxton Supreme V	C57F	1981	Lock, Croydon, 2002
VMX234X	Leyland Tiger TRCTL11/3R	Plaxton Supreme V	C53F	1981	Draper, Sidcup, 2002
SPY374X	Leyland Leopard PSU5C/4R	Plaxton Supreme V	C57F	1982	Harrington, Bedworth, 2004
AIW257	Leyland Tiger TRCTL11/3R	Van Hool Alizée	C48FT	1982	Boomerang Bus, Tewkesbury, 2003
JDE973X	Leyland Tiger TRCTL11/3R	Plaxton Supreme VI Express	C57F	1982	Taylors, Tintinhull, 2004
YSU923	Ford R1115	Plaxton Paramount 3200	C53F	1983	Harrington's, Bedworth, 1996
312KTT	Ford R1115	Plaxton Paramount 3200	C53F	1983	Harrington's, Bedworth, 1996
A726SDV	Leyland Tiger TRCTL11/2R	Duple Laser	C53F	1984	Cook's Coaches, Wellington, 2004
HIL2897	DAF SB2300DHTD585	Plaxton Paramount 3200	C53F	1984	Stevens, Modbury, 1999
A131DTO	Volvo Citybus B10M-50	Marshall	B45/33F	1984	Arriva Midlands, 2005
B137GAU	Volvo Citybus B10M-50	East Lancs	B45/31F	1984	Arriva Midlands, 2005
B630DDW	Bedford YNT	Plaxton Paramount 3200	C53F	1985	Oakley Coaches, 2000
LIL6148	Leyland Tiger TRCTL11/3RZ	Plaxton Paramount 3200 III	C57F	1986	Taylors, Tintinhull, 2004
HIL4966	Mercedes-Benz 609D	Whittaker Europa	C21F	1987	Stevens, Modbury, 1999
E809MOU	Mercedes-Benz 811D	Optare StarRider	B33F	1988	FirstGroup, 2004
E817MOU	Mercedes-Benz 811D	Optare StarRider	B33F	1988	FirstGroup, 2004
E39SBO	Dennis Javelin 11m	Duple 320	C53F	1988	Bebb, Llantwit Fardre, 1989
E40SBO	Dennis Javelin 11m	Duple 320	C53F	1988	Bebb, Llantwit Fardre, 1989
E347EVH	DAF SB3000DKV601	Van Hool Alizée	C51FT	1988	Eagle, Bristol, 2005
E351EVH	DAF SB3000DKV601	Van Hool Alizée	C51FT	1988	Eagle, Bristol, 2005
G841DVX	Ford Transit VE6	G&M	B16F	1990	Kingsbridge Senior Citizens, 2004
G179PAO	Mercedes-Benz 709D	Alexander Sprint	B25F	1990	Stagecoach North West, 2002
G184PAO	Mercedes-Benz 709D	Alexander Sprint	B25F	1990	Stagecoach North West, 2002
G186PAO	Mercedes-Benz 709D	Alexander Sprint	B25F	1990	EST Bus, Landow, 2002

Tally Ho! has been a long-time enthusiast for the Bristol LH. Now only three examples remain, represented here in a line-up of the type at Lee Mill depot. *Mark Bailey*

Recent coach acquisitions by Tally Ho! have included a trio of Irizar Century-bodied Scanias. Previously with Blue Iris MLZ2391 was at a typically overcast Cheltenham Gold Cup meeting in 2004. *Dave Heath*

JCZ3604	Mercedes-Benz 709D	Alexander Sprint	B25F	1990	Stagecoach North West, 2001
G253TSL	Mercedes-Benz 709D	Alexander Sprint	B25F	1990	Stagecoach South, 2002
PBZ7052	Dennis Javelin 11m	Duple 320	BC68F	1991	Holmeswood Coaches, 2002
J780NHA	LDV 400	LDV	M16	1992	Wills, Kingsbridge, 2003
J616KCU	Dennis Dart 9.8m	Wright Handybus	B40F	1992	Dart Buses, Paisley, 2002
J618KCU	Dennis Dart 9.8m	Wright Handybus	B40F	1992	Dart Buses, Paisley, 2002
K309YKG	Mercedes-Benz 811D	Wright Nimbus	B33F	1992	Stagecoach, 2004
K423ARW	Mercedes-Benz 811D	Wright Nimbus	B33F	1993	Stagecoach, 2004
K544RWP	LDV 400	Zodiac	M16	1993	Wills, Kingsbridge, 2003
L322AUT	Mercedes-Benz 709D	Alexander Sprint	B25F	1994	Sureline, Portland, 2004
M583WLV	Dennis Dart 9.8m	Marshall C37	B40F	1994	Halton Buses, 2001
M584WLV	Dennis Dart 9.8m	Marshall C37	B40F	1994	Halton Buses, 2001
MLZ2392	Scania K113CRB	Irizar Century 12.35	C49FT	1994	The King's Ferry, Gillingham, 2002
MLZ2391	Scania K113CRB	Irizar Century 12.35	C49FT	1995	Blue Iris, Nailsea, 2002
KIW6512	Toyota Coaster HZB50R	Caetano Optimo III	C21F	1995	Reliant, Heather, 2004
M297LOD	Ford Transit VE6	Ford	M16	1995	Devon CC, 2004
N151MTG	Mercedes-Benz 811D	UVG Wessex	B31F	1995	Stagecoach, 2004
MLZ2393	Scania K113CRB	Irizar Century 12.35	C53F	1996	Buddens, Romsey, 2002
WDR598	Dennis Javelin 12m	Plaxton Première 320	C53F	1996	Stort Valley, Stansted, 2002

Previous registrations:

312KTT	TUK665Y, HBZ2459	LIL6148	D85UCK
A726SDV	A159MNE, HAZ3346	LUB512P	LUB512P, 641UTO
AIW257	WBV541Y, 6449WF, 8921WF, 4529WF	MLZ2391	M495XWF, M18LUE, M495XWF
DCZ2307	CNA827T	MLZ2392	M2KFC, M623UKO
DNT717T	PRG961T, 289MPU	MLZ2393	N919DWJ
E347EVH	E347EVH, 613WHT	NIL4842	JGO336T
E351EVH	E351EVH, 94SHU	PBZ7052	H52FDB
HIL2897	A351RUA	VMX234X	ORN341X, TIL9835
HIL4966	E201WMB	WDR598	P423JDT
JCZ2604	G568PRM	YSU923	BLJ717Y, HBZ4299
KIW6512	N3HCT, N381OGH		

Web: www.tallyhocoaches.com
Depots: East Way, Lee Mill Industrial Estate, Ivybridge; Union Road, Kingsbridge and Station Yard Industrial Estate, Kingsbridge

The South West Bus Handbook

TARGET TRAVEL

Dealtop (Plymouth) Ltd, 17 Walkham Industrial Estate, Burrington Way, Plymouth, PL5 3LS

LPB500	Bedford OB	Duple Vista	C29F	1949	First Western National, 1999
B674CBD	Fiat 60F10	Caetano Beja	C18F	1985	Phillips, Totnes, 1998
D542GFH	DAF SB2300 DHS585	Plaxton Paramount 3200 III	C53F	1987	Chester, Plymouth, 1999
F999UGL	Ford Transit 130	Deansgate	M12	1988	First Western National, 1998
NUI1577	Mercedes-Benz 609D	Reeve Burgess Beaver	BC23F	1988	Plymouth RHA, 2001
NIL6560	Mercedes-Benz 609D	G&M	BC24FL	1989	Gullen, Quintrell Downs, 1998
CSU926	Volvo B10M-60	Plaxton Paramount 3500 III	C53F	1990	Stagecoach Cheltenham, 1998
WCR819	Volvo B10M-60	Plaxton Paramount 3500 III	C47FT	1991	Dorset Travel Services, 2000
PJI3354	Volvo B10M-60	Plaxton Paramount 3500 III	C47FT	1991	Dorset Travel Services, 2000
NUI1588	Dennis Dart 9.8m	Reeve Burgess Pointer	B40F	1992	Travel Dundee, 2003
NUI1599	Dennis Dart 9.8m	Reeve Burgess Pointer	B40F	1992	Travel Dundee, 2003
K179SLY	Mercedes-Benz 410D	?	M15	1992	MCH, Uxbridge, 1998
L853WDS	Mercedes-Benz 709D	Dormobile Routemaker	B29F	1994	Hutchinson, Easingwold, 2003
L76DPE	Mercedes-Benz 709D	Crystals	B27F	1994	Crystals, Dartford, 2003
L168EKR	Mercedes-Benz 711D	Crystals	B27F	1994	Crystals, Dartford, 2003
4011LJ	Volvo B12T	Jonckheere Deauville 45	C36FT	1994	Chester, Plymouth, 1999
M359LFX	Scania K113CRB	Van Hool Alizée HE	C49FT	1995	Yellow Buses, Bournemouth, 2002
M360LFX	Scania K113CRB	Van Hool Alizée HE	C49FT	1995	Yellow Buses, Bournemouth, 2002
M364LFX	Scania K113CRB	Van Hool Alizée HE	C49FT	1995	Yellow Buses, Bournemouth, 2002
M365LFX	Scania K113CRB	Van Hool Alizée HE	C49FT	1995	Yellow Buses, Bournemouth, 2002
M12YCL	Scania K113CRB	Van Hool Alizée HE	C49FT	1995	Yellow Buses, Bournemouth, 2002
N3YCL	Scania K113CRB	Irizar Century 12.35	C49FT	1996	Yellow Buses, Bournemouth, 2002

Acquired from Travel Dundee, NUI1588 is a Dennis Dart with Reeve Burgess Pointer body. When pictured it still carried the index mark J853TRW though it has since been registered. It is seen on route 53 to Plympton Langage. *Mark Bailey*

Target Travel's coach fleet includes Scania K113, registered N3YCL, one of several acquired from Yellow Coaches, the coaching arm of Yellow Buses of Bournemouth. This coach has Irizar Century bodywork and is pictured while on an excursion to London. *Dave Heath*

N481RTA	LDV 400	G&M	M15	1995	City of Plymouth, 2004	
N94BNF	Mercedes-Benz 709D	Plaxton Beaver	B25F	1996	Blue Bus, Bolton, 2004	
N95BNF	Mercedes-Benz 709D	Plaxton Beaver	B25F	1996	Blue Bus, Bolton, 2004	
R338NRU	Volvo B10M-62	Berkhof Axial 50	C49FT	1997	Yellow Buses, Bournemouth, 2004	
R265THL	MAN 18.350	Neoplan Transliner	C39FT	1997	Peter Carol, Bristol, 2002	
R341LPR	Scania K113CRB	Irizar Century 12.35	C34FT	1997	Yellow Buses, Bournemouth, 2002	
S398TNE	Toyota Coaster BB50R	Caetano Optimo IV	C21F	1998	Thompson, Bournemouth, 2003	
C17MEO	MAN 24.400 12m	Noge Catalan 370	C32FT	1998	Shamrock, Pontypridd, 2004	
S3HJC	MAN 18.350	Neoplan Transliner	C38FT	1999	Home James, Totton, 2002	
T325RTT	LDV Convoy	LDV School bus	M16	1999	Uffculme School, 2004	
T297PDF	LDV Convoy	LDV	M16	1999	Outward Bound school, ?, 2004	
T301PDF	LDV Convoy	LDV / Target	M16	1999	Powys CC, 2004	
X315WFX	Mercedes-Benz 614D	Crest	BC24F	2000	Yellow Buses, Bournemouth, 2004	

Previous registrations:

4011LJ	L702SUA, 4WA, L965NWW	NIL6560	F861ATH
C17MEO	S602VAY	NUI1577	F689OFJ
CSU926	G534LWU	NUI1588	J853TRW
D542GFH	D287XCX, PSV111	NUI1599	J997UAC
K179SLY	K149SDF, MCH85	PJI3354	H818AHS
M364LFX	M364LFX, YXI7923	R265THL	R265THL, ROI6774
M365LFX	M365LFX, MUI4841	WCR819	H815AHS, PJI3354, H371VCG

The South West Bus Handbook

TAW & TORRIDGE

Taw & Torridge - Loverings

Taw & Torridge Coaches Ltd, Merton Garage, Merton, Okehampton, EX20 3ED

Reg	Chassis	Body	Config	Year	History
ODV287P	Volvo B58-56	Duple Dominant	C53F	1975	Newquay Motors, 1986
NOK43	Volvo B58-61	Plaxton Supreme III	C57F	1976	Park's of Hamilton,
VAB893R	Bristol LHS6L	Plaxton Supreme III	C53F	1976	Coombe Hill, Salisbury, 1989
JCW517S	Volvo B58-56	Plaxton Supreme III	C53F	1978	Abbott, Blackpool, 2001
AFJ740T	Bristol LH6L	Plaxton Supreme III Express	C43F	1979	Grey Cars, Exeter, 1992
AFJ742T	Bristol LH6L	Plaxton Supreme III Express	C43F	1979	Bordon International, 1992
DMJ374T	Bedford YMT	Duple Dominant II	C53F	1979	Tanners, Sibford Gower, 1983
JMJ134V	Ford R1114	Duple Dominant II	C53F	1980	Tarka Travel, Bideford, 1989
RLN230W	Bristol LHS6L	Plaxton Supreme V	C31F	1980	British Airways, Heathrow, 1996
PJI4713	Bristol LHS6L	Plaxton Supreme V	C33F	1981	British Airways, Heathrow, 1996
TIW7681	Bedford YMQ	Plaxton Supreme IV	C35F	1981	Bromyard Bus Company, 1999
509HUO	Volvo B58-61	Van Hool Aragon	C49FT	1981	Lowland, 1993
6986RU	Van Hool T815	Van Hool Alizée	C49FT	1982	Tourist, Figheldean, 1989
676GDV	Volvo B10M-61	Jonckheere Jubilee	C51FT	1983	Wood, Oldbury, 2002
FAZ7273	Volvo B10M-61	Jonckheere Jubilee	C49FT	1983	Kentishman, Swanley, 2003
B588XNO	Volvo B10M-61	Berkhof Esprite 340	C53F	1984	Embling, Maidenhead, 2003
895FXA	Bova FHD12.280	Bova Futura	C49FT	1985	Robinson, Stewkeley, 1997
C546BHY	Ford Transit 190	Dormobile	B16F	1986	Badgerline, 1994
C550BHY	Ford Transit 190	Dormobile	B16F	1986	Badgerline, 1994
D100XRY	MAN MT8.136	GG Smith Whippet	B28F	198	Crudge, Honiton, 2001
E365HFG	Volvo B10M-61	Plaxton Paramount 3500 III	C53F	1988	Torr, Nottingham, 2004
407JWO	Scania K112CRB	Jonckheere Jubilee P50	C49FT	1988	Hayward, Horndean, 1998
G391PNV	Volvo B10M-60	Plaxton Expressliner	C46FT	1990	Torr, Nottingham, 2004
J130LVM	DAF 400	Deansgate	M16	1991	Tally Ho!, Kingsbridge, 2001
J318LNL	DAF 400	Autobus Classique	M16	1992	Lloyd, Shouldham, 2003
JLZ3073	Volvo B10M-60	Plaxton Excalibur	C50F	1992	Loverings, Coombe Martin, 2004
JLZ3074	Volvo B10M-60	Plaxton Excalibur	C50F	1992	Loverings, Coombe Martin, 2004

Most of the Van Hool coaches imported to Britain and Ireland have bodies built on traditional chassis from suppliers such as Volvo, Scania and DAF. For the left-hand drive European and American markets, the products are constructed integrally. Since the early 1980s some integral Van Hool coaches have been imported with right-hand drive. Here, 6986RU is a Van Hool T815 coach, is seen in Taw & Torridge colours.
Robert Edworthy

The short version of the Bristol LH, the LHS, has always been associated with the west country more than any other part of Britain. Here RLN230W, an example with Plaxton Supreme V coachwork is seen in Taw & Torridge colours. This coach was new to British Airways where it was used to ferry crew between the offices and aircraft. *Robert Edworthy*

K400TAW	Dennis Javelin 8.5m	Wadham Stringer Vanguard II	BC34FA	1993	MoD (75KK350), 2003
JLZ3082	Toyota Coaster HDB30R	Caetano Optimo II	C18F	1993	Loverings, Coombe Martin, 2004
L924NWW	Volvo B10M-60	Plaxton Excalibur	C50F	1994	Loverings, Coombe Martin, 2004
M134UWY	Volvo B10M-62	Plaxton Première 350	C53F	1995	Loverings, Coombe Martin, 2004
M68UWB	DAF 400	Crystals	M16	1994	Hilton, Newton-le-Willows, 2002
N219HWX	Volvo B10M-62	Plaxton Première 350	C53F	1996	Loverings, Coombe Martin, 2004
N220HWX	Volvo B10M-62	Plaxton Première 350	C53F	1996	Loverings, Coombe Martin, 2004
N226HWX	Volvo B10M-62	Plaxton Première 350	C53F	1996	Loverings, Coombe Martin, 2004
775HOD	Dennis Javelin GX 12m	Berkhof Excellence 1000	C53F	1996	Dunn-Line, Nottingham, 1999
R10TAW	Dennis Javelin GX 12m	Neoplan Transliner	C49FT	1998	
R612HMW	Ford Transit	Robin Hood	M8	1998	Hertz, Heathrow, 2003
R927LAA	Volvo B10M-62	Plaxton Excalibur	C53F	1998	Loverings, Coombe Martin, 2004
T402VHO	Volvo B10M-62	Plaxton Excalibur	C49FT	1999	Loverings, Coombe Martin, 2004
A4EXC	Volvo B10M-62	Plaxton Excalibur	C49FT	1999	Excelsior, Bournemouth, 2004
X301AKY	MAN 18.350	Neoplan Transliner	C49FT	2000	Ashall's Coaches, Clayton, 2004
X509HNR	MAN 18.350	Neoplan Transliner	C49FT	2000	Cummer, Galway, 2004
Y25TAW	Bova FHD12-370	Bova Futura	C49FT	2001	

Previous registrations:

407JWO	E518KNV		JLZ3074	J726CWT
509HUO	RHS2W		JLZ3082	K596VBC
676GDV	ONV652Y, 349LVO, ONV652Y, TIL8148		M68UWB	M68UWB, 935BRU
775HOD	N870XMO		NOK43	NGB5P
895FXA	C104TFP, 4542VU, C104TFP		ODV287P	KTT316P, 676GDV
6986RU	NOX740X		PJI4713	RLN231W
E365HFG	E597UHS, KAZ6914, WSV491		R927LAA	A10XEL
FAZ7273	A625DCU, OIL8656, A922MSH, 319BHR, A427XOS, OIB2884, A311XHE		T402VHO	A1XEL
			TIW7681	NPC387W, TIW7681, 81CW271(EI)
JLZ3073	J732CWT		X509HNR	01G2067

Depots: Grange Lane, Oakhampton and Merton Garage, Merton
Web: www.tawandtorridge.co.uk

The South West Bus Handbook

TAYLORS

Taylors Coach Travel Ltd, Townsend Garage, Tintinhull, Yeovil, BA22 8PF

CYA614X	Leyland Tiger TRCTL11/3R	Plaxton Supreme V	C53F	1982	First Southern National, 2002
YPD116Y	Leyland Tiger TRCTL11/2R	Duple Dominant IV Express	C53F	1983	First Southern National, 2002
FNM854Y	Leyland Tiger TRCTL11/3R	Plaxton Paramount 3200	C53F	1983	First Somerset and Avon, 2003
HHJ372Y	Leyland Tiger TRCTL11/3R	Alexander TE	B53F	1983	First Somerset and Avon, 2003
HHJ376Y	Leyland Tiger TRCTL11/3R	Alexander TE	C53F	1983	First Somerset and Avon, 2003
A696OHJ	Leyland Tiger TRCTL11/2R	Alexander TE	C53F	1983	First Somerset and Avon, 2003
A897KCL	Leyland Tiger TRCTL11/3R	Plaxton Paramount 3200 E	C53F	1983	First Southern National, 2002
C457HAK	Volvo B10M-61	Plaxton Paramount 3200 II	C53F	1985	Spring, Evesham, 2003
RIL1057	Volvo B10M-61	Van Hool Alizée	C53F	1988	First Southern National, 2000
E755HJF	Dennis Javelin 12m	Duple 320	C57F	1988	Powell, Ledbury, 2001
TJI4683	DAF MB230LB615	Plaxton Paramount 3500 III	C53F	1988	Cunningham, Northampton, 2002
F729JWD	Leyland Swift LBM6T/2RS	Wadham Stringer Vanguard II	BC33F	1988	Royal Blue, Kingskerswell, 2000
F869YWX	Leyland Swift LBM6T/2RS	Reeve Burgess Harrier	BC37F	1988	Smith, Darenth, 2001
F791GNA	Leyland Tiger TRCTL11/3RARZ	Duple 320	C53F	1989	Newbury Coaches, Ledbury, 2001
WJI1414	DAF SB3000DKV585	Van Hool Alizée	C57F	1990	Cerbydau Cenarth, 2000
K150PHW	Dennis Javelin 10m	Wadham Stringer Vanguard II	BC60F	1992	MoD (77KK73), 2004
RJX318	Bova FHD12-340	Bova Futura	C55F	1994	The King's Ferry, Gillingham, 2001
M379CGN	Mercedes-Benz 410D	Crest	C16F	1995	Golden Boy, Hoddesdon, 2002
752FUV	Volvo B10M-62	Van Hool Alizée	C53F	1996	Shearings, 2003
P224KTP	Iveco EuroMidi CC95.E.18	Indcar EC03	C35F	1996	Botley, Bishops Waltham, 2001
FD03YOC	Irisbus Scolabus 150E24	Vehixel	BC68F	2003	PMP, Luton, 2004
FG03JBE	Irisbus Scolabus 150E24	Vehixel	BC68F	2003	PMP, Luton, 2004
FJ53ZSZ	Irisbus Scolabus 150E24	Vehixel	BC68F	2003	PMP, Luton, 2004
WU53ESG	LDV Convoy	LDV	M16	2003	

Previous registrations:

752FUV	N704UVR		K150PHW	K808CSC
A696OHJ	A696OHJ, UFX940		RIL1057	E313OPR
A897KCL	A897KCL, 620HOD		RJX318	L7KFC, L485HKN
CYA614X	CYA614X, TPR354		TJI4683	E642KCX
F729JWD	88M2013		WJI1414	G965KJX
FNM754Y	FNM754Y, KFX791		YPD116Y	YPD116Y, TJI4683

web: www.taylorscoachtravel.co.uk
Depots: Townsend Garage, Tintinhull and Lynx Trading Estate, Yeovil.

Taylors was acquired by the Cawlett Group which included Southern National and North Devon Red Bus. However, after their sale to First, a change in policy led to Taylors regaining its independence. Among the fleet which comprises mainly contract vehicles, is Bova Futura RJX318, seen at Tintinhull. *Robert Edworthy*

THAMESDOWN

Thamesdown Transport Ltd, Corporation Street, Swindon, SN1 1DU

69-73		Dennis Dominator DDA1033		East Lancs		B45/31F	1990		
69	H969XHR	70	H970XHR	71	H971XHR	72	H972XHR	73	H973XHR
75	F603RPG		Dennis Dominator DDA1026		East Lancs	B45/30F	1989	Arriva Southern Counties, 1998	

101-110		Dennis Dart 8.5m		Plaxton Pointer		B33F	1993		
101	K101OMW	104	K104OMW	106	K106OMW	108	K108OMW	110	K110OMW
102	K102OMW								

111-119		Dennis Dart 9.8m		Plaxton Pointer		B40F	1994		
111	M711BMR	113	M113BMR	115	M115BMR	117	M117BMR	119	M119BMR
112	M112BMR	114	M114BMR	116	M116BMR	118	M118BMR		

120-128		Dennis Dart 9.8m		Plaxton Pointer		B40F	1995		
120	XMW120	122	N122JHR	124	N124JHR	126	N126LMW	128	N128LMW
121	N121JHR	123	N123JHR	125	N125LMW	127	N127LMW		

129	XBZ7729	Dennis Dart 9.8m	Plaxton Pointer	B40F	1995	Isle of Man Transport, 2000	
130	XBZ7730	Dennis Dart 9.8m	Plaxton Pointer	B40F	1995	Isle of Man Transport, 2000	
131	XBZ7731	Dennis Dart 9.8m	Plaxton Pointer	B40F	1994	Isle of Man Transport, 2000	
132	XBZ7732	Dennis Dart 9.8m	Plaxton Pointer	B40F	1994	Isle of Man Transport, 2000	
141	R314NGM	Dennis Dart SLF	Plaxton Pointer 2	N37F	1997	The King's Ferry, Gillingham, 2000	
142	R315NGM	Dennis Dart SLF	Plaxton Pointer 2	N37F	1997	The King's Ferry, Gillingham, 2000	
143	R317NGM	Dennis Dart SLF	Plaxton Pointer 2	N37F	1997	The King's Ferry, Gillingham, 2000	
144	R319NGM	Dennis Dart SLF	Plaxton Pointer 2	N37F	1997	The King's Ferry, Gillingham, 2000	
145	JAM145E	Daimler CVG6/30	Northern Counties	B40/30F	1967		

One of the few TransBus Super Pointers to carry the TransBus oval badge, 214, WX04CZK is seen on route 1A in Swindon centre. This 11.3 metre version is one of eighteen operated by Thamesdown. *Dave Heath*

Park & Ride route 901 in Swindon is provided by Thamesdown using three Super Pointer Darts. Illustrating the livery applied to these is 198, WV02NNA, seen in the town. *Phillip Stephenson*

151-158			Dennis Dart SLF		Plaxton Pointer		B41F	1996		
151	P151SMW	153	P153SMW	155	P155SMW	157	P157SMW	158	P158SMW
152	P152SMW	154	P154SMW	156	P156SMW				

159	P159VHR		Dennis Dart SLF		Plaxton Pointer 2		N41F	1997		
160	P160VHR		Dennis Dart SLF		Plaxton Pointer 2		N41F	1997		
161	P161VHR		Dennis Dart SLF		Plaxton Pointer 2		N41F	1997		
162	S162BMR		Dennis Dart SLF		Plaxton Pointer 2		N38F	1998		
163	T163RMR		Dennis Dart SLF		Plaxton Pointer 2		N40F	1999		
164	T164RMR		Dennis Dart SLF		Plaxton Pointer 2		N40F	1999		
165	T165RMR		Dennis Dart SLF		Plaxton Pointer 2		N40F	1999		
175	KMW175P		Daimler Fleetline CRG6LX		Eastern Coach Works		O43/31F	1976		
180	S838VAG		Dennis Dart SLF 11.7m		Plaxton Pointer SPD		N45F	1998	Plaxton demonstrator, 2000

181-191			Dennis Dart SLF 11.7m		Plaxton Pointer SPD		N45F	1998-2000 *184-6 are N41F		
181	S181BMR	184	S184BMR	186	S186BMR	188	V188EAM	190	V190EAM
182	S182BMR	185	S185BMR	187	V187EAM	189	V189EAM	191	V191EAM
183	S183BMR								

192-197			Dennis Dart SLF 11.7m		Plaxton Pointer 2		N41F	2001		
192	Y192YMR	194	Y194YMR	195	Y195YMR	196	Y196YMR	197	Y197YMR
193	Y193YMR								

198-210			Dennis Dart SLF 11.7m		Plaxton Pointer SPD		N41F	2002-03		
198	WV02NNA	201	WU52YWE	204	WU52YWH	207	WU52YWL	209	WX03YFD
199	WV02NNB	202	WU52YWF	205	WU52YWJ	208	WU52YWM	210	WX03YFE
200	WV02NNC	203	WU52YWG	206	WU52YWK				

211-215			TransBus Dart SLF 11.7m		TransBus Super Pointer		N41F	2004		
211	WX03ZNS	212	WX04CZH	213	WX04CZJ	214	WX04CZK	215	WX04CZL

| 216 | BVR59T | Leyland Fleetline FE30AGR | Northern Counties | | B43/32F | 1978 | GM Buses, 1989 | |
| 217 | BVR89T | Leyland Fleetline FE30AGR | Northern Counties | | B43/32F | 1978 | GM Buses, 1989 | |

262-266
			Leyland Fleetline FE30AGR		Alexander AL		B43/31F	1980	Yellow Buses, Bournemouth, 2000	
262	GRU162V	263	GRU163V	264	GRU164V	265	GRU165V	266	GRU166V	

267-275
			Leyland Fleetline FE30AGR		Alexander AL		B43/31F	1980-81	Yellow Buses, Bournemouth, 2002-04	
267	GRU167V	269	MFX169W	271	MFX171W	273	MFX173W	275	MFX175W	
268	GRU168V	270	MFX170W	272	MFX172W	274	MFX174W			

| 281 | F81ODX | Dennis Dominator DDA1019 | East Lancs | | B45/31F | 1988 | Ipswich Buses, 2004 | |

299-305
			Leyland Fleetline FE30AGR		Eastern Coach Works		B43/31F	1978-80		
299	UMR199T	301	BMR201V	303	BMR203V	304	BMR204V	305	BMR205V	
300	UMR200T	302	BMR202V							

Ancillary vehicle:
| 383 | OHR183R | Leyland Fleetline FE30AGR | Eastern Coach Works | | O-F | 1977 | Mobile workshop and tree-lopper | |

Previous registrations:
XBZ7729	MAN14A, M410XTC
XBZ7730	MAN15D, M409XTC
XBZ7731	CMN76X, M505XTC
XBZ7732	CMN78X, M506XTC

Named vehicles:- 69 *Western Pathfinder*; 70 *Western Explorer*; 71 *Western Pioneer*; 72 *Western Crusader*; 73 *Western Venturer*; 75 *Western Talisman*; 101 *Blackbird*; 102 *Bullfnch*; 104 *Cormorant*; 106 *Goldfinch*; 108 *Kingfisher*; 110 *Peacock*; 111 *Dog Star*; 112 *Lode Star*; 113 *Morning Star*; 114 *Polar Star*; 115 *Red Star*; 116 *Rising Star*; 117 *Royal Star*; 118 *Shooting Star*; 119 *Western Star*; 121 *Evening Star*; 122 *Knight of the Garter*; 123 *Knight of the Thistle*; 124 *Knight of St Patrick*; 125 *Knight of the Bath*; 126 *Knight of St John*; 127 *Knight of the Golden Fleece*; 128 *Knight of the Grand Cross*; 129 *County of Gloucester*; 130 *County of Oxford*; 131 *County of Berks*; 132 *County of Wilts*; 141 *Sir Daniel Gooch*; 142 *Armstrong*; 143 *William Dean*; 144 *G J Churchward*; 151 *Saint Ambrose*; 152 *Saint Andrew*; 153 *Saint Augustine*; 154 *Saint Bartholomew*; 155 *Saint Benedict*; 156 *Saint Bernard*; 157 *Saint Cuthbert*; 158 *Saint David*; 159 *Saint Agatha*; 160 *Saint Catherine*; 161*St Helena*; 162 *Saint Dunstan*; 163 *Saint Gabriel*; 164 *Saint George*; 165 *Saint Nicholas*; 175 *Isambard Kingdom Brunel*; 180 *Caerphilly Castle*; 181 *Eclipse*; 182 *Vanguard*; 183 *Formidable*; 184 *Albion*; 185 *Avenger*; 186 *Benbow*; 187 *Caradoc*; 188 *Centaur*; 189 *Champion*; 190 *Cockade*; 191 *Daring*; 192 *Despatch*; 193 *Diadem*; 194 *Dragon*; 195 *Druid*; 196 *Glory*; 197 *Magnificent*; 198 *Cambrian*; 199 *Foxhound*; 200 *Goliath*; 201 *Salzgitter*; 202 *Ocotal*; 203 *Pontorson*; 204 *Grenville*; 205 *Greyhound*; 206 *Hercules*; 207 *Hermes*; 208 *High Flyer*; 209 *Intrepid*; 210 *Jupiter*; 211 *Torun - City of Copernicus*; 212 *Kelly*; 213 *Magpie*; 214 *Majestic*; 215 *Swindon*; 281 *Helmingham Hall*.

Special liveries: (Park & Ride) 198-200; (Hospital Express) 201-203
web: www.thamesdown-transport.co.uk

The latest arrivals with Thamesdown are further 11.3metre Darts, this time produced by TransBus. The last of the batch has been painted in a gold livery to celebrate the centenary of the transport business in Swindon. The bus, 215, WX04CZL, was shown to the enthusiasts at Alton in July 2004. *Richard Godfrey*

TILLEY'S

P A & L A Tilley, The Coach Station, Wainhouse Corner, Bude, EX23 0AZ

TIL1262	Dennis Javelin 10m	Wadham Stringer Vanguard II	BC47FL	1993	LB Lewisham, 2004
TIL1255	Dennis Javelin GX 12m	Marcopolo Explorer	C50FT	1995	Eagles & Crawford, Mold, 2003
TIL1253	Marshall Midibus	Marshall MM	N29F	1996	Glyn Williams, Pontllanfraith, 2002
TIL1254	Marshall Midibus	Marshall MM	N29F	1996	Glyn Williams, Pontllanfraith, 2002
TIL1257	Dennis Javelin GX 12m	Marcopolo Explorer	C50FT	1997	Chalfont, Southall, 2001
TIL1260	Dennis Javelin GX 12m	Caetano Algarve 2	C53F	1997	Metroline, 2001
TIL5081	Dennis Javelin 10m	Berkhof Axial	C39F	1997	Richmond, Barley, 2004
TIL1258	Dennis Javelin GX 12m	Neoplan Transliner	C53F	1998	Londoners, Nunhead, 2002
TIL1259	Iveco EuroRider 391E.12.35	Beulas Stergo ε	C53F	1999	Grangeville, Gravesend, 2003
TIL1261	Optare Solo M850	Optare	N30F	2000	
TIL1256	MAN 13.220	Marcopolo Continental 330	C37F	2001	
TIL1263	Iveco EuroMidi CC100E21F/P	Indcar Maxim 2	C29F	2004	

Previous registrations:

TIL1253	P402KAV		TIL1259	T284CJU
TIL1254	P410KAV		TIL1260	P771BJF
TIL1255	M715HBC		TIL1261	W676DDN
TIL1256	from new		TIL1262	K954OPX
TIL1257	P559BAY		TIL1263	-
TIL1258	R7LON		TIL5081	P626WMJ, 426YRA

One of the early integral low-floor buses was produced by Marshalls as a 9-metre 29 seater. Two are still used by Tilleys and TIL1253 is seen in Launceston during June 2004 having operated the service from North Petherwin, route 225. *Mark Bailey*

TRATHENS

Trathens Travel Services Ltd, Walkham Park, Burrington Way, Plymouth, PL5 3LS

Part of Park's Motor Group

15	KSK984	Volvo B12T	Jonckheere Monaco	C57/14CT	2002	Park's of Hamilton, 2002
16	KSK985	Volvo B12T	Jonckheere Monaco	C57/14CT	2002	Park's of Hamilton, 2002
17	KSK986	Volvo B12T	Jonckheere Monaco	C57/14CT	2002	Park's of Hamilton, 2002
-	290WE	Volvo B10M-53	Van Hool Astral	C10/6CT	1984	Express Travel, Perth, 1993
-	B469FCS	Volvo B10M-61	Van Hool Astral	C12/6CT	1984	Deeble, Darleyford, 1995
473	LSK473	Volvo B12T	Van Hool Astrobel	C10/6FT	1998	
481	LSK481	Volvo B12T	Van Hool Astrobel	C10/6CT	1998	
498	LSK498	Volvo B12T	Van Hool Astrobel	C57/14CT	1998	
499	LSK499	Volvo B12T	Van Hool Astrobel	C57/14CT	1998	
503	LSK503	Volvo B10M-62	VDL Jonckheere Mistral 50	C51FT	2004	
504	LSK504	Volvo B10M-62	VDL Jonckheere Mistral 50	C51FT	2004	
505	LSK505	Volvo B10M-62	VDL Jonckheere Mistral 50	C51FT	2004	
511	LSK511	Volvo B12T	Van Hool Astrobel	C57/14CT	1997	
512	LSK512	Volvo B12T	Van Hool Astrobel	C57/14CT	1997	
513	YN51XMW	Neoplan Skyliner N122/3	Neoplan	C57/18CT	2001	
514	YN51XMX	Neoplan Skyliner N122/3	Neoplan	C57/18CT	2001	
515	YN51XMK	Neoplan Skyliner N122/3	Neoplan	C57/18CT	2002	
516	YN51XML	Neoplan Skyliner N122/3	Neoplan	C57/18CT	2002	
517	YN51XMZ	Neoplan Skyliner N122/3	Neoplan	C57/18CT	2001	

Trathens' principal operations are for National Express for whom they currently perform all the duties requiring double-deck coaches. To meet this need a fleet of Volvo coaches with a mix of Jonckheere and Van Hool bodywork has been augmented with a large batch of Neoplan Skyliners. Illustrating the Skyliner is 522, YN51XMJ, seen passing through Exeter en route to Paignton. *Mark Bailey*

During 2004 the single-deck fleet received a batch of new VDL Jonckheere Mistral-bodied Volvos. These carry cherished index marks initially used by Trathens' parent company, Park's of Hamilton. 507, LSK507, is seen in Exeter before heading off for London. *Phillip Stephenson*

518	YN51XMC	Neoplan Skyliner N122/3	Neoplan	C57/18CT	2001	
519	YN51XMD	Neoplan Skyliner N122/3	Neoplan	C57/18CT	2001	
520	YN51XME	Neoplan Skyliner N122/3	Neoplan	C57/18CT	2001	
521	YN51XMH	Neoplan Skyliner N122/3	Neoplan	C57/18CT	2001	
522	YN51XMJ	Neoplan Skyliner N122/3	Neoplan	C57/18CT	2001	
523	YN51XMU	Neoplan Skyliner N122/3	Neoplan	C57/18CT	2001	
524	YN51XMV	Neoplan Skyliner N122/3	Neoplan	C57/18CT	2001	
611	LSK611	Volvo B12T	Van Hool Astrobel	C10/6CT	1995	Park's of Hamilton, 1996
612	LSK612	Volvo B12T	Van Hool Astrobel	C10/6CT	1995	Park's of Hamilton, 1996
613	LSK613	Volvo B12T	Van Hool Astrobel	C10/6CT	1993	
614	LSK614	Volvo B12T	Jonckheere Monaco	C10/6CT	1994	Park's of Hamilton, 1996
615	LSK615	Volvo B12T	Jonckheere Monaco	C10/6CT	1994	Park's of Hamilton, 1996
645	HSK645	Volvo B12B	VDL Jonckheere Mistral 50	C49FT	2005	
646	HSK646	Volvo B12B	VDL Jonckheere Mistral 50	C49FT	2005	
647	HSK647	Volvo B12B	VDL Jonckheere Mistral 50	C49FT	2005	
648	HSK648	Volvo B12B	VDL Jonckheere Mistral 50	C49FT	2005	
649	HSK649	Volvo B12B	VDL Jonckheere Mistral 50	C49FT	2005	
650	HSK650	Volvo B12B	VDL Jonckheere Mistral 50	C49FT	2005	
651	HSK651	Volvo B10M-62	Jonckheere Mistral 50	C53F	2003	Park's of Hamilton, 2003
652	HSK652	Volvo B10M-62	Jonckheere Mistral 50	C53F	2003	Park's of Hamilton, 2003
653	HSK653	Volvo B10M-62	Jonckheere Mistral 50	C53F	2003	Park's of Hamilton, 2003
812	LSK812	Volvo B12T	Van Hool Astrobel	C10/6CT	1994	Park's of Hamilton, 1996
814	LSK814	Volvo B12T	Van Hool Astrobel	C10/6CT	1994	Park's of Hamilton, 1996

HSK654

Previous registrations:

290WE	B418CGG	LSK511	P926KYC
B469FCS	B320HSC, FXU355, LSK825	LSK512	P927KYC
LSK473	R262OFJ	LSK611	LSK831
LSK481	R263OFJ	LSK612	LSK832
LSK498	R261OFJ	LSK613	L977KDT
LSK499	R264OFJ		

Livery: White (private hire and National Express); Grey/multi ("Stariders" - band bus specification).

TRURONIAN

Truronian Ltd, 24 Lemon Street, Truro, Cornwall TR1 2LS

AFJ771T	Bristol VRT/SL3/6LXB	Eastern Coach Works	B43/31F	1979	Tally Ho!, Kingsbridge, 1996
BKE857T	Bristol VRT/SL3/6LXB	Eastern Coach Works	B43/31F	1979	Arriva Southern Counties, 1998
PRC849X	Bristol VRT/SL3/6LXB	Eastern Coach Works	B43/31F	1981	Trent, 1991
PRC856X	Bristol VRT/SL3/6LXB	Eastern Coach Works	B43/31F	1981	Trent, 1991
TPL762X	Leyland Tiger TRBL11/2R	Plaxton Supreme V Express	C53F	1982	Vale of Manchester, 1997
HWU885Y	Volvo B10M-61	Plaxton Paramount 3200	C53F	1983	Buzzlines, Hythe, 2005
C812BYY	Leyland Olympian ONLXB/1RH	Eastern Coach Works	B42/30F	1986	Arriva London, 2001
C819BYY	Leyland Olympian ONLXB/1RH	Eastern Coach Works	B42/30F	1986	Arriva London, 2001
C24CHM	Leyland Olympian ONLXB/1RH	Eastern Coach Works	B42/30F	1986	Arriva London, 2001
C83CHM	Leyland Olympian ONLXB/1RH	Eastern Coach Works	B42/30F	1986	Arriva London, 2001
C87CHM	Leyland Olympian ONLXB/1RH	Eastern Coach Works	B42/30F	1986	Arriva London, 2001
F315VCV	Mercedes-Benz 609D	Reeve Burgess Beaver	DP25F	1988	
JIL7904	Volvo B10M-60	Plaxton Paramount 3200 III	C49FT	1990	DMA, Tudhoe, 2002
L995VAF	Ford Transit VE6	Ford	M14	1994	
260ERY	Volvo B10M-62	Caetano Algarve 2	C49FT	1994	
L725WCV	Mercedes-Benz 811D	Plaxton Beaver	B31F	1994	
L726WCV	Mercedes-Benz 811D	Plaxton Beaver	B31F	1994	
M373CRL	Volvo B10M-62	Plaxton Première 320	C46FT	1995	
N212KBJ	Mercedes-Benz 711D	Autobus Classique	BC24F	1995	Galloway, Mendelsham, 2000
N166KAF	Dennis Dart 9.8m	Plaxton Pointer	B37F	1996	
N167KAF	Dennis Dart 9.8m	Plaxton Pointer	B37F	1996	
N168KAF	Dennis Dart 9.8m	Plaxton Pointer	B37F	1996	
N169KAF	Dennis Dart 9.8m	Plaxton Pointer	B37F	1996	
N170KAF	Mercedes-Benz 711D	Plaxton Beaver	C25F	1996	
P452SCV	Dennis Dart SLF	Plaxton Pointer	B34F	1997	
P453SCV	Dennis Dart SLF	Plaxton Pointer	B34F	1997	
P455SCV	Dennis Dart SLF	Plaxton Pointer	B34F	1997	
R1TRU	Volvo B10M-62	Van Hool T9 Alizée	C49FT	1998	
S549SCV	Dennis Dart SLF	Plaxton Pointer MPD	N29F	1998	
S889RRL	Ford Transit	Ford	M8	1999	

Carrying *Corlink* livery, TransBus Mini Pointer KU52RXJ is one of the buses which Truronian operates on behalf of Cornwall council. It is seen in Truro while operating route T7 to Redruth.
Mark Bailey

T32JCV	Dennis Dart SLF	Plaxton Pointer 2	NC32F	1999	
T34JCV	Dennis Dart SLF	Plaxton Pointer 2	NC32F	1999	
T35JCV	Dennis Dart SLF	Plaxton Pointer 2	NC32F	1999	
T12TRU	Dennis Dart SLF	Plaxton Pointer 2	N29F	1999	
T2TRU	Volvo B10M-62	Plaxton Excalibur	C49FT	1999	
W3TRU	Volvo B10M-62	Plaxton Panther	C49FT	2000	
W4TRU	Mercedes-Benz Vario 0814	Plaxton Cheetah	C27F	2000	
Y1EDN	Dennis Dart SLF	Plaxton Pointer 2	N37F	2001	
Y2EDN	Dennis Dart SLF	Plaxton Pointer 2	N37F	2001	
Y5TRU	Volvo B10M-62	Plaxton Panther	C49FT	2001	
AN02EDN	TransBus Enviro 300	TransBus 300	N44F	2002	
BN02EDN	TransBus Enviro 300	TransBus 300	N44F	2002	
CN02EDN	TransBus Enviro 300	TransBus 300	N44F	2002	
DN02EDN	TransBus Enviro 300	TransBus 300	N44F	2002	
EN02EDN	TransBus Enviro 300	TransBus 300	N44F	2002	
WK02XLT	Mercedes-Benz Sprinter 110cdi	GM	M7L	2002	Operated for Cornwall CC
WK52LZA	Mercedes-Benz Sprinter 110cdi	GM	M7L	2002	Operated for Cornwall CC
KU52RXJ	TransBus Dart SLF 8.8m	TransBus Mini Pointer	N29F	2003	Operated for Cornwall CC
WK52WKV	TransBus Dart SLF 8.8m	TransBus Mini Pointer	N29F	2003	
TT03TRU	TransBus Dart SLF 10.2m	TransBus Pointer	N37F	2003	
WK03CXS	Irisbus Scolabus 150E04	Vehixel	B61FL	2003	Operated for Cornwall CC
WK03EKH	Irisbus Scolabus 150E04	Vehixel	B64F	2003	
WK04AOW	Irisbus Scolabus 150E04	Vehixel	B67F	2004	
TT04TRU	Volvo B12B	Plaxton Panther	C49FT	2004	
TU04TRU	Optare Solo M950	Optare	N33F	2004	
T77TRU	Optare Solo M950	Optare	N33F	2004	
TL54TVL	Optare Solo M880	Optare	N29F	2004	
TT54TVL	Optare Solo M880	Optare	N29F	2004	
T20TVL	Optare Solo M880	Optare	N29F	2004	
TO54TRU	Optare Solo M880	Optare	N29F	2004	

Previous registrations:
260ERY   L339WAF   JIL7904   G504EFX, A4EXC, G371GJT

Special livery: Yellow (school bus) or red (buses); green (Eden / Helston Branchline)
Web: www.truronian.co.uk
Depots: Flambards, Helston & Newham Industrial Estate, Truro

Truronian operates the courtesy services at the Eden Project for which five TransBus Enviro buses was acquired. These vehicles have a dedicated livery and distinctive marks, illustrated by DN02EDN. *Mark Bailey*

TURNERS

Turners Coachways (Bristol) Ltd, 59 Days Road, St Phillips, Bristol, BS2 0QS

3138DP	Leyland Tiger TRCTL11/3LZ	Plaxton Derwent 2	BC70F	1986	MoD (82KF21), 1998
110LHW	Leyland Tiger TRCTL11/3LZ	Plaxton Derwent 2	BC70F	1987	MoD (82KF29), 1998
XHY256	Leyland Tiger TRCTL11/3LZ	Plaxton Derwent 2	BC56F	1987	MoD (87KF17), 1998
73WAE	Leyland Tiger TRCTL11/3LZ	Plaxton Derwent 2	BC70F	1987	MoD (87KF38), 1998
G826XWS	Leyland Tiger TRCTL11/3LZ	Plaxton Derwent 2	BC56F	1989	MoD (03KJ28), 1998
G829XWS	Leyland Tiger TRCTL11/3LZ	Plaxton Derwent 2	BC56F	1989	MoD (03KJ23), 1998
OYY3	Volvo B10M-60	Van Hool Alizée	C57F	1990	North Mymms, Potters Bar, 1993
K5CJT	Toyota Coaster HDB30R	Caetano Optimo II	C21F	1992	
K18LUE	Volvo B10M-60	Jonckheere Deauville 45	C53F	1995	Tarhum, Nailsea, 2003
K6CJT	Volvo B10M-60	Van Hool Alizée	C57F	1993	
K7CJT	Volvo B10M-60	Van Hool Alizée	C57F	1993	
L8CJT	Volvo B10M-60	Van Hool Alizée	C49FT	1994	
L9CJT	Volvo B10M-60	Van Hool Alizée	C49FT	1994	
M10CJT	Volvo B10M-62	Jonckheere Deauville 45	C53F	1995	Park's of Hamilton, 1996
M11CJT	Volvo B10M-62	Jonckheere Deauville 45	C49FT	1995	Park's of Hamilton, 1996
M12CJT	Volvo B10M-62	Jonckheere Deauville 45	C53F	1995	Park's of Hamilton, 1996
M13CJT	Volvo B10M-62	Jonckheere Deauville 45	C45FT	1995	Park's of Hamilton, 1996
M165XHW	Dennis Javelin 12m	Wadham Stringer Vanguard III	BC57F	1995	MoD (CX57AA), 2003
M20CJT	Dennis Javelin 12m	Wadham Stringer Vanguard III	BC57F	1995	MoD (CX73AA), 2003
(CX54AA)	Dennis Javelin 12m	Wadham Stringer Vanguard III	BC57F	1995	MoD (CX54AA), 2003
M396TRC	Dennis Javelin 12m	Wadham Stringer Vanguard III	BC57F	1995	MoD (CX65AA), 2003
M463SMO	Dennis Javelin 12m	Wadham Stringer Vanguard III	BC57F	1995	MoD (CX70AA), 2003
N599OAE	Dennis Javelin 8.5m	Wadham Stringer Vanguard III	BC35F	1996	MoD (ER46AA), 2003
N813OAE	Dennis Javelin 8.5m	Wadham Stringer Vanguard III	BC35F	1996	MoD (GE53AA), 2003
N823OAE	Dennis Javelin 12m	Wadham Stringer Vanguard III	BC57F	1996	MoD (EC54AA), 2003
N966OAE	Dennis Javelin 12m	Wadham Stringer Vanguard III	BC57F	1996	MoD (EC55AA), 2003
MIL8583	Toyota Coaster HDB30R	Caetano Optimo II	C21F	1996	

X70CJT is a Volvo B10M with Jonckheere Mistral 50 bodywork. It is seen in London on the Albert Embankment.
Colin Lloyd

Turners is another operator to make use of former MoD buses for school contracts. Nine Dennis Javelins and six Leyland Tigers are currently operated. Illustrating the latter is D78JHY, which has gained the mark 3138DP since this picture was taken. *Robert Edworthy*

N14CJT	Volvo B10M-62	Plaxton Excalibur	C49FT	1996	Tillingbourne, Cranleigh, 2001	
P15CJT	Volvo B10M-62	Plaxton Première 320	C57F	1997		
P16CJT	Volvo B10M-62	Plaxton Première 320	C57F	1997		
R2CJT	Volvo B10M-62	Jonckheere Mistral 50	C49FT	1997		
R3CJT	Volvo B10M-62	Jonckheere Mistral 50	C49FT	1997		
R18CJT	Volvo B10M-62	Plaxton Première 320	C57F	1998		
R19CJT	Volvo B10M-62	Plaxton Première 320	C57F	1998		
R30CJT	Mercedes-Benz O1120L	Optare/Ferqui Solera	C35F	1998		
R111CJT	Mercedes-Benz O404	Hispano Vita	C49FT	1998	Powner, Burbage, 2003	
R90CJT	Scania K113TRB	Irizar Century 12.37	C49FT	1998	Halcyon, Hull, 2001	
S50CJT	Volvo B10M-62	Berkhof Axial 50	C49FT	1998		
S60CJT	Volvo B10M-62	Berkhof Axial 50	C49FT	1998		
X70CJT	Volvo B10M-62	Jonckheere Mistral 50	C49FT	2000		
X80CJT	Volvo B10M-62	Jonckheere Mistral 50	C49FT	2000		
W17CJT	Volvo B7R	Plaxton Prima	C53F	2000	TransBus demonstrator, 2002	
AT02CJT	Volvo B7R	Jonckheere Modulo	C53F	2002		
BT02CJT	Volvo B7R	Jonckheere Modulo	C53F	2002		
GT02CJT	Toyota Coaster BB50R	Caetano Optimo V	C21F	2002	Z Cars, Bristol, 2004	
CJ53CJT	Iveco EuroRider 391.12.35	Beulas Stergo ε	C49FT	2003		
DT04CJT	Scania K114EB4	Irizar Century 12.35	C49FT	2004		
ET04CJT	Scania K114EB4	Irizar Century 12.35	C49FT	2004		
FT04CJT	Scania K114EB4	Irizar InterCentury 12.32	C57F	2004		
HT04CJT	Mercedes-Benz Sprinter 413cdi	Onyx	M16	2004		
KT54CJT	Scania K114EB4	Irizar Century 12.35	C53FT	2004		

Previous registrations:

73WAE	E787NOU	M12CJT	KSK977, M985HHS
110LHW	D202JHY	M13CJT	KSK985, M987HHS
		M20CJT	M250XWS
		MIL8583	N14CJT
3138DP	82KF21, D78JHY	N14CJT	A5XEL, N997THO, MIL8583
GT02CJT	W302UVV	OYY3	G879ARO
K18LUE	K921RGE	R90CJT	R278RRH
M10CJT	LSK825, M983HHS	R111CJT	R310HTF
		W17CJT	W38DOE
M11CJT	LSK821, M984HHS	XHY256	E691NOU

Livery: Silver and blue

The South West Bus Handbook

TURNER'S TOURS

AR & ME Turner and SL & PC Gilson, 1 Fore Street, Chulmleigh, EX17 7BR

NMJ283V	Volvo B58-56	Plaxton Supreme IV	C53F	1980	Horseshoe, Kempston, 1991
HAX331W	Ford R1114	Plaxton Supreme IV	C53F	1980	Bennetts, Gloucester, 1997
YUY94W	Ford R1114	Plaxton Supreme IV	C53F	1980	North Somerset, Nailsea, 2001
AEF260Y	Ford R1014	Plaxton Paramount 3200	C35F	1983	Compass Royston, Stockton, 1985
GIL5107	Volvo B10M-56	Plaxton Paramount 3200	C53F	1983	
458FTA	Volvo B10M-61	Plaxton Paramount 3200	C49F	1984	Horseshoe, Kempston, 1991
GIL5711	Volvo B10M-61	Plaxton Paramount 3200	C53F	1985	Horseshoe, Kempston, 1991
D851UTA	Dodge G13	Wadham Stringer	BC38F	1986	MoD (80KF56), 1996
D928UTA	Dodge G13	Wadham Stringer	BC38F	1986	MoD (80KF38), 1997
PIL6577	Volvo B10M-61	Caetano Algarve	C49FT	1986	Chiltern Queens, Woodcote, 2001
LBZ2939	Volvo B10M-61	Plaxton Paramount 3200 III	C49FT	1987	Ralph's, Langley, 1996
F515SCW	Mercedes-Benz 407D	Reeve Burgess	BC15F	1988	Mellor, Harrow, 2000
GIL5109	Volvo B10M-60	Plaxton Paramount 3200 III	C53F	1989	Dawlish Coaches, 2001
G506VYE	Dennis Dart 8.5m	Duple Dartline	BC21F	1990	Boomerang Bus, Tewkesbury, 2004
H458UGO	Dennis Dart 8.5m	Carlyle Dartline	B28F	1990	Arriva North West, 2002
VAZ2533	Volvo B10M-60	Jonckheere Deauville P50	C49FT	1991	Limebourne, Battersea, 1998
J398GKH	Dennis Dart 9m	Plaxton Pointer	NC30F	1992	Metroline, 2001
K892CSX	Dennis Dart 9.8m	Alexander Dash	B40F	1992	Epsom Coaches, 2001
K437OKH	Dennis Dart 9m	Plaxton Pointer	B34F	1992	Metroline, 2002

Two of the five Dennis Darts operated by Turner's Tours have Plaxton Pointer bodywork. J398GKH is seen taking a break in Exeter bus station following a duty on route 374 from Chulmleigh. *Mark Bailey*

L535YCC	Volvo B10M-62	Jonckheere Deauville P50	C49FT	1994	Vale of Llangollen, 2002
L537YCC	Volvo B10M-62	Jonckheere Deauville P50	C49FT	1994	Vale of Llangollen, 2002
M619ORJ	Volvo B10M-62	Jonckheere Deauville 45	C49FT	1995	Shearings, 1999
M629KVU	Volvo B10M-62	Jonckheere Deauville 45	C49FT	1995	Shearings, 1999
R190SUT	Volvo B10M-62	Jonckheere Mistral	C49FT	1998	Mayne, Buckie, 2001
R404FWT	Volvo B10M-62	Plaxton Première 350	C49FT	1998	Wallace Arnold, 2005
T544EUB	Volvo B10M-62	Plaxton Première 350	C49FT	1999	Wallace Arnold, 2003
W627FUM	Volvo B10M-62	Plaxton Première 350	C48FT	2000	Wallace Arnold, 2003
Y79CDS	Volvo B10M-62	Jonckheere Mistral 50	C49FT	2001	Trathens, Plymouth, 2004
FP02ZNV	LDV Convoy	LDV	M16	2002	-, 2005

(handwritten: W 652 FUM)

Previous registrations:

458FTA	A943VMH	L537YCC	L6VLT, VLT55
GIL5107	EFJ573Y	LBZ2939	D251HFX
GIL5109	F453WFX, XEL6S, F788MAA	PIL6577	C690KDS, SEL7X, C114PUJ
GIL5711	B27BMC	R190SUT	R190SUT, R555GSM
HAX331W	HAX335W	VAZ2533	H61XBD
L535YCC	L5VLT, LVT22	Y79CDS	LSK503

Depot: Langley Lane, Chulmleigh and Fore Street, Chulmleigh.
Web: www.turnerstours.co.uk

WEAVERBUS

RG & JE Weaver, 1 Hazeldown Avenue, Weymouth, DT3 6HT

G515VYE	Dennis Dart 8.5m	Duple Dartline	BC28F	1990	London United, 2000

Weaverbus is a single vehicle operation that runs the local route between Weymouth and Crossway. New to London Buses as DT15, G515VYE, is one of the early examples of only sixty built by Duple before the body design was sold to Carlyle Works.
Tony Wilson

WEBBERBUS

Webber - www.webber - Bryants

Webberbus Ltd, The Garage, Whaddon Cross, Minehead, TA24 7DR

Reg	Chassis	Body	Config	Year	History
MYD217V	DAF MB200DKFL500	Duple Dominant II	C50F	1980	Morley, Minehead, 1999
SND282X	Leyland Leopard PSU5D/4R	Duple Dominant IV	C50F	1981	Hookways, Meeth, 2001
FHS762X	Volvo B58-61	Duple Dominant IV	C57F	1982	Girlings, Plymouth, 2002
RIL6849	Leyland Tiger TRCTL11/3R	Plaxton Paramount 3200	C53F	1984	Filer, Ilfracombe, 2000
B73FGT	Leyland Tiger TRCTL11/3R	Duple Laser	C48FT	1985	Morley, Minehead, 2000
B247KUX	DAF MB200DKFL600	Caetano Algarve	C53F	1985	M Line, Byfleet, 2000
C906GYD	Ford Transit	Robin Hood	B16F	1986	First Southern National, 1998
511SKM	Leyland Tiger TRCTL11/3RZ	Duple 340	C50FT	1987	Baker, Yeovil, 2001
E604CDS	Volvo B10M-61	Plaxton Paramount 3500 III	C53F	1987	Repton, New Haw, 2000
F404DUG	Volvo B10M-61	Plaxton Paramount 3500 III	C53F	1989	Richmond, Barley, 1999
H159EJU	Dennis Javelin 12m	Duple 320	C53FT	1991	Woodfin, Bolton, 2004
K601JYA	Ford Transit	Ford	M11	1993	private owner, 2000
K262AWL	LDV 400	LDV	M11	1993	-, 2001
L424ANP	LDV 400	Premier	M16	1994	Stevens, Withycombe, 1998
L670YTT	DAF 400	DAF	M16	1994	van conversion, 2000
M962TKL	Ford Transit VE6	Devon	B16F	1995	Kent CC, 2002
M968TKL	Ford Transit VE6	Devon	B16F	1995	Kent CC, 2002
M974TKL	Ford Transit VE6	Devon	B16F	1995	Kent CC, 2002
M416VYD	Volvo B10M-62	Van Hool Alizée	C49FT	1995	Armchair, Brentford, 2002
M418VYD	Volvo B10M-62	Van Hool Alizée	C49FT	1995	Armchair, Brentford, 2002
M908OVR	Dennis Javelin GX 12m	Neoplan Transliner	C53F	1995	Clarke, Hemel Hempstead, 2004
P728ADV	LDV Convoy	LDV	M16	1997	private owner, 1998
P73RFB	Ford Transit	Ford	M16	1998	
T979OGA	Mercedes-Benz Vario O814	Mellor	BC33F	1999	DAC, St Ann's Chapel, 2002
T46RJL	Mercedes-Benz Vario O814	Autobus Nouvelle 2	BC29F	1999	Weavaway, Newbury, 2002
W322MKY	Scania L94IB	Irizar InterCentury 12.32	C49FT	2000	Bus Eireann, 2004
WA52MTE	Bova Futura FHD12.340	Bova Futura	C53F	2003	
WA03EYR	Bova Futura FHD12.340	Bova Futura	C53F	2003	

Pictured in its home town of Minehead, Webberbus' F404DUG represents the coach fleet. New to Wallace Arnold Tours, it is a Volvo B10M with Plaxton Paramount 3500 body. *Bill Potter*

A fleet of five Scolabus school buses is operated by Webberbus. Pictured in this pre-delivery photograph is one of the five operated in conjunction with Somerset County Council. The old-established firm of Bryants of Williton was acquired in December 2004. Bryants was well-known to steam engine enthusiasts, as their depot is next door to the West Somerset railway workshop and Williton station. *Irisbus*

WA54FSF	Irisbus Scolabus 150E24	Vehixel		B67F	2004	
WA54GOE	Irisbus Scolabus 150E24	Vehixel		B67F	2004	
WA54GPJ	Irisbus Scolabus 150E24	Vehixel		B67F	2004	
WA54GPK	Irisbus Scolabus 150E24	Vehixel		B67F	2004	
WA54LSX	Irisbus Scolabus 150E24	Vehixel		B67F	2004	

Bryants

D970RNC	Volvo B10M-61	Plaxton Paramount 3200 II	C53F	1987	Clarkes of London, 1996
E331UYC	Mercedes-Benz 609D	Reeve Burgess	BC25F	1987	
E574WOK	Renault G10	Wadham Stringer Vanguard	B38F	1988	MoD (64KG09), 1998
E133PLJ	Bedford YNT	Plaxton Paramount 3200 III	C53F	1988	Buckland, Hurst, 1989
UJI3793	Volvo B10M-61	Van Hool Alizée H	C53F	1988	Phillips, Crediton, 1999
YXI7381	Volvo B10M-61	Van Hool Alizée H	C53F	1989	Skills, Nottingham, 1999
JIL2018	Volvo B10M-61	Plaxton Paramount 3500 III	C53F	1990	Ideal, Watford, 1994
H123TYD	Dennis Javelin 11m	Plaxton Paramount 3200 III	C53F	1990	
H124TYD	Dennis Javelin 11m	Plaxton Paramount 3200 III	C53F	1990	
J173BYD	Leyland Tiger TRCTL10/3RZ	Plaxton 321	C53F	1991	
J41EYB	Volvo B10M-60	Plaxton Paramount 3200 III	C53F	1991	Denslow, Chad, 1995
N832MAM	Dennis Javelin GX	Plaxton Première 350	C53F	1996	Ellison. Ashton Keynes, 2003
P285LJH	Volvo B10M-62	Plaxton Première 350	C53F	1997	Bus Eireann, 2003
P532CLJ	Volvo B10M-62	Plaxton Première 320	C49FT	1997	Excelsior, Bournemouth, 1998

Previous registrations:

511SKM	D135HML	W322MKY	?
JIL2018	G83RGG	UJI3793	E443RCV
P285LJH	96D42516	YXI7381	F743ENE
P532CLJ	A8EXC		

Depots: Brue Avenue, Colly Lane Ind Est, Bridgwater; Brunel Way, Minehead; Whaddon Cross, Minehead and Station Road, Williton.

WESSEX BUS

G A Douglass, 43 Norfolk Road, Weymouth, DT4 0QF

	D463CKV	Freight Rover Sherpa	Rootes	B16F	1986	Charlton, Weymouth, 1998
	DNZ5130	Mercedes-Benz 811D	Optare StarRider	B26F	1989	Stagecoach London, 2001
	H882LOX	Mercedes-Benz 811D	Carlyle	B31F	1990	2 Travel, Swansea, 2004
	L289SEM	Iveco TurboDaily 59-10	Wadham Stringer	M8L	1994	MB Liverpool, 2001
w	L292SEM	Iveco TurboDaily 59-10	Wadham Stringer	M8L	1994	MB Liverpool. 2001
	L293SEM	Iveco TurboDaily 59-10	Wadham Stringer	M8L	1994	MB Liverpool. 2001
	N573OUH	Mercedes-Benz 811D	Plaxton Beaver	B29F	1995	Islwyn, 2004
	RIL8110	Mercedes-Benz 410D	G&M	M16	1997	Bawden, Truro, 2004
	P786VYS	LDV Convoy	LDV	M16	1997	City of Glasgow, 2002
	S804LPY	Fiat Ducato	?	M8L	1998	private owner, 2002

Previous registrations:
DNZ 5130   G106 KUB   RIL8110   R211GRL, R6LEY

Depot: Surrey Close, Granby Industrial Estate, Weymouth

Representing the pink-liveried Wessex Bus is Freight Rover Sherpa D463CKV. It is now approaching its twentieth year of service, a time-frame somewhat longer than the five years expected lifespan for this type of vehicle. It was one of the early pioneers of then NBC minibus revolution of the mid 1980s. *Phillip Stephenson*

WESTERN GREYHOUND

Western Greyhound Ltd, 14 East Street, Newquay, TR7 1BH

WSV537	Volvo B10M-61	Van Hool Alizée	C50FT	1986	Mitchell, Birmingham, 2002
DSU107	Volvo B10M-60	Van Hool Alizée	C49FT	1992	Shearings, 1999
ULL933	Volvo B10M-60	Van Hool Alizée	C49FT	1992	Shearings, 1999
TFO319	Volvo B10M-60	Van Hool Alizée	C53F	1993	Worthing Coaches, 2002

500	S100PAF	Mercedes-Benz Vario 0814	Plaxton Beaver 2	B31F	1998	Hambly of Kernow, 2004
501	S501SRL	Mercedes-Benz Vario 0814	Plaxton Beaver 2	B27F	1999	
502	S502SRL	Mercedes-Benz Vario 0814	Plaxton Beaver 2	BC27F	1999	
503	S503SRL	Mercedes-Benz Vario 0814	Plaxton Beaver 2	BC27F	1999	
507	R807HWS	Mercedes-Benz Vario 0814	Plaxton Beaver 2	BC33F	1998	Andybus, Tetbury, 2003
508	R808HWS	Mercedes-Benz Vario 0814	Plaxton Beaver 2	BC33F	1998	Andybus, Tetbury, 2003
509	R809HWS	Mercedes-Benz Vario 0814	Plaxton Beaver 2	BC33F	1998	Andubus, Tetbury, 2003
510	R810HWS	Mercedes-Benz Vario 0814	Plaxton Beaver 2	BC33F	1998	Andybus, Tetbury, 2003
518	S18RED	Mercedes-Benz Vario 0814	Plaxton Beaver 2	B27F	1999	Hazell, Northlew, 2003
520	S20WGL	Mercedes-Benz Vario 0814	Plaxton Beaver 2	BC33F	1998	Cerbydau Carreglefn, 2003
529	W29WGL	Mercedes-Benz Vario 0814	Plaxton Beaver 2	B31F	2001	Brylaine, Boston, 2002
530	S30ARJ	Mercedes-Benz Vario 0814	Plaxton Beaver 2	BC33F	1998	Andybus, Tetbury, 2001
531	V31WGL	Mercedes-Benz Vario 0814	Plaxton Beaver 2	BC28F	1999	Countryliner, Guildford, 2003
533	X33WGL	Mercedes-Benz Vario 0814	Plaxton Beaver 2	BC33F	2001	Wilson, Rhu, 2003
534	S34BMR	Mercedes-Benz Vario 0814	Plaxton Beaver 2	BC33F	1998	Andybus, Tetbury, 2001
540	V40WGL	Mercedes-Benz Vario 0814	Plaxton Cheetah	C31F	1999	Countryliner, Guildford, 2002
544	W44WGL	Mercedes-Benz Vario 0814	Plaxton Beaver 2	BC33F	2000	Brylaine, Boston, 2002
550	W50MBH	Mercedes-Benz Vario 0814	Plaxton Beaver 2	BC33F	2000	Brylaine, Boston, 2002
551	WK51AVP	Mercedes-Benz Vario 0814	Plaxton Beaver 2	BC33F	2001	
552	WK51HNF	Mercedes-Benz Vario 0814	Plaxton Beaver 2	BC33F	2002	
553	WK53BNA	Mercedes-Benz Vario 0814	Plaxton Beaver 2	BC33F	2003	
554	WK53BNB	Mercedes-Benz Vario 0814	Plaxton Beaver 2	BC33F	2003	
555	WK53BND	Mercedes-Benz Vario 0814	Plaxton Beaver 2	BC33F	2003	
560	WK02BUS	Mercedes-Benz Vario 0814	Plaxton Beaver 2	BC33F	2002	Mitchell, Plean, 2004
561	WK51BUF	Mercedes-Benz Vario 0814	Plaxton Beaver 2	BC33F	2001	Hutchinson, Easingwold, 2003
562	WK53EUT	Mercedes-Benz Vario 0814	Plaxton Beaver 2	BC33F	2003	
563	WK53EUU	Mercedes-Benz Vario 0814	Plaxton Beaver 2	BC33F	2003	
564	WK04CUA	Mercedes-Benz Vario 0814	Plaxton Beaver 2	BC33F	2004	
565	WK04CUC	Mercedes-Benz Vario 0814	Plaxton Beaver 2	BC33F	2004	
566	WK54BHL	Mercedes-Benz Vario 0814	Plaxton Beaver 2	BC33F	2004	
567	WK54BHN	Mercedes-Benz Vario 0814	Plaxton Beaver 2	BC33F	2004	
568	WK54BHO	Mercedes-Benz Vario 0814	Plaxton Beaver 2	BC33F	2004	
569	WK54BHP	Mercedes-Benz Vario 0814	Plaxton Beaver 2	BC33F	2004	

The start of 2005 has seen the last Plaxton Beaver 2 built without the now required disability features. The vehicle, with dummy registration WGL1, is seen shortly after delivery. *Plaxton*

Western Greyhounds' main double-decks are all Olympians. However, seven older buses are retained for special event work. One of these, Bristol VR JWV259W, is seen heading for Sunnyside Holiday Park in Newquay during August 2004. *Mark Bailey*

570	WK05CFD	Mercedes-Benz Vario O814	Plaxton Beaver 2	BC33F	2005	
571	WK05CFE	Mercedes-Benz Vario O814	Plaxton Beaver 2	BC33F	2005	
572	WK05CFF	Mercedes-Benz Vario O814	Plaxton Beaver 2	BC33F	2005	
600	N600WGL	Volvo Olympian	Alexander RH	BC43/--F	1995	National Express, West Drayton, 2002
624	D824UTF	Leyland Olympian ONLXB/1RH	Eastern Coach Works	BC39/21F	1986	Peacock, Eston, 2003
633	F633LMJ	Leyland Olympian ONCL10/1RZ	Alexander RH	B47/32F	1988	Arriva The Shires, 2002
635	F635LMJ	Leyland Olympian ONCL10/1RZ	Alexander RH	B47/32F	1988	Arriva The Shires, 2002
638	F638LMJ	Leyland Olympian ONCL10/1RZ	Alexander RH	B47/32F	1988	Arriva The Shires, 2002
649	WLT649	Leyland Olympian ONCL10/1RV	Eastern Coach Works	BC42/30F	1985	Go-Northern, 2003
665	XOD665	Leyland Olympian ONLXB/1R	Eastern Coach Works	BC41/23F	1984	Arriva The Shires, 2002

Special event vehicles:

2748	EOO590	Bristol FLF6G	Eastern Coach Works	B38/32R	1962	Sanders, South Benfleet, 2003
1783	783DYE	AEC Routemaster R2RH	Park Royal	O36/28R	1964	Ensignbus (Bath Bus), 2004
2648	NMY648E	AEC Routemaster R2RH	Park Royal	B32/24R	1967	preservation, 2004
347	MHJ347F	Leyland Titan PD3/4	East Lancs	B41/32R	1967	Stephensons, Rochford, 2003
119	CJH119V	Bristol VRT/SL3/6LXB	Eastern Coach Works	O43/31F	1980	Fitzpatrick, Bristol, 2003
259	JWV259W	Bristol VRT/SL3/6LXB	Eastern Coach Works	B43/31F	1981	Brighton & Hove, 2000
82	LUA282V	Leyland Leopard PSU5D/4R	Plaxton Supreme IV	C53F	1980	Gill, Wadebridge, 1998

Previous registrations:

DSU107	J232NNC	TFO319	THL291Y, 1056AR, LBH460Y, JIL5289
N600WGL	N124YRW	W44WGL	W965JNF
S20WGL	S135UEY	W50MBH	W969JNF
TFO319	HSK646, L656ADS	WK51BUF	PX51ELJ
ULL933	J234NNC	WK02BUS	SL02COU
UWR498	?	WLT649	C523LJR
V31WGL	V451FOT	WSV537	C28VJF, LIW3459
V40WGL	V991DNB	XOD665	A110FDL, WDL748, A701DDL
W29WGL	W968JNF	X33WGL	X437JHS

Web: westerngreyhound.com
Depots: St Austell Street, Summercourt.
Outstations: Newquay (Greenacres, Trevarrian and Sunnyside Holiday Park, Quintrell Downs), Delabole (Tregath Farm), Bodmin (Priory Road), Padstow (Trecerus Industrial Estate) and Wadebridge (Kestle Quarry, Sladesbridge) .

The South West Bus Handbook

WESTWARD TRAVEL

MC & LC Simmons, 10 The Chipping, Kingswood, Wotton-under-Edge, GL12 8RT

18		VWX350X	Bova EL26/581	Bova Europa	C51F	1982	Wallace Arnold, 1987
20		HBH416Y	Leyland Tiger TRCTL11/3R	Plaxton Paramount 3200	C53F	1983	Stevens, Bristol, 1991
21	w	DPV881	Bova EL26/581	Bova Europa	C53F	1981	Braid, Prestwood, 1990
22		A930JOD	Leyland Tiger TRCTL11/3R	Plaxton Paramount 3200	C57F	1983	Snell, Newton Abbot, 1992
26		URB161S	Bristol VRT/SL3/6LXB	Eastern Coach Works	B45/28F	1977	Bugler, Bristol, 1994
27		VPF287S	Bristol VRT/SL3/6LXB	Eastern Coach Works	B45/28F	1978	Red Bus, Clyst Honiton, 1995
28		EAP989V	Bristol VRT/SL3/6LXB	Eastern Coach Works	B45/28F	1980	City of Oxford, 1996
27		XPG295Y	DAF MB200DKTL600	Plaxton Supreme V	C57F	1982	Garrett, Newton Abbot, 1992
28		9996WX	Volvo B10M-61	Van Hool Alizée	C50FT	1983	Park's of Hamilton, 1993
30		A661UHY	Bova FLD12-250	Bova Futura	C53F	1984	Clayton, Leicester, 1995
31		F281ENV	Leyland Tiger TRCTL11/3ARZ	Plaxton Paramount 3200 III	C53F	1988	Wainfleet, Nuneaton, 1997
33		E650KCX	DAF SB2300DHTD585	Plaxton Paramount 3500 III	C57F	1988	Burtons, Haverhill, 1998
34		KRU844W	Bristol VRT/SL3/6LXB	Eastern Coach Works	B45/28F	1980	A-Bus, Bristol, 1998
35		A611XKU	Leyland Tiger TRCTL11/3R	Plaxton Paramount 3200	C57F	1983	First Avon, 1998
36		C828EHU	Leyland Tiger TRCTL11/3LZ	Wadham Stringer Vanguard II	BC68F	1985	MoD (37KC10), 1999
38		LHT730P	Bristol VRT/SL3/6LXB	Eastern Coach Works	B45/28F	1976	Eagle, Bristol, 2001
		TAZ4992	Leyland Royal Tiger RTC	Leyland Doyen	C49FT	1987	A-Bus, Bristol, 2002
		F617VNH	LAG Panoramic G355Z	LAG	C49FT	1989	Dearnley, Littleton, 2002

Previous registrations:
DPV881	URW702X	F617VNH	F617VNH, 6769FM
F281ENV	F203HSO, MIW5788	TAZ4992	D801NBO

Many of the remaining Bristol VRs are to be found with West Country operators. Westward Travel operates five, including URB161S, an example that was new to East Midland. *Robert Edworthy*

F T WILLIAMS TRAVEL

F T Williams, Dolcoath Industrial Park, Dolcoath Road, Camborne, TR14 8RA

XPG295Y	DAF MB200DKTL600	Plaxton Supreme V	C57F	1982	Garrett, Newton Abbot, 1992
9996WX	Volvo B10M-61	Van Hool Alizée	C50FT	1983	Park's of Hamilton, 1993
B710EOF	Volvo B10M-53	Jonckheere Jubilee P90	C54/13CT	1985	Travellers Choice, Carnforth, 2001
A516VKG	Leyland Olympian ONTL11/2Rsp Eastern Coach Works		C45/28F	1985	Boomerang Bus, Tewkesbury, 2004
PJI4983	Leyland Olympian ONTL11/2Rsp Eastern Coach Works		C45/28F	1985	Tims Travel, Sheerness, 2003
511HCV	Volvo B10M-61	Plaxton Paramount 3500 II	C53F	1985	St Buryan Garage, St Buryan,
C105AFX	Volvo B10M-61	Plaxton Paramount 3200 II	C53F	1986	Safeguard, Guildford, 1997
E920EAY	Volvo B10M-61	Plaxton Paramount 3500 III	C53F	1987	Stevens, Colchester, 1997
PJI5014	Volvo B10M-61	Van Hool Alizée	C50FT	1987	Eastville, Bristol, 1999
739JUA	DAF MB230LB615	Van Hool Alizée H	C53FT	1988	Countryliner, Guildford, 2004
CJZ6782	Volvo B10M-60	Ikarus Blue Danube	C53F	1989	KATS, Bedwas, 2003
F276WAF	Volvo B10M-60	Van Hool Alizée	C49FT	1989	Dawlish Coaches, 2002
RIL3706	Volvo B10M-60	Jonckheere Deauville P599	C51F	1990	Knowles, Paignton, 2000
H165DJU	Volvo B10M-60	Duple 340	C53FT	1990	Jennings, Bude, 1998
H215LOM	Scania N113DRB	Alexander RH	B45/31F	1990	The King's Ferry, Gillingham, 2003
H217LOM	Scania N113DRB	Alexander RH	B45/31F	1990	The King's Ferry, Gillingham, 2003
H794FAF	Dennis Javelin 11SDA1923	Wadham Stringer Vanguard II	BC40FL	1990	Cornwall Disabled Association, 2000
H823GAF	Peugeot Talbot Express	Dormobile	M14L	1991	Cornwall CC, 1996
H128NWO	Peugeot Talbot Freeway	Peugeot Talbot	M11L	1991	Gwent CC, 1998
J283TOJ	Peugeot Talbot Freeway	Peugeot Talbot	M7L	1992	LB Hillingdon, 2002
J953SBU	Dennis Dart 9.8SDL3012	Northern Counties Paladin	BC31D	1992	D&J Travel, Silvertown, 1997
K593PCV	Renault Trafic	Devon	M7L	1993	private owner, 1998
L872WCV	Peugeot Talbot Express	Devon Conversions	M8	1994	Cornwall CC, 2000
L917NWW	Volvo B10M-60	Van Hool Alizée	C48FT	1994	Bakers, Weston-super-Mare, 2002
M417VYD	Volvo B10M-60	Van Hool Alizée	C49FT	1995	Armchair, Brentwood, 2002
M883LNF	Iveco Daily 49-10	Mellor	B18L	1995	Rochdale MBC, 2003
M608UUR	Peugeot Boxer	G&M	M5L	1995	private owner, 1998

Pictured in Boscastle while on an excursion, 511HCV is a Volvo B10M with Plaxton Paramount bodywork. The livery is principally all white. *J C Walton*

Local services around Redruth are provided by F T Williams. Pictured operating route 317, a service also known as the Tesco link, Iveco P347FOL illustrates the G&M conversion to the Daily 49, that gives the van a higher roofline. *Mark Bailey*

N290VDA	LDV 400	Bedwas	BC16FL	1996	LB Harrow, 2003	
P695JOM	Iveco TurboDaily 59-12	Cunliffe	BC24FL	1996	Sandwell UA, 2004	
P791JKW	Ford Transit	Ford	M14	1996	Gibson, Coventry, 2001	
P125MOV	LDV Convoy	LDV	M16	1997	Stevens, Penzance, 2003	
P133KOJ	LDV Convoy	LDV	M16	1997	British Car Rentals, 2001	
P476NCR	LDV Convoy	G&M	M15	1997	Baker, Duloe, 2004	
P479OGV	LDV Convoy	LDV	M16	1997	British Car Rentals, 2001	
P292CPH	Peugeot Boxer	G&M	M5L	1997	private owner, 2001	
P878VYJ	Peugeot Boxer	G&M	M6L	1997	private owner, 2001	
P347FOL	Iveco Daily 49-10	G&M	B19F	1997	Pete's Travel, West Bromwich, 2001	
R271UES	Iveco Daily 40-10	-	M14L	1998	Angus UA, 2002	
R272UES	Iveco Daily 40-10	-	M14L	1998	Angus UA, 2002	
R230DHU	Iveco Daily 40-10	-	M-	1998	private owner, 2002	
R746VNT	LDV Convoy	LDV	M16	1998	Sixt Kenning, 2001	
R552JAF	Fiat Ducato	Oughtred & Harrison	M16	1998	-, 2002	
BX04NAE	Mercedes-Benz 1836RL	Mercedes-Benz Touro	C49FT	2004	Evobus demonstrator, 2004	
BX04NCA	Mercedes-Benz 1836RL	Mercedes-Benz Touro	C49FT	2004		
WA04MHE	Mercedes-Benz Vario O815	Sitcar Beluga	C29F	2004		

Previous registrations:

511HCV	C483HAK	L917NWW	L917NWW, B17APT
739JUA	F619HGO	M417VYD	M417VYD, B12APT
9996WX	TCV137Y	PJI4983	B577LPE
B710EOF	B710EOF, LSU939	PJI5014	D616MVR
CJZ6782	F108SSE, 1223PL, F127JNH, CJZ2778	RIL3706	G141MNH, RIL3707

YELLOW BUSES

Yellow Buses - Dorset Travel

Bournemouth Transport Ltd, Mallard Road, Bournemouth, BH8 4PN

110	HF04JWJ	Volvo B7TL		East Lancs Vyking		N43/31F	2004	
111	HF04JWK	Volvo B7TL		East Lancs Vyking		N43/31F	2004	
112	HF04JWL	Volvo B7TL		East Lancs Vyking		N43/31F	2004	
138	VJT138S	Leyland Fleetline FE30ALR		Alexander AL		CO43/31F	1978	
140	VJT140S	Leyland Fleetline FE30ALR		Alexander AL		CO43/31F	1978	
176	MFX176W	Leyland Fleetline FE30AGR		Alexander AL		B43/31F	1981	
180	HF03ODU	Volvo B7TL		Wrightbus Eclipse		N47/31F	2003	
181	HF03ODV	Volvo B7TL		Wrightbus Eclipse		N47/31F	2003	
182	HF03ODW	Volvo B7TL		Wrightbus Eclipse		N47/31F	2003	
183	HF04JWD	Volvo B7TL		Wrightbus Eclipse		N45/31F	2004	
184	HF04JWE	Volvo B7TL		Wrightbus Eclipse		N45/31F	2004	
185	HF04JWG	Volvo B7TL		Wrightbus Eclipse		N45/31F	2004	

200-204 Volvo Citybus B10M-50 East Lancs BC43/33F 1986

200	D200ELJ	201	C201YPR	202	D202ELJ	203	D203ELJ	204	D204ELJ

205-214 Volvo Citybus B10M-50 Alexander RH B47/33F 1988-89

205	E205GCG	207	E207GCG	209	E209GCG	211	F211WRU	213	F213WRU
206	E206GCG	208	E208GCG	210	F210WRU	212	F212WRU	214	F214WRU

251-269 Dennis Dominator DDA1033 East Lancs B47/33F 1990-92

251	H251JJT	255	H255JJT	259	H259MFX	264	H264MFX	267	J267SPR
252	H252JJT	256	H256JJT	261	H261MFX	265	H265MFX	268	J268SPR
		257	H257JJT	262	H262MFX	266	J266SPR	269	J269SPR
254	H254JJT	258	H258MFX	263	H263MFX				

270-278 Dennis Trident 2-axle East Lancs Lolyne N51/33F 1999

270	T270BPR	272	T272BPR	274	T274BPR	276	T276BPR	278	T278BPR
271	T271BPR	273	T273BPR	275	T275BPR	277	T277BPR		

Yellow Buses evolved from Bournemouth Corporation. One of the recent arrivals is Wrightbus Eclipse 181, HF03ODV, one of six such buses in the fleet based on the Volvo B7TL. *Gerry Mead*

East Lancs is one of the coachbuilders prepared to produce open-top buses. Following East Lancs' success with orders in Spain and Paris, Yellow Buses now operate three convertible Vyking models. In summer guise, 430, HJ02HFA is seen heading for Christchurch. In spring 2005 the Yellow Buses business was approaching new ownership having been offered for sale by it local authority owners. *Tony Wilson*

310	HF53OBG	Volvo B12B	TransBus Paragon Expressliner	C49FT	2003			
311	HF53OBH	Volvo B12B	TransBus Paragon Expressliner	C49FT	2003			
312	HF54JUJ	Volvo B12B	Plaxton Paragon Expressliner	C49FT	2004			
313	HF54JUK	Volvo B12B	Plaxton Paragon Expressliner	C49FT	2004			
314	HF54JUL	Volvo B12B	Plaxton Paragon Expressliner	C49FT	2004			
315	HF54KXH	Volvo B12B	Caetano Enigma	C49FT	2005			
316	HF54KXJ	Volvo B12B	Caetano Enigma	C49FT	2005			
317	HF54KXK	Volvo B12B	Caetano Enigma	C49FT	2005			
326	R326NRU	Volvo B10M-62	Van Hool T9 Alizée	C49FT	1998			
327	R327NRU	Volvo B10M-62	Van Hool T9 Alizée	C49FT	1998			
329	R329NRU	Volvo B10M-62	Van Hool T9 Alizée	C49FT	1998			
330	T330AFX	Volvo B10M-62	Van Hool T9 Alizée	C49FT	1999			
331	T331AFX	Volvo B10M-62	Van Hool T9 Alizée	C49FT	1999			
352	P352ARU	Scania K113TRB	Van Hool Alizée	C49FT	1997			
354	R354NRU	Volvo B10M-62	Van Hool T9 Alizée	C49FT	1998			
355	R355NRU	Volvo B10M-62	Van Hool T9 Alizée	C49FT	1998			
381	W381UEL	Scania L94IB	Van Hool T9 Alizée	C49FT	2000			
382	W382UEL	Scania L94IB	Van Hool T9 Alizée	C49FT	2000			
383	W383UEL	Scania L94IB	Van Hool T9 Alizée	C49FT	2000			
384	W384UEL	Scania L94IB	Van Hool T9 Alizée	C49FT	2000			
390	R998FNW	DAF DE33WSSB3000	Ikarus Blue Danube	C51FT	1998	Whippet Cs, Bournemouth, 2000		

401-406   Dennis Lance 11SDA3107   East Lancs   B48F   1993

401w	L401BFX	403w	L403BFX	404w	L404BFX	405w	L405BFX	406t	L406BFX
402t	L402BFX							

411-418   Volvo B7TL   East Lancs Vyking   N45/31F   2001

411	Y411CFX	413	Y413CFX	415	Y415CFX	417	Y417CFX	418	Y418CFX
412	Y412CFX	414	Y414CFX	416	Y416CFX			

420-428   Volvo B7TL   East Lancs Vyking   N45/31F   2002-03

420	HJ02HFD	422	HJ02HFF	424	HJ02HFH	427	HF03ODS	428	HF03ODT
421	HJ02HFE	423	HJ02HFG	426	HF03ODR			

430	HJ02HFA		Volvo B7TL		East Lancs Vyking		OC45/31F 2002		
431	HJ02HFB		Volvo B7TL		East Lancs Vyking		CO45/31F 2002		
432	HJ02HFC		Volvo B7TL		East Lancs Vyking		CO45/31F 2002		

451-462			Dennis Dart 9.8SDL3054		East Lancs		B40F	1995	
451	M451LLJ	454	M454LLJ	457	M457LLJ	459	M459LLJ	461	M461LLJ
452	M452LLJ	455	M455LLJ	458	M458LLJ	460	M460LLJ	462	M462LLJ
453	M453LLJ	456	M456LLJ						

463-472			Dennis Dart 9.8SDL3054		East Lancs		B40F	1996	
463	N463TPR	465	N465TPR	467	N467TPR	469	N469TPR	471	N471TPR
464	N464TPR	466	N466TPR	468	N468TPR	470	N470TPR	472	N472TPR

473	P473BLJ		Dennis Dart SLF	East Lancs Spryte	N32F	1997
474	P474BLJ		Dennis Dart SLF	East Lancs Spryte	N32F	1997

475-482			Dennis Dart SLF		East Lancs Spryte		N37F	1998	
475	R475NPR	477	R477NPR	479	R479NPR	481	R481NPR	482	R482NPR
476	R476NPR	478	R478NPR	480	R480NPR				

Special event vehicles:						
112	DLJ112L	Daimler Fleetline CRL6	Alexander AL	B43/31F	1973	
143	AJT143T	Leyland Fleetline FE30ALR	Alexander AL	B43/31F	1978	
245	ADV299A	Leyland Atlantean PDR1/1	Metro-Cammell	CO44/31F	1961	Leisurelink, Newhaven, 1996
248	928GTA	Leyland Atlantean PDR1/1	Metro-Cammell	CO44/31F	1961	Leisurelink, Newhaven, 1996

Ancillary vehicles:						
107	MUD27W	Leyland Leopard PSU3F/4R	Willowbrook Warrior	TV	1981	Brighton & Hove, 1999

Previous registrations:
ADV299A   925GTA

Not really the weather for tourists, as rain-covered Dart 459, M459LLJ waits time on route 10. It is one of twelve dating from 1995 with an adaptation of the East Lancs EL2000 body. *Dave Heath*

Vehicle index

Reg	Operator	Reg	Operator	Reg	Operator	Reg	Operator
24THU	Eagle of Bristol	1434HP	Hookways	A610THV	Applegate		
29DRH	Rover	2091MX	Grey Cars	A611XKU	Westward Travel		
73WAE	Turners Coachways	2411KR	Eagle of Bristol	A649THV	South Gloucestershire		
74DRH	Rover	2603HP	Hookways	A661UHY	Westward Travel		
86JBF	Castleways	3138DP	Turners Coachways	A675DCN	Centurion		
108GYC	Redwoods	3271CD	C J Down	A693TPO	Bluebird		
110LHW	Turners Coachways	3315HP	Hookways	A696OHJ	Taylors		
120JRB	Quantock MS	3427HP	Hookways	A703THV	Swanbrook		
152EKH	Arleen	3504CD	C J Down	A707GPR	Mike's Travel		
194WHT	Bakers Dolphin	3594CD	C J Down	A710SDV	Safeway		
223TUO	Hookways	3655NE	Quantock MS	A726SDV	Tally Ho!		
237AJB	Roselyn	3785HP	Hookways	A799REO	South West Coaches		
239AJB	Roselyn	4011LJ	Target Travel	A887SYE	South Gloucestershire		
241AJB	Roselyn	4415HP	Hookways	A892SYE	South Gloucestershire		
241KRO	C J Down	4691HP	Hookways	A897KCL	Taylors		
260ERY	Truronian	4708RU	Barry's	A898SYE	South Gloucestershire		
280OHT	Buglers	4846HP	Hookways	A900SUL	Swanbrook		
290WE	Trathens	5351HP	Hookways	A926SUL	Swanbrook		
298HPK	Barry's	5448CD	C J Down	A930JOD	Westward Travel		
312KTT	Tally Ho!	6130EL	Eagle of Bristol	A943SYE	South Gloucestershire		
315MWL	Bakers Dolphin	6185RU	Hookways	A958SYF	Swanbrook		
338EDV	Mike's Travel	6740HP	Hookways	A983NYC	Safeway		
340MYA	Bakers Dolphin	6986RU	Taw & Torridge	AA52EFA	Applegate		
362KHT	Barry's	7346HP	Hookways	AAP648T	Currian's		
407JWO	Taw & Torridge	7740KO	Bakers Dolphin	ACH53A	Alexcars		
426VNU	Buglers	7876HP	Hookways	ACH80A	Alexcars		
458FTA	Turners Tours	8405CD	C J Down	ACZ1133	Hatts Europa		
466DHN	Quantock MS	8515CD	C J Down	ADV299A	Yellow Buses		
471BET	Barry's	8933CD	C J Down	ADV854A	Quantock MS		
501BTA	Quantock MS	9743HP	Hookways	AEF260Y	Turners Tours		
503BTA	Quantock MS	9878HP	Hookways	AFE719A	Quantock MS		
508AHU	Hopley's	9880HP	Hookways	AFH390T	Roselyn		
509HUO	Taw & Torridge	9891CD	C J Down	AFJ734T	Shaftesbury & District		
511HCV	F T Williams	990XYA	Hookways	AFJ740T	Taw & Torridge		
511SKM	Webberbus	9996WX	F T Williams	AFJ742T	Taw & Torridge		
513SRL	Currian's	9996WX	Westward Travel	AFJ771T	Truronian		
516ACH	Alexcars	A2XCL	Excelsior	AHN455B	Quantock MS		
539WCV	Hamblys of Kernow	A2XEL	Excelsior	AHW198V	A Bus		
569EFJ	Quantock MS	A3XCL	Excelsior	AHW199V	Citytour		
572CNW	Quantock MS	A3XEL	Excelsior	AIW257	Tally Ho!		
586PHU	Buglers	A4EXC	Taw & Torridge	AJ03LXD	Hatts Europa		
640UAF	Hopley's	A4XEL	Excelsior	AJ04BUS	Andybus		
647PYC	Roselyn	A5XEL	Excelsior	AJA132	Quantock MS		
654JHU	Bluebird	A6ECS	Ebley Bus	AJH854T	Roselyn		
660FHU	Arleen	A6XEL	Excelsior	AJT143T	Shamrock Buses		
672DYA	Alexcars	A7XCL	Excelsior	AJT143T	Yellow Buses		
676GDV	Taw & Torridge	A7XEL	Excelsior	AN02EDN	Truronian		
704BYL	Somerbus	A8EXC	Excelsior	ANA5T	Quantock MS		
708RHN	Blue Iris	A8XCL	Excelsior	ANA155Y	Axe Valley		
710VCV	Hamblys of Kernow	A9ECS	Ebley Bus	ANA158Y	DAC Coaches		
728FDV	Roselyn	A9EXC	Excelsior	ANA565Y	Citytour		
739JUA	F T Williams	A9XCL	Excelsior	ANZ3607	Beeline		
748JTA	Hookways	A12EXC	Excelsior	ANZ4372	South West Coaches		
751CRT	Caradon Riviera	A13EXC	Excelsior	ANZ4373	South West Coaches		
752FUV	Taylors	A14FRX	Bluebird	ANZ4374	South West Coaches		
761CRT	Caradon Riviera	A15FRX	Bluebird	AP03BUS	A Bus		
775HOD	Taw & Torridge	A16EFA	Applegate	AP03BUZ	A Bus		
789FAY	Hookways	A16GVC	Glenvic	AP04BUS	A Bus		
791WHT	Bakers Dolphin	A17GVC	Glenvic	AP53BUS	A Bus		
800XPC	Peter Carol	A18EFA	Applegate	APM114T	Quantock MS		
816SHW	Somerbus	A18EXC	Excelsior	APT834S	Quantock MS		
832JYA	Beeline	A18GVC	Glenvic	ASV900	Safeway		
838AFM	Quantock MS	A19EFA	Applegate	AT02CJT	Turners Coachways		
890ADV	Quantock MS	A35AWA	Mid Devon	ATK153W	Roselyn		
890CVJ	Geoff Willetts	A109EPA	South West Coaches	ATK156W	Roselyn		
895FXA	Taw & Torridge	A130EPA	South West Coaches	ATK157W	Roselyn		
904DRH	Rover	A131DTO	Tally Ho!	AUP651L	Blue Motors		
924CRT	Caradon Riviera	A158EPA	Coombs Travel	AVK142V	A Bus		
928GTA	Yellow Buses	A168PAE	Roselyn	AVK156V	A Bus		
931DHT	Eagle of Bristol	A256VYC	South West Coaches	B5GBD	Dukes Travel		
958VKM	Bakers Dolphin	A342MWD	APL Travel	B7BEN	Bennett		
969EHW	A Bus	A462ODY	Quantock MS	B21AUS	Ebley Bus		
972EHW	A Bus	A516VKG	F T Williams	B45DNY	Centurion		

130   The South West Bus Handbook

One of the early Bova's delivered following the coachbuilders entry into the VDL Group is BC04BBC, seen while in London. The Bova is available in several length, and was one of the first 15-metre examples to be seen in the other European countries that permit such a length. *Dave Heath*

B73FGT	Webberbus	BAZ6516	Hatts Europa	BX54EBD	Bennett
B87WUV	Axe Valley	BAZ7326	Cooks Coaches	BX54EBF	Bennett
B120UUD	Swanbrook	BC04BBC	Bluebird	BX54EBG	Bennett
B137GAU	Tally Ho!	BC51BBC	Bluebird	BX54EBL	Dawlish Coaches
B149WUL	Swanbrook	BEO731V	Polperro Tram Co 4	BX54ECA	Peter Carol
B152TRN	Shamrock Buses	BFR958Y	Applegate	BX54ECE	Peter Carol
B175VDV	Plymouth Citybus	BHZ6984	South Gloucestershire	BX54ECT	Peter Carol
B176VDV	Plymouth Citybus	BHZ6985	South Gloucestershire	BYC802B	Centurion
B209REL	Barry's	BHZ6986	South Gloucestershire	BYC828B	Arleen
B221WUL	Swanbrook	BHZ6987	South Gloucestershire	BYD795X	South West Coaches
B234RRU	Blue Motors	BHZ6988	South Gloucestershire	BYX186V	Swanbrook
B247KUX	Webberbus	BHZ8804	K W Beard	BYX239V	Currian's
B289KPF	Coombs Travel	BJV590	Barnes	C1EGO	Eurotaxis
B469FCS	Trathens	BKE857T	Truronian	C17MEO	Target Travel
B477UNB	Barry's	BKH983T	Roselyn	C28EUH	South Gloucestershire
B588XNO	Taw & Torridge	BMR201V	Thamesdown	C29EUH	South Gloucestershire
B630DDW	Tally Ho!	BMR202V	Thamesdown	C30EUH	South Gloucestershire
B674CBD	Target Travel	BMR203V	Thamesdown	CZ4CHM	Truronian
B710EOF	F T Williams	BMR204V	Thamesdown	C83CHM	Truronian
B726OBC	Hookways	BMR205V	Thamesdown	C105AFX	F T Williams
B863XYR	Shamrock Buses	BN02EDN	Truronian	C110DWR	Berkeley
B865XYR	Shamrock Buses	BNZ4922	Beeline	C112DWR	Berkeley
B866XYR	Shamrock Buses	BT02CJT	Turners Coachways	C122PNV	Caradon Riviera
B883YTC	South Gloucestershire	BU03SSK	DAC Coaches	C142SPB	Swanbrook
B888PDY	Alexcars	BU54AJP	A Bus	C178ECK	Shamrock Buses
B892UAS	A Bus	BUI4646	Ebley Bus	C201YPR	Yellow Buses
B893UAS	A Bus	BUR438T	Quantock MS	C219FMF	Berry's
B895UAS	A Bus	BVA787V	Caradon Riviera	C312NRC	Applegate
B896UAS	A Bus	BVR59T	Thamesdown	C314NRC	Applegate
B899UAS	A Bus	BVR89T	Thamesdown	C407VVN	Sureline
B910SPR	Berry's	BW03ZUB	Hatts Europa	C432VGX	Bakers Dolphin
B991YTC	Centurion	BW03ZUC	Hatts Europa	C440BUV	Currian's
BA02EFA	Applegate	BW03ZVA	Hatts Europa	C457HAK	Taylors
BAS562	Quantock MS	BX02CME	Castleways	C481YWY	Shamrock Buses
BAS563	Quantock MS	BX04NAE	F T Williams	C516DND	Sureline
BAS564	Quantock MS	BX04NCA	F T Williams	C546BHY	Taw & Torridge
BAZ6170	Hatts Europa	BX53OMD	Applegate	C550BHY	Taw & Torridge

The South West Bus Handbook

Reg	Operator	Reg	Operator	Reg	Operator	Reg	Operator
C637LFT	Beaumont Travel	DNT717T	Tally Ho!	F193UGL		St Ives Mini	
C660JAT	Caradon Riviera	DNZ5043	Beeline	F198JKL		Mid Devon	
C680KDS	Bluebird	DNZ5130	Wessex Bus	F202HSO		Safeway	
C680KFM	St Ives Mini	DPV65D	Quantock MS	F210WRU		Yellow Buses	
C681EHU	South Gloucestershire	DPV881	Westward Travel	F211WRU		Yellow Buses	
C812BYY	Truronian	DSU107	Western Greyhound	F212WRU		Yellow Buses	
C819BYY	Truronian	DT04CJT	Turners Coachways	F213DCC		Ebley Bus	
C822EHU	South Gloucestershire	E39SBO	Tally Ho!	F213WRU		Yellow Buses	
C828EHU	Westward Travel	E40SBO	Tally Ho!	F214WRU		Yellow Buses	
C849CSN	Caradon Riviera	E42ODE	Berkeley	F215DCC		Hookways	
C87CHM	Truronian	E131KGM	Berry's	F221DCC		Hookways	
C906GYD	Webberbus	E133PLJ	Webberbus	F232DWF		Dawlish Coaches	
C930LMW	Blue Motors	E156OMD	South Gloucestershire	F249YTJ		South Gloucestershire	
CAZ2749	Quantock MS	E169XWF	Geoff Willetts	F254MGB		Coach House	
CFN121	Quantock MS	E181AUJ	Glenvic	F275AWW		Sureline	
CHG545	Quantock MS	E205GCG	Yellow Buses	F276WAF		F T Williams	
CHL772	Quantock MS	E206GCG	Yellow Buses	F281ENV		Westward Travel	
CHZ4714	K W Beard	E207GCG	Yellow Buses	F301RUT		River Link	
CHZ9055	Mike's Travel	E208GCG	Yellow Buses	F306JTY		South Gloucestershire	
CJ53CJT	Turners Coachways	E209GCG	Yellow Buses	F309JTY		South Gloucestershire	
CJZ3681	DAC Coaches	E219WBG	South Gloucestershire	F309RMH		Cottrell's	
CJZ6782	F T Williams	E296OMG	Dawlish Coaches	F310JTY		South Gloucestershire	
CLV85X	Beaumont Travel	E300BWL	Beaumont Travel	F311JTY		South Gloucestershire	
CLZ8307	Arleen	E303BWL	Beaumont Travel	F312JTY		Marchants	
CN02EDN	Truronian	E318STG	Andybus	F315VCV		Truronian	
CNZ3829	Hatts Europa	E322PMD	Marchants	F329GYA		South West Coaches	
CRO671K	Quantock MS	E323PMD	Marchants	F387FYC		South West Coaches	
CSU926	Target Travel	E323UUB	Beeline	F404DUG		Webberbus	
CSU938	Hookways	E324PMD	Marchants	F425DUG		Coach House	
CWR512Y	Marchants	E325BVO	DAC Coaches	F432OBK		Buglers	
CYA181J	Quantock MS	E325CTT	Sewards	F441DUG		Barry's	
CYA614X	Taylors	E325PMD	Swanbrook	F449XFX		South West Coaches	
D35ALR	Berkeley	E331UYC	Webberbus	F450XFX		South West Coaches	
D65RMW	South West Coaches	E347EVH	Tally Ho!	F476WFX		Berry's	
D86VDV	Sewards	E351EVH	Tally Ho!	F484MTA		Dartline	
D100XRY	Taw & Torridge	E365HFG	Taw & Torridge	F512LTT		Dawlish Coaches	
D160UGA	Cottrell's	E402TVC	Caradon Riviera	F515SCW		Turners Tours	
D200ELJ	Yellow Buses	E416YYB	South West Coaches	F538LUF		South Gloucestershire	
D202ELJ	Yellow Buses	E458CGM	Mike's Travel	F544LUF		South Gloucestershire	
D203ELJ	Yellow Buses	E461CGM	South Gloucestershire	F578SHT		South West Coaches	
D204ELJ	Yellow Buses	E477SON	Cottrell's	F600GVO		Plymouth Citybus	
D215JHY	Eurotaxis	E565YYA	Safeway	F601GVO		Plymouth Citybus	
D241OOJ	Caradon Riviera	E574WOK	Webberbus	F602GVO		Plymouth Citybus	
D260HFX	Berry's	E604CDS	Webberbus	F603GVO		Plymouth Citybus	
D272BJB	Hatts Europa	E650KCX	Westward Travel	F603RPG		Thamesdown	
D327TRN	Coombs Travel	E660XND	Eurotaxis	F604GVO		Plymouth Citybus	
D353RCY	Dartline	E716CPC	Hookways	F605GVO		Plymouth Citybus	
D434OWO	Dartline	E755HJF	Taylors	F606GVO		Plymouth Citybus	
D434OWO	Target Travel	E758XYB	South West Coaches	F607GVO		Plymouth Citybus	
D463CKV	Wessex Bus	E809MOU	Tally Ho!	F617VNH		Westward Travel	
D504NDA	Blue Motors	E817MOU	Tally Ho!	F633LMJ		Western Greyhound	
D542GFH	Target Travel	E845YYA	South West Coaches	F635LMJ		Western Greyhound	
D603MVR	Grey Cars	E906UNW	Grey Cars	F638LMJ		Western Greyhound	
D615ASG	Somerbus	E907UNW	Grey Cars	F693GYD		South West Coaches	
D649NYC	South West Coaches	E920EAY	F T Williams	F714EUG		Hookways	
D706YHK	South Gloucestershire	E995KJF	Mike's Travel	F729JWD		Taylors	
D726VAM	Andybus	EAP989V	Westward Travel	F734USF		South West Coaches	
D759UTA	Sewards	EBM448T	Quantock MS	F791GNA		Taylors	
D778NYG	Hookways	ECZ4634	South West Coaches	F869YWX		Taylors	
D824UTF	Western Greyhound	EEH902Y	Marchants	F875RFP		Coach House	
D825PUK	Blue Motors	EGV695Y	South West Coaches	F909UPR		Grey Cars	
D851UTA	Turners Tours	EJR118W	A Bus	F997KCU		South West Coaches	
D928UTA	Turners Tours	ELZ2062	Safeway	F999UGL		Target Travel	
D930LYC	DAC Coaches	EMW893	Quantock MS	FA02CJV		DAC Coaches	
D947ARE	Country Bus	EN02EDN	Truronian	FAZ7273		Taw & Torridge	
D970RNC	Webberbus	ENF573Y	DAC Coaches	FD03YOC		Taylors	
DAD200T	Tally Ho!	ER05BUS	Somerbus	FDF965		Pulham's	
DAD600Y	Mike's Travel	ESK812	South Gloucestershire	FDV417V		Quantock MS	
DBV132Y	Shamrock Coaches	ET04CJT	Turners Coachways	FDV837V		Ebley Bus	
DBV31H	Ebley Bus	EWS739W	A Bus	FE52HFR		Applegate	
DCA528X	Michaels	F50ACL	Plymouth Citybus	FG03JBE		Taylors	
DCK219	Quantock MS	F51ACL	Plymouth Citybus	FH53DRH		Rover	
DCZ2307	Tally Ho!	F77MFJ	Dawlish Coaches	FHS762X		Webberbus	
DH02DRH	Rover	F81ONX	Thamesdown	HIL6783		St Ives Mini	
DKZ4602	South West Coaches	F105SSE	Grey Cars	FIL9220		Currian's	
DLJ112L	Yellow Buses	F134JHO	South West Coaches	FIL9270		Eagle of Bristol	
DMJ374T	Taw & Torridge	F167UDG	K W Beard	FJ53ZSZ		Taylors	
DN02EDN	Truronian	F183UFH	Cottrell's	FJ54ZCV		Marchants	

Reg	Operator	Reg	Operator	Reg	Operator	Reg	Operator
FJ54ZCX	Marchants	G907VKJ	Coach House	H342UWT	South Gloucestershire		
FMO949	Quantock MS	G921WGS	Beaumont Travel	H343UWX	South Gloucestershire		
FN02VCF	Bakers Dolphin	G958VBC	Dartline	H344UWX	South Gloucestershire		
FN02VCK	Bakers Dolphin	G992VWV	South Gloucestershire	H345UWX	South Gloucestershire		
FN03DXY	Excelsior	G993VWV	South Gloucestershire	H346JFX	Hookways		
FN03DXZ	Excelsior	GBU2V	James Bevan	H346UWX	South Gloucestershire		
FN03DYA	Excelsior	GBU6V	Cottrell's	H347CKP	Coach House		
FN03DYB	Excelsior	GBU7V	Cottrell's	H347UWX	South Gloucestershire		
FNM854Y	Taylors	GBU8V	Axe Valley	H356WWX	South Gloucestershire		
FNZ5636	Faresaver	GIB5970	Safeway	H357WWX	South Gloucestershire		
FNZ7649	Faresaver	GIL3113	Grey Cars	H362BDV	Hamblys of Kernow		
FP02ZNV	Turners Tours	GIL5107	Turners Tours	H422GPM	South Gloucestershire		
FP53JYB	James Bevan	GIL5109	Turners Tours	H423GPM	Swanbrook		
FT04CJT	Turners Coachways	GIL5711	Turners Tours	H437BVU	DAC Coaches		
FVM191V	Blue Motors	GJZ6083	Faresaver	H458UGO	Turners Tours		
FX51AXP	Michaels	GL03PUL	Pulham's	H460WWY	South Gloucestershire		
G38KAK	Barry's	GL52PUL	Pulham's	H476UYD	Cooks Coaches		
G46RGG	Berry's	GL53PUL	Pulham's	H484BND	South West Coaches		
G50ONN	Marchants	GLZ7465	South West Coaches	H533YCX	Safeway		
G104EOG	South Gloucestershire	GOU908	Hookways	H534RKG	DAC Coaches		
G105APC	Hookways	GRU162V	Thamesdown	H538ETT	South West Coaches		
G115TNL	Ebley Bus	GRU163V	Thamesdown	H544FVN	South Gloucestershire		
G128TJA	South Gloucestershire	GRU164V	Thamesdown	H642GRO	Coombs Travel		
G159EOG	South Gloucestershire	GRU165V	Thamesdown	H651UWR	Cottrell's		
G167XJF	Mid Devon	GRU166V	Thamesdown	H655DKO	Barry's		
G170FJC	Beaumont Travel	GRU167V	Thamesdown	H672ATN	Barry's		
G170XJF	Roselyn	GRU168V	Thamesdown	H683NEF	Swanbrook		
G174EOG	South Gloucestershire	GSU344	Caradon Riviera	H756WWW	South Gloucestershire		
G176FJC	Beaumont Travel	GSU372	Quantock MS	H757WWW	South Gloucestershire		
G177EOG	South Gloucestershire	GSU678	Quantock MS	H781GTA	Faresaver		
G179PAO	Tally Ho!	GT02CJT	Turners Coachways	H794FAF	F T Williams		
G184PAO	Tally Ho!	GWN432	Quantock MS	H823GAF	F T Williams		
G186PAO	Tally Ho!	GYE261W	South Gloucestershire	H843NOC	Ebley Bus		
G221VDX	Shaftesbury & District	GYE557W	Axe Valley	H853OWN	Rover		
G222KWE	Country Bus	H4GBD	Dukes Travel	H882LOX	Wessex Bus		
G230FJC	Ebley Bus	H5GBD	Dukes Travel	H886LOX	Ebley Bus		
G247CLE	Dukes Travel	H6GBD	Dukes Travel	H888LOX	Ebley Bus		
G250CPS	Coach House	H7GBD	Dukes Travel	H889LOX	Ebley Bus		
G253TSL	Tally Ho!	H8GBD	Dukes Travel	H913FTT	Shaftesbury & District		
G276WFU	Sewards	H9GBD	Dukes Travel	H914XGA	DAC Coaches		
G290XFH	Geoff Willetts	H10GBD	Dukes Travel	H932DRJ	Cottrell's		
G293CLE	Bennett	H23JMJ	Ebley Bus	H937DRJ	Geoff Willetts		
G296EOG	South Gloucestershire	H24GRE	Ebley Bus	H969XHR	Thamesdown		
G330XRE	Brean & Berrow	H34HBG	South Gloucestershire	H970XHR	Thamesdown		
G340KWE	Applegate	H97PVW	Swanbrook	H971XHR	Thamesdown		
G391PNV	Taw & Torridge	H104CHG	Ebley Bus	H972XHR	Thamesdown		
G444NYC	South West Coaches	H105CHG	Ebley Bus	H973XHR	Thamesdown		
G451XJH	Ebley Bus	H119PVW	Swanbrook	H980PTW	South Gloucestershire		
G501XOR	Barry's	H123TYD	Webberbus	H986PTW	South Gloucestershire		
G506VYE	Turners Tours	H124TYD	Webberbus	HAX331W	Turners Tours		
G515VYE	Weaverbus	H128NWO	F T Williams	HAZ2963	Buglers		
G517MYD	Barry's	H137PVW	Swanbrook	HAZ3346	Cooks Coaches		
G524YAE	Eurotaxis	H156HAC	Pulham's	HAZ3540	Eurotaxis		
G525YAE	Eurotaxis	H159EJU	Webberbus	HBH416Y	Westward Travel		
G612OTV	Plymouth Citybus	H165DJU	F T Williams	HBZ4676	Cooks Coaches		
G614OTV	Plymouth Citybus	H170SAB	South West Coaches	HDF661	Pulham's		
G615OTV	Plymouth Citybus	H177GTT	Plymouth Citybus	HF03ODR	Yellow Buses		
G621OTV	Plymouth Citybus	H178GTT	Plymouth Citybus	HF03ODS	Yellow Buses		
G623OTV	Eurotaxis	H203LOM	Bennett	HF03ODT	Yellow Buses		
G629XWS	Bennett	H207LOM	Bennett	HF03ODU	Yellow Buses		
G640CHF	Plymouth Citybus	H215LOM	F T Williams	HF03ODV	Yellow Buses		
G643CHF	Plymouth Citybus	H217LOM	F T Williams	HF03ODW	Yellow Buses		
G680YLP	Pulham's	H226TCP	Quantock MS	HF04JWD	Yellow Buses		
G693NUB	Coombs Travel	H251JJT	Yellow Buses	HF04JWE	Yellow Buses		
G699NUB	Coombs Travel	H252JJT	Yellow Buses	HF04JWG	Yellow Buses		
G713HOP	Eastwood	H254JJT	Yellow Buses	HF04JWJ	Yellow Buses		
G717HOP	Eastwood	H255JJT	Yellow Buses	HF04JWK	Yellow Buses		
G782XAE	Andybul	H256JJT	Yellow Buses	HF04JWL	Yellow Buses		
G783XWS	Eurotaxis	H257JJT	Yellow Buses	HF53OBG	Yellow Buses		
G800PTT	Dartline	H258MFX	Yellow Buses	HF53OBH	Yellow Buses		
G823KWF	South Gloucestershire	H259MFX	Yellow Buses	HF54JUJ	Yellow Buses		
G826XWS	Turners Coachways	H261MFX	Yellow Buses	HF54JUK	Yellow Buses		
G828XWS	Eurotaxis	H262MFX	Yellow Buses	HF54JUL	Yellow Buses		
G829XWS	Turners Coachways	H263MFX	Yellow Buses	HF54KXH	Yellow Buses		
G840UDV	South Gloucestershire	H264MFX	Yellow Buses	HF54KXJ	Yellow Buses		
G841DVX	Tally Ho!	H265MFX	Yellow Buses	HF54KXK	Yellow Buses		
G896TGG	Ebley Bus	H337TYG	South Gloucestershire	HHJ372Y	Taylors		
G900TJA	South Gloucestershire	H341UWT	South Gloucestershire	HHJ376Y	Taylors		

HHU146V	Bakers Dolphin	J398GKH	Turners Tours	K104SFJ	Plymouth Citybus
HIB7178	Barnes	J412LLK	Centurion	K105OMW	Sureline
HIL2897	Tally Ho!	J430PPF	South Gloucestershire	K105SFJ	Plymouth Citybus
HIL3188	South Gloucestershire	J511LRY	Hookways	K106OMW	Thamesdown
HIL3451	Citytour	J571PRU	Coach House	K107SFJ	Plymouth Citybus
HIL3471	Buglers	J601KCU	Safeway	K108OMW	Thamesdown
HIL4966	Tally Ho!	J601WHJ	South Gloucestershire	K108SFJ	Plymouth Citybus
HIL5697	South West Coaches	J606WHJ	South Gloucestershire	K109OMW	Sureline
HIL7621	Caradon Riviera	J616KCU	Tally Ho!	K109SFJ	Plymouth Citybus
HIL7772	Safeway	J618KCU	Tally Ho!	K110OMW	Thamesdown
HIL8518	Shaftesbury & District	J622HMH	Axe Valley	K110SFJ	Plymouth Citybus
HJ02HFA	Yellow Buses	J656REY	Dukes Travel	K112XRU	Andybus
HJ02HFB	Yellow Buses	J688MFE	Castleways	K150PHW	Taylors
HJ02HFC	Yellow Buses	J689MFE	Castleways	K164FYG	Axe Valley
HJ02HFD	Yellow Buses	J734KBC	Centurion	K179SLY	Target Travel
HJ02HFE	Yellow Buses	J780NHA	Tally Ho!	K186HTV	Eastwood
HJ02HFF	Yellow Buses	J807KHD	Dukes Travel	K205GMX	APL Travel
HJ02HFG	Yellow Buses	J819EYC	Berry's	K216SUY	James Bevan
HJ02HFH	Yellow Buses	J824MOD	Dartline	K227WNH	Hookways
HJA965E	Quantock MS	J825MOD	Dartline	K237SUY	James Bevan
HKL819	Quantock MS	J853KHD	Hatts Europa	K239FAW	South Gloucestershire
HLZ4439	Dukes Travel	J870FGX	Dartline	K262AWL	Webberbus
HSK645	Trathens	J953SBU	F T Williams	K271BRJ	Eurotaxis
HSK646	Trathens	J988TVU	South Gloucestershire	K301WTA	Plymouth Citybus
HSK647	Trathens	J995GCP	Dukes Travel	K309YKG	Tally Ho!
HSK648	Trathens	JAM145E	Thamesdown	K326PHT	South Gloucestershire
HSK649	Trathens	JAZ9910	Michaels	K327PHT	South Gloucestershire
HSK650	Trathens	JBZ4909	Caradon Riviera	K331RCN	Axe Valley
HSK651	Trathens	JCW517S	Taw & Torridge	K338FYG	Cooks Coaches
HSK652	Trathens	JCZ3604	Tally Ho!	K345PJR	Ebley Bus
HSK653	Trathens	JDE973X	Tally Ho!	K365TJF	Faresaver
HT04CJT	Turners Coachways	JDR661F	Polperro Tram Co	K371FRY	South Gloucestershire
HUD495W	Roselyn	JDV754	Blue Motors	K400TAW	Taw & Torridge
HUD501W	Roselyn	JEO587X	Ebley Bus	K423ARW	Tally Ho!
HUO510	Quantock MS	JEY124Y	Marchants	K424WUT	Bennett
HVU247N	Quantock MS	JFJ875	Quantock MS	K427HWY	Caradon Riviera
HWU885Y	Truronian	JFM575	Quantock MS	K437OKH	Turners Tours
IAZ2314	Hopley's	JFR3W	Shamrock Buses	K458YPK	Sewards
IDZ8561	Faresaver	JFR10W	Shamrock Buses	K496SUS	Eurotaxis
IIB8903	Ebley Bus	JFR11W	Shamrock Buses	K505RJX	Hatts Europa
IUI4360	Bakers Dolphin	JFR13W	Shamrock Buses	K518RJX	Eagle of Bristol
J21GCX	Bennett	JG9938	Quantock MS	K522EFL	Country Bus
J41EYB	Webberbus	JIB1451	Barnes	K526EFL	Coach House
J42VWO	Hookways	JIL2018	Webberbus	K537CWN	Travel Filer's
J61NJT	Coach House	JIL3959	Hatts Europa	K539CWN	Travel Filer's
J80BUS	A Bus	JIL3967	C J Down	K544RWP	Tally Ho!
J93UBL	Coach House	JIL7714	Eastwood	K562YFJ	Sewards
J112DUV	Sureline	JIL7904	Truronian	K589VBC	Bennett
J114DUV	Sureline	JIL8319	South West Coaches	K590VBC	Applegate
J120SPF	South Gloucestershire	JJD511D	Quantock MS	K593PCV	F T Williams
J127DGC	Sewards	JLJ402	Quantock MS	K601JYA	Webberbus
J129GMP	Somerbus	JLZ3043	Beeline	K622YVN	South Gloucestershire
J130LVM	Taw & Torridge	JLZ3073	Taw & Torridge	K623YVN	South Gloucestershire
J173BYD	Webberbus	JLZ3074	Taw & Torridge	K624YVN	South Gloucestershire
J173CNU	Beaumont Travel	JLZ3082	Taw & Torridge	K625YVN	South Gloucestershire
J205KTT	DAC Coaches	JMJ134V	Taw & Torridge	K628YVN	South Gloucestershire
J210KTT	Beaumont Travel	JSK261	Plymouth Citybus	K695RNR	South Gloucestershire
J211DYL	Centurion	JSK262	Plymouth Citybus	K712RNR	Bennett
J215OCW	South Gloucestershire	JSK264	Plymouth Citybus	K714PHU	Eurotaxis
J229JJR	Ebley Bus	JSK265	Plymouth Citybus	K721HYA	Coombs Travel
J243MFP	Citytour	JTE546	Quantock MS	K722HYA	Coombs Travel
J266SPR	Yellow Buses	JTL150T	Quantock MS	K727UTT	Hatts Europa
J267SPR	Yellow Buses	JUI1717	Cooks Coaches	K729GBE	Hookways
J268SPR	Yellow Buses	JUO992	Quantock MS	K744RBX	Sewards
J269SPR	Yellow Buses	JVH378	Quantock MS	K775UTT	Dartline
J271TTX	Coombs Travel	K3BUS	Grey Cars	K803WFJ	Andybus
J272NNC	Coombs Travel	K5CJT	Turners Coachways	K809WPF	Barry's
J275NNC	Coombs Travel	K6CJT	Turners Coachways	K835HUM	Safeway
J278NNC	Coombs Travel	K7CJT	Turners Coachways	K854ODY	Dukes Travel
J283TOJ	F T Williams	K18AND	Rover	K859ODY	Dukes Travel
J297NNB	South Gloucestershire	K18LUE	Turners Coachways	K878UDB	Faresaver
J302BVO	Dukes Travel	K30ARJ*	Andybus	K879UDB	South Gloucestershire
J303BVO	Dukes Travel	K101SFJ	Plymouth Citybus	K882UDB	Dukes Travel
J304DVO	Dukes Travel	K102OMW	Thamesdown	K892CSX	Turners Tours
J305BVO	Dukes Travel	K102SFJ	Plymouth Citybus	K922UFX	Dawlish Coaches
J318LNL	Taw & Torridge	K103SFJ	Plymouth Citybus	K926TTA	Mid Devon
J348GKH	Beaumont Travel	K104OMW	Thamesdown	K945OPX	Rover
J369YWB	South Gloucestershire	K104PHW	Caradon Riviera	K977RLW	Barry's

K989TOD	Country Bus	L233HRF	Faresaver	LAZ5826	South West Coaches
KAU573V	Bakers Dolphin	L238OYC	Berry's	LBD921V	Ebley Bus
KAZ6911	Hookways	L251YOD	Plymouth Citybus	LBZ2571	Dartline
KFM767	Quantock MS	L257YOD	Plymouth Citybus	LBZ2939	Turners Tours
KFM893	Quantock MS	L258YOD	Plymouth Citybus	LDB756	Quantock MS
KGJ603D	Shaftesbury & District	L289SEM	Wessex Bus	LDD488	Pulham's
KHL460W	Tally Ho!	L292SEM	Wessex Bus	LEN616	Barry's
KIW4489	Dartline	L293SEM	Wessex Bus	LFM302	Quantock MS
KIW6512	Tally Ho!	L302YOD	Plymouth Citybus	LFM717	Quantock MS
KJD410P	Tally Ho!	L303AUT	Sureline	LFM734	Quantock MS
KJD413P	Tally Ho!	L306AUT	Sureline	LHT730P	Westward Travel
KLZ1148	K W Beard	L307AUT	Sureline	LIB1180	Caradon Riviera
KLZ1149	K W Beard	L312AUT	Sureline	LIB3903	Barnes
KLZ3240	South West Coaches	L316AUT	Faresaver	LIB6445	Berkeley
KMW175P	Thamesdown	L317AUT	Sureline	LIL2167	South West Coaches
KOO791V	A Bus	L318AUT	Faresaver	LIL3060	Hatts Europa
KOO792V	A Bus	L322AUT	Tally Ho!	LIL4348	Mid Devon
KOO793V	A Bus	L336DTG	Travel Filer's	LIL6148	Tally Ho!
KRU844W	Westward Travel	L345ATA	Dartline	LIL6537	Dartline
KSK984	Trathens	L360ANR	Cooks Coaches	LIL6538	Dartline
KSK985	Trathens	L376JBD	Beaumont Travel	LIL7802	Dartline
KSK986	Trathens	L378JBD	Beaumont Travel	LIL7818	DAC Coaches
KSU454	Currian's	L379JBD	Beaumont Travel	LIL8052	Dartline
KT54CJT	Turners Coachways	L401BFX	Yellow Buses	LIL8876	Dartline
KTA986V	Quantock MS	L402BFX	Yellow Buses	LIL9017	Dartline
KTF594	Quantock MS	L403BFX	Yellow Buses	LIL9168	Barnes
KTL25V	Ebley Bus	L404BBC	Eurotaxis	LIL9174	Mid Devon
KU52RXJ	Truronian	L404BFX	Yellow Buses	LIL9843	Marchants
KUB97	Grey Cars	L405BBC	Eurotaxis	LIL9990	Dartline
KVF248V	Hopley's	L405BFX	Yellow Buses	LJH665	Quantock MS
KX04HPN	Cooks Coaches	L406BFX	Yellow Buses	LOD495	Carmel
KX04HPP	Cooks Coaches	L407BBC	Eurotaxis	LPB500	Target Travel
KX04HPU	Cooks Coaches	L422CPB	Faresaver	LSK473	Trathens
KX04HPV	Cooks Coaches	L422WHR	Dartline	LSK481	Trathens
KX04HPY	Cooks Coaches	L423CPB	Faresaver	LSK498	Trathens
KX04HPZ	Cooks Coaches	L424ANP	Webberbus	LSK499	Trathens
KYA284Y	South West Coaches	L433CPJ	South Gloucestershire	LSK503	Trathens
KYV685X	Axe Valley	L463RDN	Bennett	LSK504	Trathens
L2POW	Berkeley	L479BUE	Dartline	LSK505	Trathens
L6ABC	Blue Motors	L486HKN	Sewards	LSK511	Trathens
L8CJT	Turners Coachways	L519EHD	Bennett	LSK512	Trathens
L9CJT	Turners Coachways	L524BDH	Hatts Europa	LSK611	Trathens
L18LUE	Blue Iris	L535YCC	Turners Tours	LSK612	Trathens
L32OKV	Cooks Coaches	L537YCC	Turners Tours	LSK613	Trathens
L3RDC	Eurotaxis	L543JFS	Country Bus	LSK614	Trathens
L55BUS	South West Coaches	L543YUS	Marchants	LSK615	Trathens
L76DPE	Target Travel	L549EHD	Quantock MS	LSK812	Trathens
L84CNY	South Gloucestershire	L552EHD	Carmel	LSK814	Trathens
L110UHF	Coombs Travel	L589BFJ	Mid Devon	LTA755	Hatts Europa
L112YOD	Plymouth Citybus	L657MFL	South Gloucestershire	LTY553X	Bakers Dolphin
L113YOD	Plymouth Citybus	L667PWT	Centurion	LUB512P	Tally Ho!
L114YOD	Plymouth Citybus	L670YTT	Webberbus	LUI1512	Dukes Travel
L115YOD	Plymouth Citybus	L687PYD	South West Coaches	LUI1519	Barry's
L116YOD	Plymouth Citybus	L688PYD	South West Coaches	LUI2527	South West Coaches
L117YOD	Plymouth Citybus	L691WHY	Coombs Travel	LUI2528	South West Coaches
L118YOD	Plymouth Citybus	L694JEC	Beeline	LUI2529	South West Coaches
L119YOD	Plymouth Citybus	L703JSC	Eurotaxis	LUI4653	Barry's
L120YOD	Plymouth Citybus	L725WCV	Truronian	LUI5601	Alexcars
L121YOD	Plymouth Citybus	L726WCV	Truronian	LUI5812	Barry's
L122YOD	Plymouth Citybus	L776RWW	South Gloucestershire	LUI9952	Caradon Riviera
L123YOD	Plymouth Citybus	L778RWW	South Gloucestershire	LUI9953	Caradon Riviera
L124YOD	Plymouth Citybus	L779RWW	South Gloucestershire	LUI9954	Caradon Riviera
L125YOD	Plymouth Citybus	L796DTT	Dawlish Coaches	LUI9955	Caradon Riviera
L126YOD	Plymouth Citybus	L807ORD	South West Coaches	LUI9956	Caradon Riviera
L151FRJ	Faresaver	L810TFY	Axe Valley	LUI9957	Caradon Riviera
L168EKR	Target Travel	L853WDS	Target Travel	LUI9958	Caradon Riviera
L182PMX	Dawlish Coaches	L858COD	Dartline	LUI9959	Caradon Riviera
L187DDW	Eastwood	L865TFB	South West Coaches	LUI9961	Caradon Riviera
L193OVO	Dawlish Coaches	L866BEA	Country Bus	LUI9962	Caradon Riviera
L194OVO	Swanbrook	L872WCV	F T Williams	LUI9964	Caradon Riviera
L195OVO	Swanbrook	L882MWB	Coombs Travel	LUI9965	Caradon Riviera
L202MHL	Pulham's	L917NWW	F T Williams	LUI9966	Caradon Riviera
L210OYC	South West Coaches	L920NWW	Roselyn	LUI9967	Caradon Riviera
L211OYC	South West Coaches	L924NWW	Taw & Torridge	LUI9968	Caradon Riviera
L225BUT	Carmel	L948CTT	Arleen	LWS116Y	Roselyn
L226JFA	St Ives Mini	L969UHU	Caradon Riviera	LYA315V	South West Coaches
L228HRF	Faresaver	L995VAF	Truronian	M6HAT	Hatts Europa
L231HRF	Faresaver	LAZ2370	Barry's	M8HAT	Hatts Europa

The South West Bus Handbook

Latterly with Arrive North East, F312JTY has received a new set of high-back seating for its school role with Marchants. It is seen showing off its new colours. *Robert Edworthy*

M9FUG	Cottrell's	M116BMR	Thamesdown	M273HOD	Plymouth Citybus
M10CJT	Turners Coachways	M117BMR	Thamesdown	M274HOD	Plymouth Citybus
M11CJT	Turners Coachways	M118BMR	Thamesdown	M276FNS	Faresaver
M12CJT	Turners Coachways	M119BMR	Thamesdown	M289CAM	Cooks Coaches
M12YCL	Target Travel	M122YCM	Faresaver	M297LOD	Tally Ho!
M13CJT	Turners Coachways	M127HOD	Plymouth Citybus	M301TSF	Eurotaxis
M18LUE	Blue Iris	M128HOD	Plymouth Citybus	M304KOD	Plymouth Citybus
M20CJT	Turners Coachways	M129HOD	Plymouth Citybus	M305KOD	Plymouth Citybus
M30ARJ	Andybus	M130HOD	Plymouth Citybus	M311EEA	Arleen
M39LOA	Coach House	M131HOD	Plymouth Citybus	M321VET	Barry's
M39WUR	Faresaver	M132HOD	Plymouth Citybus	M325KRY	Roselyn
M41WUR	Faresaver	M134UWY	Taw & Torridge	M345TDO	DAC Coaches
M42HSU	Roselyn	M153XHW	Hatts Europa	M345UVX	Cooks Coaches
M42WUR	Faresaver	M158KOD	Dartline	M359LFX	Target Travel
M45GRY	Eurotaxis	M164LNC	Dukes Travel	M360LFX	Target Travel
M46GRY	Eurotaxis	M165XHW	Turners Coachways	M364LFX	Target Travel
M46POL	South Gloucestershire	M166WTJ	Sureline	M365LFX	Target Travel
M47GRY	Eurotaxis	M193TMG	Faresaver	M373CRL	Truronian
M48GRY	Eurotaxis	M198TKJ	Beaumont Travel	M379CGN	Taylors
M51HOD	Plymouth Citybus	M201TYB	Berry's	M396TRC	Turners Coachways
M52HOD	Plymouth Citybus	M231XWS	Coombs Travel	M411BEY	Faresaver
M53HOD	Plymouth Citybus	M236KNR	Faresaver	M412BEY	Faresaver
M68UWB	Taw & Torridge	M248NNF	A Bus	M413ALU	Country Bus
M91JHB	Cooks Coaches	M259CDE	APL Travel	M413RND	A Bus
M93BOU	Andybus	M261HOD	Plymouth Citybus	M414ALU	Country Bus
M101SWG	South West Coaches	M262HOD	Plymouth Citybus	M416VYD	Webberbus
M102BLE	South Gloucestershire	M263HOD	Plymouth Citybus	M417VYD	F T Williams
M102SWG	South West Coaches	M264HOD	Plymouth Citybus	M418VYD	Webberbus
M103CYR	South West Coaches	M265HOD	Plymouth Citybus	M419VYD	South Gloucestershire
M103SWG	South West Coaches	M266HOD	Plymouth Citybus	M451LLJ	Yellow Buses
M104SWG	South West Coaches	M267HOD	Plymouth Citybus	M452LLJ	Yellow Buses
M107BLE	South Gloucestershire	M268HOD	Plymouth Citybus	M463LLJ	Yellow Buses
M108BLE	South Gloucestershire	M269HOD	Plymouth Citybus	M454HPG	Faresaver
M112BMR	Thamesdown	M270HOD	Plymouth Citybus	M454JPA	Sureline
M113BMR	Thamesdown	M271HOD	Plymouth Citybus	M454LLJ	Yellow Buses
M114BMR	Thamesdown	M272HOD	Plymouth Citybus	M455LLJ	Yellow Buses
M115BMR	Thamesdown	M272POS	Glenvic	M456LLJ	Yellow Buses

Displaced by new arrivals with Dublin bus, a number of these Olympians are now entering service with English operators. Seen in Cheltenham still in its former colours, H97PVW also carries the Swanbrook name.
Robert Edworthy

M457HPG	Faresaver	M711BMR	Thamesdown	MFX174W	Thamesdown
M457LLJ	Yellow Buses	M740RCP	Bluebird	MFX175W	Thamesdown
M458LLJ	Yellow Buses	M741RCP	Bluebird	MFX176W	Yellow Buses
M459EDH	Faresaver	M745ARP	Coombs Travel	MIB6310	Barnes
M459JPA	Sureline	M756XET	Marchants	MIL2066	Grey Cars
M459LLJ	Yellow Buses	M775RCP	Eagle of Bristol	MIL2088	Grey Cars
M460JPA	Sureline	M799EUS	Faresaver	MIL2175	Michaels
M460LLJ	Yellow Buses	M805RCP	Eagle of Bristol	MIL3010	Grey Cars
M461LLJ	Yellow Buses	M809RCP	Bennett	MIL3012	Grey Cars
M462LLJ	Yellow Buses	M823HNS	Travel Filer's	MIL4680	Hookways
M463SMO	Turners Coachways	M825HNS	Travel Filer's	MIL5237	APL Travel
M464JPA	Country Bus	M842TYC	Cooks Coaches	MIL5577	Mid Devon
M485VST	South Gloucestershire	M843TYC	Cooks Coaches	MIL5578	Mid Devon
M503ALP	South Gloucestershire	M845CWS	Buglers	MIL5579	Mid Devon
M504ALP	South Gloucestershire	M861TYC	South Gloucestershire	MIL5991	Mid Devon
M505ALP	South Gloucestershire	M862TYC	South Gloucestershire	MIL5992	Mid Devon
M533BLU	Hookways	M883LNF	F T Williams	MIL5993	Mid Devon
M549XHC	Alexcars	M887WWB	Alexcars	MIL6682	Mid Devon
M569SRE	Mike's Travel	M908OVR	Webberbus	MIL6684	Mid Devon
M572TYB	Coombs Travel	M935XKA	Eurotaxis	MIL6804	Barnes
M573TYB	Coombs Travel	M943JBO	Pulham's	MIL7609	C J Down
M582KTG	Cooks Coaches	M944JBO	Pulham's	MIL7611	C J Down
M583WLV	Tally Ho!	M960TKL	Beaumont Travel	MIL8328	South Gloucestershire
M584WLV	Tally Ho!	M962TKL	Webberbus	MIL9751	Travel Filer's
M587KTT	Dawlish Coaches	M965LDV	Mid Devon	MJH280L	Mid Devon
M590GRY	Bluebird	M968TKL	Webberbus	MLZ2391	Tally Ho!
M608RCP	Ebley Bus	M968TYG	Cooks Coaches	MLZ2392	Tally Ho!
M608UUR	F T Williams	M974TKL	Webberbus	MLZ2393	Tally Ho!
M619ORJ	Turners Tours	M981HNS	Roselyn	MOD642	Grey Cars
M629KVU	Turners Tours	M998XRF	Faresaver	MP51BUS	Eurotaxis
M638KVU	Bakers Dolphin	MAZ6792	South West Coaches	MUD27W	Yellow Buses
M646HFJ	Dartline	MCO658	Plymouth Citybus	MUR217L	Quantock MS
M646OOM	Eurotaxis	MFX169W	Thamesdown	MW52PZP	South Gloucestershire
M657COR	Hatts Europa	MFX170W	Thamesdown	MW52PZR	South Gloucestershire
M681HGG	Hookways	MFX171W	Thamesdown	MX04DSV	Somerbus
M685MRP	Bluebird	MFX172W	Thamesdown	MX51TJY	Coach House
M702HBC	Alexcars	MFX173W	Thamesdown	MXX398	Shaftesbury & District

The South West Bus Handbook

MYD217V	Webberbus	N282PDV	Plymouth Citybus	N991FWT	Carmel
N2RED	Redwoods	N283PDV	Plymouth Citybus	N993FWT	Eagle of Bristol
N3ARJ	Andybus	N283VDA	Country Bus	N998KUS	Carmel
N3YCL	Target Travel	N284PDV	Plymouth Citybus	NBZ1360	Barnes
N4RDC	Alexcars	N286PDV	Plymouth Citybus	NDB356	Quantock MS
N9LON	APL Travel	N287PDV	Plymouth Citybus	NDD672	Pulham's
N14CJT	Turners Coachways	N287VDA	Country Bus	NFB113R	A Bus
N18LUE	Blue Iris	N288PDV	Plymouth Citybus	NFX133P	Sureline
N24EYB	South Gloucestershire	N289PDV	Plymouth Citybus	NFX134P	Quantock MS
N27YJW	Country Bus	N290VDA	F T Williams	NFX135P	Sureline
N28YJW	Country Bus	N307UTT	Plymouth Citybus	NFX136P	Sureline
N30AJRJ	Andybus	N308OGJ	Bakers Dolphin	NFX137P	Sureline
N31YJW	Country Bus	N312HUM	Eurotaxis	NHG541	Somerbus
N34YJW	Country Bus	N320BYA	Berry's	NIB5595	Barnes
N35YJW	Country Bus	N344OBC	Cooks Coaches	NIB8459	Safeway
N36YJW	Country Bus	N346OBC	Faresaver	NIL4842	Tally Ho!
N37YJW	Country Bus	N347OBC	Dukes Travel	NIL4981	Bakers Dolphin
N40TCC	Dartline	N348OBC	Dukes Travel	NIL4982	Bakers Dolphin
N43ENW	Coombs Travel	N349OBC	Dukes Travel	NIL4983	Bakers Dolphin
N88LUE	Blue Iris	N350OBC	Sureline	NIL4984	Bakers Dolphin
N94BNF	Target Travel	N351OBC	Sureline	NIL4985	Bakers Dolphin
N95BNF	Target Travel	N352OBC	Faresaver	NIL4986	Bakers Dolphin
N101HGO	Marchants	N410WJL	Coombs Travel	NIL4987	C J Down
N101UTT	Plymouth Citybus	N456VOD	Cooks Coaches	NIL4988	C J Down
N102UTT	Plymouth Citybus	N457VOD	Cooks Coaches	NIL5381	Bakers Dolphin
N103UTT	Plymouth Citybus	N463TPR	Yellow Buses	NIL5382	Bakers Dolphin
N104UTT	Plymouth Citybus	N464TPR	Yellow Buses	NIL5652	DAC Coaches
N105UTT	Plymouth Citybus	N465TPR	Yellow Buses	NIL6560	Target Travel
N107UTT	Plymouth Citybus	N466TPR	Yellow Buses	NIL7278	Cooks Coaches
N108UTT	Plymouth Citybus	N467TPR	Yellow Buses	NIL8255	Glenvic
N109UTT	Plymouth Citybus	N468TPR	Yellow Buses	NIL8259	Glenvic
N110UTT	Plymouth Citybus	N469TPR	Yellow Buses	NIL9886	Beeline
N112UTT	Plymouth Citybus	N470TPR	Yellow Buses	NIW8290	Hookways
N121JHR	Thamesdown	N471TPR	Yellow Buses	NIW8794	Currian's
N122JHR	Thamesdown	N472TPR	Yellow Buses	NKU962X	Caradon Riviera
N123DNV	Beeline	N481RTA	Target Travel	NLJ271	Quantock MS
N123JHR Thamesdown		N482BFY	Eurotaxis	NMJ283V	Turners Tours
N124JHR	Thamesdown	N512MWV	Barry's	NNC854P	Quantock MS
N125LMW	Thamesdown	N536SJF	Hopley's	NNN9P	Quantock MS
N126LMW	Thamesdown	N541CYA	Coombs Travel	NOK43	Taw & Torridge
N127LMW	Thamesdown	N542BFY	Eurotaxis	NPA228W	Safeway
N128LMW	Thamesdown	N573OUH	Wessex Bus	NSU205	Mid Devon
N151MTG	Tally Ho!	N586OAE	Eurotaxis	NTT575W	Currian's
N157MTG	Dukes Travel	N599OAE	Turners Coachways	NUB93V	Quantock MS
N160MTG	Dukes Travel	N600WGL	Western Greyhound	NUD106L	Citytour
N166KAF	Truronian	N602JGP	Faresaver	NUI1577	Target Travel
N167KAF	Truronian	N603JGP	Faresaver	NUI1588	Target Travel
N168KAF	Truronian	N605DOR	Coombs Travel	NUI1599	Target Travel
N169KAF	Truronian	N609DWT	Coombs Travel	NUI1602	Bakers Dolphin
N170KAF	Truronian	N614DKR	Cooks Coaches	NUI5155	Alexcars
N195EMJ	Faresaver	N614DKR	Cooks Coaches	NUI5167	South West Coaches
N199DYB	Berry's	N627BWG	Eurotaxis	NUW557Y	Shaftesbury & District
N201DYB	Dawlish Coaches	N653THO	James Bevan	NYC398V	Arleen
N202DYB	Dawlish Coaches	N722DKJ	Hatts Europa	OAZ1372	Brean & Berrow
N212KBJ	Truronian	N751DAK	Travel Filer's	OBO631X	Hookways
N219HWX	Taw & Torridge	N754CYA	South Gloucestershire	ODF561	Pulham's
N220HWX	Taw & Torridge	N758CYA	Berry's	ODV287P	Taw & Torridge
N222LFR	Andybus	N770VTT	Sewards	ODW459	Alexcars
N226HWX	Taw & Torridge	N780EUA	Faresaver	OFS668Y	South Gloucestershire
N232HWX	Coach House	N780LHY	Eagle of Bristol	OFS701Y	Bennett
N253PGD	Faresaver	N791WNE	Coach House	OFS702Y	Bennett
N265VDA	Country Bus	N813OAE	Turners Coachways	OFS912M	Brean & Berrow
N266VDA	Country Bus	N814NHS	Eurotaxis	OFV14X	Shamrock Buses
N268VDA	Country Bus	N823OAE	Turners Coachways	OFV15X	Shamrock Buses
N270KAM	Beeline	N832MAM	Webberbus	OFV19X	DAC Coaches
Country Bus		N844DKU	Mid Devon	OFV23X	Shamrock Buses
N271KAM	Beeline	N860XMO	Barry's	OHR183R	Thamesdown
N272KAM	Beeline	N873XMO	Rover	OHV707Y	Applegate
N273KAM	Beeline	N895VEG	Blue Iris	OHV766Y	South Gloucestershire
N274KAM	Beeline	N917LRL	Cooks Coaches	OHV783Y	Glenvic
N275PDV	Plymouth Citybus	N918ETM	Faresaver	OHV798Y	South Gloucestershire
N276PDV	Plymouth Citybus	N918WDV	Dartline	OIL2947	Quantock MS
N277PDV	Plymouth Citybus	N933CJA	Eurotaxis	OIL5267	Barry's
N277VDA	Country Bus	N966OAE	Turners Coachways	OIL9262	South Gloucestershire
N278PDV	Plymouth Citybus	N967BYD	Coombs Travel	OIL9263	South Gloucestershire
N279PDV	Plymouth Citybus	N967OAE	James Bevan	OIL9264	South Gloucestershire
N280PDV	Plymouth Citybus	N970BYC	Coombs Travel	OIW1319	Mid Devon
N281PDV	Plymouth Citybus	N990AEF	Eurotaxis	OJD51R	Tally Ho!

Registration	Operator	Registration	Operator	Registration	Operator	Registration	Operator
OJI4672	Barnes	P532CLJ	Webberbus	R117OFJ	Plymouth Citybus		
OLD564	Shaftesbury & District	P534PLB	Hatts Europa	R118OFJ	Plymouth Citybus		
OO04MJS	Centurion	P536YEU	Buglers	R119OFJ	Plymouth Citybus		
OTG44R	Mid Devon	P590CFH	James Bevan	R120OFJ	Plymouth Citybus		
OWO235Y	Safeway	P655EAU	Eurotaxis	R121OFJ	Plymouth Citybus		
OYY3	Turners Coachways	P665ECJ	Brean & Berrow	R122OFJ	Plymouth Citybus		
P2POW	Berkeley	P689VHU	Beeline	R123ESG	DAC Coaches		
P4BBC	Bluebird	P691LKL	Beeline	R123OFJ	Plymouth Citybus		
P6WRS	Marchants	P695JOM	F T Williams	R124OFJ	Plymouth Citybus		
P7ARL	Arleen	P725JYA	Bakers Dolphin	R125OFJ	Plymouth Citybus		
P9MCT	Buglers	P726JYA	Bakers Dolphin	R126OFJ	Plymouth Citybus		
P10TCC	Marchants	P727JYA	Berry's	R155TNN	Coombs Travel		
P15CJT	Turners Coachways	P728ADV	Webberbus	R170SUT	James Bevan		
P16CJT	Turners Coachways	P785KRV	Michaels	R179GNW	Bennett		
P50AND	Rover	P786VYS	Wessex Bus	R190SUT	Turners Tours		
P73RFB	Webberbus	P791JKW	F T Williams	R199WYD	Berry's		
P74VWO	Hatts Europa	P848REU	Cooks Coaches	R200PAR	Swanbrook		
P76VWO	APL Travel	P878VYJ	F T Williams	R201WYD	Berkeley		
P87JYC	Coombs Travel	P882FMO	Dartline	R202WYD	Berry's		
P89JYC	Coombs Travel	P928KYC	Dawlish Coaches	R208WYD	Dawlish Coaches		
P96GHE	DAC Coaches	P929KYC	Dawlish Coaches	R209WYD	Dawlish Coaches		
P97TTX	Alexcars	P934KYC	Dartline	R222AJP	A Bus		
P100SYD	Carmel	P939HVX	Dukes Travel	R230DHU	F T Williams		
P110HCH	Cooks Coaches	P944GEG	Cooks Coaches	R252EMV	Hookways		
P115HCH	Cooks Coaches	P974UKG	Country Bus	R253EMV	Hookways		
P117KBL	Cooks Coaches	PBZ7052	Tally Ho!	R254EMV	Hookways		
P125MOV	F T Williams	PDF567	Pulham's	R265THL	Target Travel		
P133KOJ	F T Williams	PHT885Y	Applegate	R271UES	F T Williams		
P151SMW	Thamesdown	PIB2470	Berry's	R272UES	F T Williams		
P152SMW	Thamesdown	PIB3360	Berry's	R275LDE	Citytour		
P153SMW	Thamesdown	PIB4019	Berry's	R300PAR	Swanbrook		
P154SMW	Thamesdown	PIL6577	Turners Tours	R309STA	Plymouth Citybus		
P155SMW	Thamesdown	PIL6581	Hookways	R314NGM	Thamesdown		
P156SMW	Thamesdown	PIL9537	Cooks Coaches	R315NGM	Thamesdown		
P157SMW	Thamesdown	PJI2803	Grey Cars	R317NGM	Thamesdown		
P158BFJ	Cooks Coaches	PJI2804	Grey Cars	R319NGM	Thamesdown		
P158SMW	Thamesdown	PJI2805	Grey Cars	R326NRU	Yellow Buses		
P159VHR	Thamesdown	PJI3354	Target Travel	R327NRU	Yellow Buses		
P160VHR	Thamesdown	PJI4713	Taw & Torridge	R329NRU	Yellow Buses		
P161VHR	Thamesdown	PJI4983	F T Williams	R338NRU	Target Travel		
P165ANR	Shaftesbury & District	PJI5013	South Gloucestershire	R341LPR	Target Travel		
P183RSC	Eurotaxis	PJI5014	F T Williams	R354NRU	Yellow Buses		
P200TCC	Castleways	PJI5016	South Gloucestershire	R355NRU	Yellow Buses		
P210JKK	Cooks Coaches	PJI6909	Hatts Europa	R360OWO	Marchants		
P211JKK	Cooks Coaches	PJI7002	Barry's	R370OWO	Marchants		
P224KTP	Taylors	POI4905	Shaftesbury & District	R372XYD	Bakers Dolphin		
P232NKK	Cooks Coaches	PRA604X	Beaumont Travel	R373XYD	Bakers Dolphin		
P285LJH	Webberbus	PRC849X	Truronian	R380OWO	Marchants		
P292CPH	F T Williams	PRC856X	Truronian	R380XYD	Berry's		
P296JHE	APL Travel	PSU527	South Gloucestershire	R404FWT	Turners Tours		
P298NLD	South Gloucestershire	R1TRU	Truronian	R418XFL	Country Bus		
P299MLD	South Gloucestershire	R2AVC	Dawlish Coaches	R419XFL	Country Bus		
P306HWG	Cooks Coaches	R2CJT	Turners Coachways	R431FWT	Marchants		
P308CTT	Plymouth Citybus	R2POW	Berkeley	R432FWT	Marchants		
P311GTO	Eurotaxis	R3CJT	Turners Coachways	R43ADV	Carmel		
P314GTO	Eurotaxis	R5WGT	K W Beard	R450YDT	Hatts Europa		
P317GTO	Eurotaxis	R6LON	Eurotaxis	R452FWT	Marchants		
P321ARU	Hatts Europa	R9HAT	Hatts Europa	R464YDT	Alexcars		
P344VWR	Dawlish Coaches	R10TAW	Taw & Torridge	R475NPR	Yellow Buses		
P347FOL	F T Williams	R13OVA	Dawlish Coaches	R476NPR	Yellow Buses		
P347VWR	James Bevan	R16BLU	DAC Coaches	R477NPR	Yellow Buses		
P351VWR	Cottrell's	R18CJT	Turners Coachways	R478NPR	Yellow Buses		
P352ARU	Yellow Buses	R18LUE	Blue Iris	R479NPR	Yellow Buses		
P429JDT	Dartline	R19CJT	Turners Coachways	R480NPR	Yellow Buses		
P452SCV	Truronian	R30ARJ	Andybus	R481NPR	Yellow Buses		
P453SCV	Truronian	R30CJT	Turners Coachways	R482NPR	Yellow Buses		
P455SCV	Truronian	R41EDW	South West Coaches	R48WUY	Marchants		
P473BLJ	Yellow Buses	R4POW	Berkeley	R500GSM	Barry's		
P473MNA	Eurotaxis	R54OCK	Beaumont Travel	R501BUA	Cooks Coaches		
P474BLJ	Yellow Buses	R57JSG	Andybus	R552JAF	F T Williams		
P474MNA	Eurotaxis	R60RED	Redwoods	R583DYG	Eurotaxis		
P476NCR	F T Williams	R90CJT	Turners Coachways	R608OTA	Sewards		
P479OGV	F T Williams	R100PAR	Swanbrook	R609OTA	Sewards		
P481CEG	Country Bus	R111CJT	Turners Coachways	R612GHJ	Coombs Travel		
P482CEG	Country Bus	R113OFJ	Plymouth Citybus	R612HMW	Taw & Torridge		
P490FOJ	Faresaver	R114OFJ	Plymouth Citybus	R614AAU	South West Coaches		
P494RHU	Cooks Coaches	R115OFJ	Plymouth Citybus	R616AAU	South West Coaches		
P525UDG	Beaumont Travel	R116OFJ	Plymouth Citybus	R616BWO	Carmel		

The South West Bus Handbook

In 1881, some time before any automobile had even been on the road, Henri Jonckheere began to build horse drawn carriages in the town of Beveren, near Roeselare in the province of West-Flanders, Belgium. This makes Jonckeere one of the longest established coachwork builders in Europe. Now part of the Dutch VDL Group, we show here Bakers Dolphin Deauville SIL6716. *Dave Heath*

R623JDV	Caradon Riviera	RCV283R	Quantock MS	ROI6774	Peter Carol
R625GFS	Eurotaxis	REO207L	Polperro Tram Co	ROI7435	Peter Carol
R627VNN	Centurion	RIB5086	C J Down	ROI8235	Peter Carol
R629YOM	Ebley Bus	RIB7874	Barnes	ROI8358	Peter Carol
R630YOM	Ebley Bus	RIB8809	Centurion	RUA452W	Marchants
R632VNN	Carmel	RIB8816	Centurion	RUA457W	Marchants
R632VYB	Bakers Dolphin	RIB8817	Centurion	RUA458W	Beaumont Travel
R652TYA	South West Coaches	RIB8819	Centurion	RUE300W	DAC Coaches
R736EGD	DAC Coaches	RIL1057	Taylors	S3HJC	Target Travel
R746VNT	F T Williams	RIL1203	Beeline	S18RED	Western Greyhound
R767HOY	Beeline	RIL1475	South West Coaches	S20WGL	Western Greyhound
R773WOB	Dartline	RIL2102	Arleen	S30ARJ	Western Greyhound
R774WOB	Dartline	RIL2103	Citytour	S34BMR	Western Greyhound
R778MFH	Bakers Dolphin	RIL3706	F T Williams	S49JFV	Glenvic
R807HWS	Western Greyhound	RIL4022	Arleen	S50CJT	Turners Coachways
R808HWS	Western Greyhound	RIL4958	C J Down	S60CJT	Turners Coachways
R809HWS	Western Greyhound	RIL6390	Shaftesbury & District	S100PAF	Western Greyhound
R810HWS	Western Greyhound	RIL6849	Webberbus	S102KJF	Bakers Dolphin
R814LFV	Buglers	RIL7643	Arleen	S111AJP	A Bus
R816LFV	Ebley Bus	RIL7644	Arleen	S127FTA	Plymouth Citybus
R843GRN	South Gloucestershire	RIL8110	Wessex Bus	S139ATA	Travel Filer's
R851SDT	Alexcars	RIL9864	K W Beard	S162BMR	Thamesdown
R872SDT	Blue Iris	RIL9865	K W Beard	S181BMR	Thamesdown
R873BKW	Hatts Europa	RJI3046	Safeway	S182BMR	Thamesdown
R879OAD	Coombs Travel	RJI4563	C J Down	S183BMR	Thamesdown
R880DGT	DAC Coaches	RJI5716	Bakers Dolphin	S184BMR	Thamesdown
R927LAA	Taw & Torridge	RJI8602	Beeline	S185BMR	Thamesdown
R964MDV	Dartline	RJI8606	Travel Filer's	S186BMR	Thamesdown
R974MGB	Coach House	RJX318	Taylors	S234FGD	Eurotaxis
R987PFT	Carmel	RK51KNV	Beeline	S344SET	Blue Iris
R990EHU	Eagle of Bristol	RLN230R	Taw & Torridge	S398TNE	Target Travel
R991HN3	Eurotaxis	RO51UVL	Eurotaxis	S400RED	Redwoods
R998FNW	Yellow Buses	RO51UWD	Eurotaxis	S462VWB	Arleen
RAZ8598	South West Coaches	ROI1229	Peter Carol	S501SRL	Western Greyhound
RBO506Y	A Bus	ROI1417	Peter Carol	S502SRL	Western Greyhound
RBO508Y	A Bus	ROI2929	Peter Carol	S503SRL	Western Greyhound

Band Buses are low capacity vehicles with exceptionally high specifications, that include accessories such as bunks, kitchens, bath and shower rooms. Trathens use several Volvo B12Ts on such duties, including Van Hool Astrobel 481, LSK481. *Colin Lloyd*

S549SCV	Truronian	SIL4460	Grey Cars	T130EFJ	Plymouth Citybus
S583VOB	South Gloucestershire	SIL4465	Cooks Coaches	T131EFJ	Plymouth Citybus
S584VOB	South Gloucestershire	SIL4470	Grey Cars	T132EFJ	Plymouth Citybus
S627ETV	South Gloucestershire	SIL5960	Mid Devon	T133EFJ	Plymouth Citybus
S639UUG	Redwoods	SIL6715	Bakers Dolphin	T134AST	South Gloucestershire
S640MGA	Coach House	SIL6716	Bakers Dolphin	T134EFJ	Plymouth Citybus
S659ETT	Bluebird	SJI8117	Hookways	T135EFJ	Plymouth Citybus
S671ETT	Dartline	SJI8285	Mid Devon	T136EFJ	Plymouth Citybus
S698RWG	Citytour	SJR617Y	Bennett	T137EFJ	Plymouth Citybus
S762XYA	APL Travel	SK51SBK	Swanbrook	T138EFJ	Plymouth Citybus
S781RNE	Dukes Travel	SN53RXC	Blue Iris	T139EFJ	Plymouth Citybus
S794JTH	Eagle of Bristol	SN53RXD	Blue Iris	T140EFJ	Plymouth Citybus
S804LPY	Wessex Bus	SND282X	Webberbus	T163RMR	Thamesdown
S838VAG	Thamesdown	SND489X	Glenvic	T164RMR	Thamesdown
S853PKH	APL Travel	SNT925H	Andybus	T165RMR	Thamesdown
S889RRL	Truronian	SPY374X	Tally Ho!	T213UCH	South Gloucestershire
S903NPO	Barry's	SRY759X	Mike's Travel	T215UCH	South Gloucestershire
S923KOD	Dartline	STW33W	A Bus	T270BPR	Yellow Buses
S924KOD	Dartline	T2RED	Redwoods	T271BPR	Yellow Buses
S925KOD	Dartline	T2TRU	Truronian	T272BPR	Yellow Buses
S926KOD	Dartline	T3RED	Redwoods	T273BPR	Yellow Buses
S944WYB	Dartline	T4POW	Berkeley	T274BPR	Yellow Buses
S995BTA	Cooks Coaches	T7BBC	Bluebird	T275BPR	Yellow Buses
SA51PVY	DAC Coaches	T12SBK	Swanbrook	T276BPR	Yellow Buses
SAZ2511	South West Coaches	T12TRU	Truronian	T277BPR	Yellow Buses
SBZ8075	Barry's	T18LUE	Blue Iris	T278BPR	Yellow Buses
SCZ9765	Glenvic	T20TVL	Truronian	T297PDF	Target Travel
SCZ9766	Beeline	T32JCV	Truronian	T301PDF	Target Travel
SF51PVU	Carmel	T34JCV	Truronian	T323UCH	South Gloucestershire
SG02VXH	Eurotaxis	T35CNN	Swanbrook	T325RTT	Target Travel
SG04XCN	DAC Coaches	T35JCV	Truronian	T330AFX	Yellow Buses
SGL498Y	Hookways	T46RJL	Webberbus	T331AFX	Yellow Buses
SIB7515	Barnes	T54AUA	Eagle of Bristol	T398VHO	Bakers Dolphin
SIB8398	Berry's	T77TRU	Truronian	T402VHO	Taw & Torridge
SIB9309	Berry's	T118UCH	South Gloucestershire	T406OWA	Travel Filer's
SIB9313	Berry's	T128EFJ	Plymouth Citybus	T419PDG	Bennett
SIL3066	Grey Cars	T129EFJ	Plymouth Citybus	T436TEU	Hatts Europa

The South West Bus Handbook

T446HRV	Alexcars	TTT165X	River Link	VIL6840		Beeline
T463UCH	South Gloucestershire	TTT170W	Plymouth Citybus	VIL9482		South West Coaches
T480RCE	Coach House	TTT171W	Plymouth Citybus	VJI8684		Caradon Riviera
T544EUB	Turners Tours	TU04TRU	Truronian	VJI8687		Hookways
T568SUF	Blue Iris	TWS914T	DAC Coaches	VJI9417		Barry's
T623KFH	APL Travel	TXI8761	Cooks Coaches	VJT138S		Yellow Buses
T623KFH	Hatts Europa	TYR95	Quantock MS	VJT140S		Yellow Buses
T708UOS	Bakers Dolphin	UCT838	Bluebird	VJY921V		Bakers Dolphin
T717UOS	DAC Coaches	UDF936	Pulham's	VMX234X		Tally Ho!
T721UOS	Bakers Dolphin	UHY384	A Bus	VN03XXG		Bennett
T761JYB	Bakers Dolphin	UIB3987	Shamrock Buses	VO03DZC		Bennett
T762JYB	Bakers Dolphin	UIB9492	Barnes	VO03DZC		Bennett
T766JYB	Berry's	UIL1335	South West Coaches	VO03DZD		Bennett
T788RDV	Cooks Coaches	UIL4705	Hookways	VO03DZE		Bennett
T825OBL	Travel Filer's	UJI1761	Swanbrook	VO03MWW		Pulham's
T892LKJ	Hatts Europa	UJI1762	Swanbrook	VPF287S		Westward Travel
T893LKJ	Hatts Europa	UJI1763	Swanbrook	VPH53S		Quantock MS
T894LKJ	Hatts Europa	UJI3791	Bakers Dolphin	VU02UVM		Castleways
T896LBF	Geoff Willetts	UJI3793	Webberbus	VU03ZPT		Hatts Europa
T905LKE	Hatts Europa	UJI3794	Dartline	VU51AXR		Eurotaxis
T920LEU	Bakers Dolphin	ULL933	Western Greyhound	VWX293X		Tally Ho!
T936YRR	Currian's	UMR199T	Thamesdown	VWX350X		Westward Travel
T953RTA	Sewards	UMR200T	Thamesdown	VX04KTK		Hatts Europa
T966ABF	Cooks Coaches	UPV487	Bakers Dolphin	VX51ABF		Dukes Travel
T979OGA	Webberbus	URB161S	Westward Travel	VX51AWO		Marchants
TAY888X	Bakers Dolphin	URM141X	Hamblys of Kernow	VX51RDO		Beaumont Travel
TAZ4992	Westward Travel	URU650X	Bluebird	VX53AVJ		Hatts Europa
TAZ6963	Buglers	USV330	Redwoods	VYD333		Quantock MS
TCZ6122	Quantock MS	USV331	Redwoods	W2BBC		Bluebird
TCZ6123	Quantock MS	USV462	Redwoods	W3TRU		Truronian
TDK686J	Quantock MS	USV474	Redwoods	W4TRU		Truronian
TDZ8157	South West Coaches	USV556	Redwoods	W17CJT		Turners Coachways
TFO319	Western Greyhound	USV620	Redwoods	W29WGL		Western Greyhound
TIB9471	Barnes	USV625	Redwoods	W31SBC		Alexcars
TIL1253	Tilleys	USV630	Redwoods	W44WGL		Western Greyhound
TIL1254	Tilleys	USV676	Redwoods	W50MBH		Western Greyhound
TIL1255	Tilleys	UWV604S	River Link	W107RTC		Berkeley
TIL1256	Tilleys	UWV614S	River Link	W157RYB		Dawlish Coaches
TIL1257	Tilleys	UWV619S	Citytour	W161CWR		Hookways
TIL1258	Tilleys	UYD950W	South West Coaches	W161RYB		Berry's
TIL1259	Tilleys	V8PCC	Cooks Coaches	W201CDN		Eagle of Bristol
TIL1260	Tilleys	V28LUE	Blue Iris	W224CDN		Quantock MS
TIL1261	Tilleys	V31WGL	Western Greyhound	W259WRV		Dartline
TIL1262	Tilleys	V40WGL	Western Greyhound	W311SDV		Plymouth Citybus
TIL1263	Tilleys	V116GWP	Beeline	W312STA		Plymouth Citybus
TIL1858	Alexcars	V181FVU	Beaumont Travel	W322MKY		Webberbus
TIL2506	Barry's	V187EAM	Thamesdown	W346VOD		Sewards
TIL2812	Mid Devon	V188EAM	Thamesdown	W347VOD		Sewards
TIL4679	Glenvic	V189EAM	Thamesdown	W371PHY		Coombs Travel
TIL5081	Tilleys	V190EAM	Thamesdown	W372PHY		Coombs Travel
TIL6878	Roselyn	V191EAM	Thamesdown	W381UEL		Yellow Buses
TIL9685	South West Coaches	V200DCC	Castleways	W382UEL		Yellow Buses
TIW7681	Taw & Torridge	V205EAL	Roselyn	W383UEL		Yellow Buses
TJF757	Castleways	V225VAL	Cooks Coaches	W384UEL		Yellow Buses
TJI4683	Taylors	V383HGG	Cooks Coaches	W391JOG		Castleways
TJT182X	Shamrock Buses	V444AJP	A Bus	W415HOB		Hatts Europa
TJT192X	Shamrock Buses	V448DYB	Coombs Travel	W416HOB		Hatts Europa
TL54TVL	Truronian	V483XJV	Dawlish Coaches	W445CFR		Travel Filer's
TMW997S	Roselyn	V600MCBC	Coach House	W453CRN		South West Coaches
TNJ995S	Citytour	V689OJW	Arleen	W454CRN		South West Coaches
TNJ996S	Citytour	V798EWF	Eurotaxis	W506EOL		Arleen
TNJ998S	Citytour	V801LWT	Eagle of Bristol	W554SJM		Hatts Europa
TO54TRU	Truronian	V844OOF	Swanbrook	W562RYC		Dawlish Coaches
TPD28S	Quantock MS	V845OOF	Swanbrook	W627FUM		Turners Tours
TPD112X	Eagle of Bristol	V852DYB	South West Coaches	W678DDN		James Bevan
TPD120X	South Gloucestershire	V888LUE	Blue Iris	W764ABV		Eurotaxis
TPL762X	Truronian	V957EOD	Travel Filer's	W818AAY		Hatts Europa
TPT6R	Quantock MS	VAB893R	Taw & Torridge	W913BEC		Carmel
TRX615	Buglers	VAD141	Pulham's	W953WDS		Eurotaxis
TSO17X	Eagle of Bristol	VAZ2533	Turners Tours	W985WDB		Eurotaxis
TSU649	Mid Devon	VBC984X	Bakers Dolphin	WA03BHW		Plymouth Citybus
TSV302	Hopley's	VCA462W	Ebley Bus	WA03BHX		Plymouth Citybus
TT03TRU	Truronian	VCA463W	Eagle of Bristol	WA03BHY		Plymouth Citybus
TT04TRU	Truronian	VDF365	Pulham's	WA03BHZ		Plymouth Citybus
TT541VL	Truronian	VDV752	Quantock MS	WA03BJE		Plymouth Citybus
TTT162W	Plymouth Citybus	VDV753	Quantock MS	WA03BJF		Plymouth Citybus
TTT163X	Roselyn	VIB3903	Barnes	WA03EYD		Berry's
TTT164X	Roselyn	VIB9378	Cooks Coaches	WA03EYR		Webberbus

The South West Bus Handbook

Reg	Operator	Reg	Operator	Reg	Operator
WA03HPZ	Barnes	WJI3726	Citytour	WYV820T	Andybus
WA03HRJ	Sewards	WJI6879	Bakers Dolphin	X33WGL	Western Greyhound
WA03JXY	Sewards	WJI6880	Bakers Dolphin	X46CNY	Beeline
WA03MGE	Plymouth Citybus	WK02BUS	Western Greyhound	X70CJT	Turners Coachways
WA03MGJ	Plymouth Citybus	WK02UHR	Currian's	X80CJT	Turners Coachways
WA03SYV	Travel Filer's	WK02XLT	Truronian	X83AAK	Bennett
WA04EWL	Barnes	WK03BTE	Hopley's	X89CNY	Carmel
WA04EWP	Carmel	WK03BTF	Hopley's	X96AHU	Beaumont Travel
WA04EWV	Barnes	WK03CXS	Truronian	X141CDV	Plymouth Citybus
WA04HNC	Sewards	WK03EKH	Truronian	X142CDV	Plymouth Citybus
WA04MHE	F T Williams	WK03ENM	Hopley's	X143CFJ	Plymouth Citybus
WA04MHF	Berry's	WK04AOW	Truronian	X149BTA	Sewards
WA04MHX	Dawlish Coaches	WK04CUA	Western Greyhound	X201CDV	Plymouth Citybus
WA51ACO	Plymouth Citybus	WK04CUC	Western Greyhound	X202CDV	Plymouth Citybus
WA51ACU	Plymouth Citybus	WK05CFD	Western Greyhound	X203CDV	Plymouth Citybus
WA51ACV	Plymouth Citybus	WK05CFE	Western Greyhound	X204CDV	Plymouth Citybus
WA51ACX	Plymouth Citybus	WK05CFF	Western Greyhound	X286DTA	Coombs Travel
WA51ACY	Plymouth Citybus	WK51AVP	Western Greyhound	X301AKY	Taw & Torridge
WA52MTE	Webberbus	WK51BUF	Western Greyhound	X314HOU	Eurotaxis
WA53ONL	DAC Coaches	WK51HNF	Western Greyhound	X315WFX	Target Travel
WA53SFY	Peter Carol	WK52LZA	Truronian	X346AVJ	Eurotaxis
WA54FSF	Webberbus	WK52VZN	Currian's	X424CFJ	Dawlish Coaches
WA54GOE	Webberbus	WK52WKV	Truronian	X436CDW	DAC Coaches
WA54GPJ	Webberbus	WK53BNA	Western Greyhound	X469XUT	Swanbrook
WA54GPK	Webberbus	WK53BNB	Western Greyhound	X499AHE	Redwoods
WA54JVV	Plymouth Citybus	WK53BND	Western Greyhound	X509HNR	Taw & Torridge
WA54JVW	Plymouth Citybus	WK53EUT	Western Greyhound	X534JOV	Rover
WA54JVX	Plymouth Citybus	WK53EUU	Western Greyhound	X541HJM	Beeline
WA54JVY	Plymouth Citybus	WK54BHL	Western Greyhound	X564CUY	K W Beard
WA54JVZ	Plymouth Citybus	WK54BHN	Western Greyhound	X574BYD	Quantock MS
WA54JWC	Plymouth Citybus	WK54BHO	Western Greyhound	X584BYD	Dawlish Coaches
WA54JWD	Plymouth Citybus	WK54BHP	Western Greyhound	X751VWR	Hatts Europa
WA54JWE	Plymouth Citybus	WLT649	Western Greyhound	X844MBM	Sureline
WA54JYX	Sewards	WP52WBZ	Centurion	X904ADF	Geoff Willetts
WA54KTT	Barnes	WP52WHG	Coombs Travel	XAN48T	Roselyn
WA54LSX	Webberbus	WP52YXA	Andybus	XBJ860	South West Coaches
WAF156	Hamblys of Kernow	WPW202S	Eagle of Bristol	XBZ4253	Arleen
WAW354Y	Mid Devon	WR02RVX	Berkeley	XBZ4254	Arleen
WB03EDE	Roselyn	WR02XXO	Andybus	XBZ4256	Arleen
WCR819	Target Travel	WSV323	South West Coaches	XBZ7729	Thamesdown
WCZ4815	Faresaver	WSV529	DAC Coaches	XBZ7730	Thamesdown
WDD17X	K W Beard	WSV537	Western Greyhound	XBZ7731	Thamesdown
WDD194	Pulham's	WSV868	South West Coaches	XBZ7732	Thamesdown
WDF946	Pulham's	WTU467W	River Link	XCZ4146	Beeline
WDK562T	Quantock MS	WU03FJY	Coombs Travel	XCZ4147	Beeline
WDR145	Buglers	WU03ZPS	Andybus	XCZ4148	Beeline
WDR598	Tally Ho!	WU03ZPY	Andybus	XCZ4149	Beeline
WFV530	Mid Devon	WU52YWE	Thamesdown	XDG614	Pulham's
WIB1444	Barnes	WU52YWF	Thamesdown	XEL158	Excelsior
WIL3621	Mid Devon	WU52YWG	Thamesdown	XEL24	Excelsior
WJ02KDF	Dawlish Coaches	WU52YWH	Thamesdown	XEL31	Excelsior
WJ02KDO	Barnes	WU52YWJ	Thamesdown	XFJ466	Dartline
WJ02KDX	DAC Coaches	WU52YWK	Thamesdown	XHK221X	A Bus
WJ02KDZ	Dartline	WU52YWL	Thamesdown	XHK222X	A Bus
WJ02KEU	Dartline	WU52YWM	Thamesdown	XHY256	Turners Coachways
WJ02VRO	Barnes	WU53ESG	Taylors	XIB1907	Beeline
WJ02VRV	Barnes	WV02ANX	Centurion	XIB3421	Barnes
WJ02YYK	Dawlish Coaches	WV02NNA	Thamesdown	XIB8380	Centurion
WJ52GNY	Plymouth Citybus	WV02NNB	Thamesdown	XIB8381	Centurion
WJ52GNZ	Plymouth Citybus	WV02NNC	Thamesdown	XIB8385	Centurion
WJ52GOA	Plymouth Citybus	WV02OGG	Coombs Travel	XIB8387	Centurion
WJ52GOC	Plymouth Citybus	WV02OGH	Coombs Travel	XIL8422	Bakers Dolphin
WJ52GOE	Plymouth Citybus	WV51RDY	Eurotaxis	XIL8423	Bakers Dolphin
WJ52GOH	Plymouth Citybus	WX03UXT	Centurion	XIL8424	Bakers Dolphin
WJ52GOK	Plymouth Citybus	WX03YFD	Thamesdown	XIL8425	Bakers Dolphin
WJ52MTO	Barnes	WX03YFE	Thamesdown	XIL8505	Brean & Berrow
WJ52MTU	Travel Filer's	WX03ZNS	Thamesdown	XIL8531	South West Coaches
WJ52MTV	Travel Filer's	WX04CZH	Thamesdown	XIL9631	Faresaver
WJI1414	Taylors	WX04CZJ	Thamesdown	XJI5457	Bakers Dolphin
WJI2321	Bakers Dolphin	WX04CZK	Thamesdown	XJI5458	Bakers Dolphin
WJI3490	Bakers Dolphin	WX04CZL	Thamesdown	XJI5459	Bakers Dolphin
WJI3491	Bakers Dolphin	WX51YGN	Eagle of Bristol	XJI6330	Bakers Dolphin
WJI3492	Bakers Dolphin	WX54PEO	Blue Iris	XJI6331	Bakers Dolphin
WJI3493	Bakers Dolphin	WXI3860	Hookways	XJI6332	Bakers Dolphin
WJI3494	Bakers Dolphin	WY04YCJ	Coombs Travel	XJI6333	Bakers Dolphin
WJI3495	Bakers Dolphin	WY04YCK	Coombs Travel	XLH570	Bakers Dolphin
WJI3496	Bakers Dolphin	WYD103W	South West Coaches	XMW120	Thamesdown
WJI3497	Bakers Dolphin	WYD104W	South West Coaches	XOD665	Western Greyhound

XPG295Y	F T Williams	Y417CFX	Yellow Buses	YK04KWB	Bennett		
XPG295Y	Westward Travel	Y418CFX	Yellow Buses	YK04KWC	Bennett		
XWY475X	Buglers	Y446AUY	Citytour	YK04KWD	Bennett		
XYC248W	South West Coaches	Y502BSF	Eurotaxis	YN03AWY	Bluebird		
Y1EDN	Truronian	Y503BSF	Eurotaxis	YN03AXS	Bennett		
Y2EDN	Truronian	Y621HHU	Coombs Travel	YN03NJE	Castleways		
Y5TRU	Truronian	Y644NYD	Plymouth Citybus	YN04AKU	Redwoods		
Y7CJD	C J Down	Y645NYD	Plymouth Citybus	YN04AWR	Redwoods		
Y7JMJ	Applegate	Y646NYD	Plymouth Citybus	YN04KWN	Cooks Coaches		
Y10RAD	Alexcars	Y647NYD	Plymouth Citybus	YN51WGX	Berry's		
Y14DLC	Dartline	Y648NYD	Plymouth Citybus	YN51XMC	Trathens		
Y25TAW	Taw & Torridge	Y683LDF	Beaumont Travel	YN51XMD	Trathens		
Y36HBT	Eurotaxis	Y736OBE	Hatts Europa	YN51XME	Trathens		
Y37HBT	Eurotaxis	Y814HUB	Hookways	YN51XMH	Trathens		
Y69HHE	Alexcars	Y818NAY	Dawlish Coaches	YN51XMJ	Trathens		
Y79CDS	Turners Tours	Y835HHE	Cooks Coaches	YN51XMK	Trathens		
Y138RDG	Citytour	Y835NAY	Dawlish Coaches	YN51XML	Trathens		
Y139RDG	Citytour	Y852SDD	Pulham's	YN51XMU	Trathens		
Y151XAE	Eagle of Bristol	Y882HAE	Beaumont Travel	YN51XMV	Trathens		
Y166GTT	Sewards	Y883HAE	Beaumont Travel	YN51XMW	Trathens		
Y192YMR	Thamesdown	Y921FDV	Cooks Coaches	YN51XMX	Trathens		
Y193YMR	Thamesdown	Y922DCY	Hopley's	YN51XMZ	Trathens		
Y194YMR	Thamesdown	YAZ6391	Shaftesbury & District	YN54LKC	Beaumont Travel		
Y195YMR	Thamesdown	YAZ6393	Shaftesbury & District	YN54LKV	Beaumont Travel		
Y196YMR	Thamesdown	YAZ6394	Shaftesbury & District	YP52BRF	Hatts Europa		
Y197YMR	Thamesdown	YAZ8922	Beeline	YPD116Y	Taylors		
Y200BCC	Bennett	YBZ9558	Arleen	YPL78T	Quantock MS		
Y201KMB	Dukes Travel	YCV500	Hamblys of Kernow	YPL92T	Quantock MS		
Y221NYA	Barnes	YDP396X	Arleen	YPL105T	Quantock MS		
Y223NYA	Hookways	YF02FWK	Cooks Coaches	YPL420T	Applegate		
Y227NYA	Bakers Dolphin	YF02SKO	Cooks Coaches	YR02UMU	Bennett		
Y228NYA	Bakers Dolphin	YF02SKV	Cooks Coaches	YR02UNY	Arleen		
Y229NYA	Bakers Dolphin	YG52CKE	Eagle of Bristol	YR52MBU	Glenvic		
Y263KNB	South Gloucestershire	YHA320	Barry's	YRY1Y	Bakers Dolphin		
Y300BCC	Bennett	YIL4529	Faresaver	YSU923	Tally Ho!		
Y313NYD	Plymouth Citybus	YIL9895	Dartline	YSV645	Barry's		
Y314NYD	Plymouth Citybus	YJ05WCX	Dartline	YSV739	Beeline		
Y334GFJ	Cooks Coaches	YJ05WCY	Dartline	YU04XJK	Beaumont Travel		
Y400BCC	Bennett	YJ05WCZ	Dartline	YUU556	Currian's		
Y411CFX	Yellow Buses	YJ54UCA	APL Travel	YUY94W	Turners Tours		
Y412CFX	Yellow Buses	YJI4610	Berkeley	YXI2730	Bakers Dolphin		
Y413CFX	Yellow Buses	YJI8594	Bluebird	YXI2732	Bakers Dolphin		
Y414CFX	Yellow Buses	YJI8595	Bluebird	YXI7381	Webberbus		
Y415CFX	Yellow Buses	YJI8596	Bluebird	YXI9528	Safeway		
Y416CFX	Yellow Buses	YK04KWA	Bennett	YYA122X	Safeway		

ISBN 1 904875 52 1

© Published by *British Bus Publishing Ltd* , April 2005

British Bus Publishing Ltd, 16 St Margaret's Drive, Telford, TF1 3PH
Telephone: 01952 255669 - Facsimile: 01952 222397